ISBN 978-1-330-80137-6
PIBN 10107217

1 MONTH OF
FREE
READING

at

www.ForgottenBooks.com

By purchasing this book you are eligible for one month membership to ForgottenBooks.com, giving you unlimited access to our entire collection of over 700,000 titles via our web site and mobile apps.

To claim your free month visit:

www.forgottenbooks.com/free107217

THE

POETICAL WORKS

OF

SIR WALTER SCOTT, Bart.

VOL. II.

MINSTRELSY.

CONTENTS

OF VOLUME SECOND.

CONTENTS.

MINSTRELSY OF THE SCOTTISH BORDER.   PART II.

ROMANTIC BALLADS.

MINSTRELSY

OF THE

SCOTTISH BORDER·

CONSISTING OF

HISTORICAL AND ROMANTIC BALLADS,

COLLECTED

IN THE SOUTHERN COUNTIES OF SCOTLAND; WITH A FEW
OF MODERN DATE, FOUNDED UPON
LOCAL TRADITION.

The songs, to savage virtue dear,
That won of yore the public ear,
Ere polity, sedate and sage,
Had quench'd the fires of feudal rage.

WARTON

VOL. II.

EDINBURGH : PRINTED BY BALLANTYNE AND CO., PAUL'S WORK.

JAMIE TELFER

OF THE FAIR DODHEAD.

There is another ballad, under the same title as the following, in which nearly the same incidents are narrated, with little difference, except that the honour of rescuing the cattle is attributed to the Liddesdale Elliots, headed by a Chief, there called Martin Elliot of the Preakin Tower, whose son, Simon, is said to have fallen in the action. It is very possible, that both the Teviotdale Scotts, and the Elliots, were engaged in the affair, and that each claimed the honour of the victory.

The Editor presumes, that the Willie Scott, here mentioned, must have been a natural son of the Laird of Buccleuch.

IT fell about the Martinmas tyde,
  When our Border steeds get corn and hay,
The Captain of Bewcastle hath bound him to ryde,
  And he's ower to Tividale to drive a prey.

The first ae guide that they met wi',
   It was high up in Hardhaughswire ;[1]
The second guide that they met wi',
   It was laigh down in Borthwick water.[2]

" What tidings, what tidings, my trusty guide ?"——
   " Nae tidings, nae tidings, I hae to thee ;
But gin ye'll gae to the fair Dodhead,[3]
   Mony a cow's cauf I'll let thee see."——

And when they cam to the fair Dodhead,
   Right hastily they clam the peel ;
They loosed the kye out, ane and a',
   And ranshackled[3] the house right weel.

Now Jamie Telfer's heart was sair,[5]
   The tear aye rowing in his ee ;
He pled wi' the Captain to hae his gear,
   Or else revenged he wad be.

The Captain turned him round and leugh ;
   Said—" Man, there's naething in thy house,

[1] Hardhaughswire is the pass from Liddesdale to the head of Teviotdale.

[2] Borthwick water is a stream, which falls into the Teviot three miles above Hawick.

[3] The Dodhead, in Selkirkshire, near Singlee, where there are still the vestiges of an old tower.

[4] *Ranshackled*—Ransacked.

[5] There is still a family of Telfers, residing near Langholm, who pretend to derive their descent from the Telfers of the Dodhead.

But ae auld sword without a sheath,
    That hardly now would fell a mouse."—

The sun wasna up, but the moon was down,
    It was the gryming[1] of a new-fa'n snaw,
Jamie Telfer has run ten myles a-foot,
    Between the Dodhead and the Stobs's Ha'.[2]

And when he cam to the fair tower yate,
    He shouted loud, and cried weel hie,
Till out bespak auld Gibby Elliot—
    " Whae's this that brings the fraye to me?"—

" It's I, Jamie Telfer, o' the fair Dodhead,
    And a harried man I think I be!
There's naething left at the fair Dodhead,
    But a waefu' wife and bairnies three."

" Gae seek your succour at Branksome Ha'.[3]
    For succour ye'se get nane frae me!
Gae seek your succour where ye paid black-mail,
    For, man, ye ne'er paid money to me."—

[1] *Gryming*—Sprinkling.

[2] Stobs Hall, upon Slitterick. [The seat of Sir William Eliott, Bart.—head of that clan.] Jamie Telfer made his first application here, because he *seems* to have paid the proprietor of the castle *black-mail*, or protection money.

[3] The ancient family-seat of the Lairds of Buccleuch, near Hawick.

Jamie has turned him round about,
  I wat the tear blinded his ee—
" I'll ne'er pay mail to Elliot again,
  And the fair Dodhead I'll never see!

" My hounds may a' rin masterless,
  My hawks may fly frae tree to tree,
My lord may grip my vassal lands,
  For there again maun I never be!"—

He has turn'd him to the Tiviot side,
  E'en as fast as he could drie,
Till he cam to the Coultart Cleugh,[1]
  And there he shouted baith loud and hie.

Then up bespak him auld Jock Grieve—
  " Whae's this that brings the fraye to me?"—
" It's I, Jamie Telfer o' the fair Dodhead,
  A harried man I trow I be.

" There's naething left in the fair Dodhead,
  But a greeting wife and bairnies three,
And sax poor ca's[2] stand in the sta',
  A' routing loud for their minnie."—[3]

" Alack a wae l" quo' auld Jock Grieve,
  " Alack ! my heart is sair for thee l

[1] The Coultart Cleugh is nearly opposite to Carlinrig, on the road
between Hawick and Mosspaul.
  [2] Ca's—Calves.—[3] Minnie—Mother.

For I was married on the elder sister,
   And you on the youngest of a' the three."

Then he has ta'en out a bonny black,
   Was right weel fed with corn and hay,
And he's set Jamie Telfer on his back,
   To the Catslockhill to tak the fraye.

And whan he cam to the Catslockhill,
   He shouted loud, and cried weel hie,
Till out and spak him William's Wat—
   " O whae's this brings the fraye to me ?"—

" It's I, Jamie Telfer of the fair Dodhead,
   A harried man I think I be !
The Captain of Bewcastle has driven my gear;
   For God's sake rise, and succour me !"—

" Alas for wae l" quoth William's Wat,
   " Alack, for thee my heart is sair l
I never cam by the fair Dodhead,
   That ever I fand thy basket bare."—

He's set his twa sons on coal-black steeds,
   Himsell upon a freckled gray,
And they are on wi' Jamie Telfer,
   To Branksome Ha' to tak the fraye.

And when they cam to Branksome Ha',
   They shouted a' baith loud and hie,

Till up and spak him auld Buccleuch,
　　Said—" Whae's this brings the fraye to me ?"—

" It's I, Jamie Telfer o' the fair Dodhead,
　　And a harried man I think I be !
There's nought left in the fair Dodhead,
　　But a greeting wife and bairnies three."—

" Alack for wae !" quoth the gude auld lord,
　　" And ever my heart is wae for thee [1]
But fye gar cry on Willie, my son,
　　And see that he come to me speedilie !

" Gar warn the water,[1] braid and wide,
　　Gar warn it sune and hastilie [1]
They that winna ride for Telfer's kye,
　　Let them never look in the face o' me [1]

" Warn Wat o' Harden, and his sons,[2]
　　Wi' them will Borthwick Water ride ;
Warn Gaudilands, and Allanhaugh,
　　And Gilmanscleugh, and Commonside.

[1] The *water*, in the mountainous districts of Scotland, is often used to express the banks of the river, which are the only inhabitable parts of the country. *To raise the water*, therefore, was to alarm those who lived along its side.

[2] The estates, mentioned in this verse, belonged to families of the name of Scott, residing upon the waters of Borthwick and Teviot, near the castle of their Chief.

" Ride by the gate at Priesthaughswire,[1]
 And warn the Currors o' the Lee ;
As ye cum down the Hermitage Slack,
 Warn doughty Willie o' Gorrinberry."—

The Scotts they rade, the Scotts they ran,
 Sae starkly and sae steadilie !
And aye the ower-word o' the thrang
 Was—" Rise for Branksome readilie !"—

The gear was driven the Frostylee up,[2]
 Frae the Frostylee unto the plain,
Whan Willie has look'd his men before,
 And saw the kye right fast drivand.

" Whae drives thir kye ?" 'gan Willie say,
 " To make an outspeckle[3] o' me ?"—
" It's I, the Captain o' Bewcastle, Willie ;
 I winna layne my name for thee."—

" O will ye let Telfer's kye gae back ?
 Or will ye do aught for regard o' me ?

[1] The pursuers seem to have taken the road through the hills of Liddesdale, in order to collect forces, and intercept the forayers at the passage of the Liddel, on their return to Bewcastle. The Ritterford and Kershope-ford, after-mentioned, are noted fords on the river Liddel.

[2] The Frostylee is a brook, which joins the Teviot, near Mosspaul.

[3] *Outspeckle*—Laughing-stock.

Or, by the faith of my body," quo' Willie Scott,
 " I'se ware my dame's cauf skin on thee!"

" I winna let the kye gae back,
   Neither for thy love, nor yet thy fear;
But I will drive Jamie Telfer's kye,
   In spite of every Scott that's here."—

" Set on them, lads!" quo' Willie than;
   " Fye, lads, set on them cruellie!
For ere they win to the Ritterford,
   Mony a toom[1] saddle there sall be!"—

Then til't they gaed, wi' heart and hand,
   The blows fell thick as bickering hail;
And mony a horse ran masterless,
   And mony a comely cheek was pale.

But Willie was stricken ower the head,
   And thro' the knapscap[2] the sword has gane;
And Harden grat for very rage,[3]
   Whan Willie on the grund lay slane.

---

[1] *Toom*—Empty.   [2] *Knapscap*—Headpiece.
[3] Of this Border laird, commonly called *Auld Wat of Harden*,
tradition has preserved many anecdotes. He was married to Mary
Scott, celebrated in song by the title of the Flower of Yarrow.
By their marriage-contract, the father-in-law, Philip Scott of Dryhope, was to find Harden in horse meat, and man's meat, at his
Tower of Dryhope, for a year and a day; but five barons pledge
themselves, that, at the expiry of that period, the son-in-law should

But he's ta'en aff his gude steel cap,
 And thrice he's waved it in the air—
The Dinlay[1] snaw was ne'er mair white
 Nor the lyart locks of Harden's hair.

" Revenge ! revenge !" auld Wat 'gan cry;
 " Fye, lads, lay on them cruellie !
We'll ne'er see Tiviotside again,
 Or Willie's death revenged sall be."—[2]

remove, without attempting to continue in possession by force ! A
notary-public signed for all the parties to the deed, none of whom
could write their names. The original is still in the charter-room
of the present Mr Scott of Harden. By the Flower of Yarrow
the Laird of Harden had six sons; five of whom survived him, and
founded the families of Harden, (now extinct,) Highchesters, (now
representing Harden,) Reaburn, Wool, and Synton. The sixth
son was slain at a fray, in a hunting-match, by the Scotts of Gilmanscleugh. His brothers flew to arms ; but the old laird secured
them in the dungeon of his tower, hurried to Edinburgh, stated
the crime, and obtained a gift of the lands of the offenders from the
Crown. He returned to Harden with equal speed, released his
sons, and showed them the charter. " To horse, lads !" cried the
savage warrior, " and let us take possession ! The lands of Gilmanscleugh are well worth a dead son." The property thus obtained continued in the family till the beginning of last century,
when it was sold, by John Scott of Harden, to Ann, Duchess of
Buccleuch. A beautiful ballad, founded on this tradition, occurs
in the Mountain Bard, a collection of legendary poetry, by Mr
James Hogg.

[1] *The Dinlay*—is a mountain in Liddesdale.

[2] [Nothing can be more striking than the picture of old Harden,
in the fight for Jamie Telfer's cattle.—*Edin. Rev.*]

O mony a horse ran masterless,
   The splinter'd lances flew on hie ;
But or they wan to the Kershope ford,
   The Scotts had gotten the victory.

John o' Brigham there was slane,[1]
   And John o' Barlow, as I heard say;
And thirty mae o' the Captain's men
   Lay bleeding on the grund that day.

The Captain was run through the thick of the thigh,
   And broken was his right leg bane ;
If he had lived this hundred years,
   He had never been loved by woman again.

" Hae back the kye !" the Captain said ;
   " Dear kye, I trow, to some they be !
For gin I suld live a hundred years,
   There will ne'er fair lady smile on me."—

Then word is gane to the Captain's bride,
   Even in the bower where that she lay,
That her lord was prisoner in enemy's land,
   Since into Tividale he had led the way.

---

[1] Perhaps one of the ancient family of Brougham, in Cumberland. The Editor has used some freedom with the original in the subsequent verse. The account of the Captain's disaster (*teste læva vulnerata*) is rather too *naïve* for literal publication.

" I wad lourd[1] have had a winding-sheet,
　　And helped to put it ower his head,
Ere he had been disgraced by the Border Scot,
　　Whan he ower Liddel his men did lead!"—

There was a wild gallant amang us a',
　　His name was Watty wi' the Wudspurs,[2]
Cried—" On for his house in Stanegirthside,[3]
　　If ony man will ride with us!"

When they cam to the Stanegirthside,
　　They dang wi' trees, and burst the door;
They loosed out a' the Captain's kye,
　　And set them forth our lads before.

There was an auld wyfe ayont the fire,
　　A wee bit o' the Captain's kin—
" Whae dar loose out the Captain's kye,
　　Or answer to him and his men?"—

" It's I, Watty Wudspurs, loose the kye,
　　I winna layne my name frae thee!
And I will loose out the Captain's kye,
　　In scorn of a' his men and he."—

　　[1] *Lourd*—Liefer; rather.
　　[2] *Wudspurs*—Hotspur, or Madspur.
　　[3] A house belonging to the Foresters, situated on the English side of the Liddel.

Whan they cam to the fair **Dodhead,**
    They were a wellcum sight to see!
For instead of his ain ten milk kye,
    Jamie Telfer has gotten thirty and three.

And he has paid the rescue shot,
    Baith wi' goud and white monie;
And at the burial o' Willie Scott,
    I wat was mony a weeping ee.[1]

[1] An article in the list of attempts upon England, fouled by the Commissioners at Berwick, in the year 1587, may relate to the subject of the foregoing ballad.

October, 1582.

Thomas Musgrave, deputy of Bewcastle, and the tenants, against	Walter Scott, Laird of Buckluth, and his complices; for	200 kine and oxen, 300 gait and sheep.

Introduction to the History of Westmoreland and Cumberland,
    p. 31.

THE

RAID OF THE REIDSWIRE.

THIS poem is published from a copy in the Bannatyne MS., in the handwriting of the Hon. Mr Carmichael, advocate. It first appeared in *Allan Ramsay's Evergreen*, but some liberties have been taken by him in transcribing it ; and, what is altogether unpardonable, the MS., which is itself rather inaccurate, has been interpolated to favour his readings ; of which there remain obvious marks.

The skirmish of the Reidswire happened upon the 7th of June, 1575, at one of the meetings held by the Wardens of the Marches, for arrangements necessary upon the Border. Sir John Carmichael, ancestor of the present Earl of Hyndford,[1] was the Scottish Warden, and Sir John Forster held that office on the English Middle March. In the course of the day, which was employed as usual in redressing wrongs, a bill, or indictment, at the instance of a Scottish complainer,

---

[1] The title of Hyndford is now extinct. 1830.

was fouled (*i. e.* found a true bill) against one **Farnstein,** a notorious English freebooter.   Forster alleged that he had fled from justice : Carmichael, considering this as a pretext to avoid making compensation for the felony, bade him " play fair !" to which the haughty English warden retorted, by some injurious expressions respecting Carmichael's family, and gave other open signs of resentment.   His retinue, chiefly men of Redes- dale and Tynedale, the most ferocious of the Eng- lish Borderers, glad of any pretext for a quarrel, dis- charged a flight of arrows among the Scots.   A warm conflict ensued, in which, Carmichael being beat down and made prisoner, success seemed at first to incline to the English side, till the Tynedale men, throwing them- selves too greedily upon the plunder, fell into disorder ; and a body of Jedburgh citizens arriving at that instant, the skirmish terminated in a complete victory on the part of the Scots, who took prisoners, the English warden, James Ogle, Cuthbert Collingwood, Francis Russell, son to the Earl of Bedford, and son-in-law to Forster, some of the Fenwicks, and several other Bor- der chiefs.   They were sent to the Earl of Morton, then Regent, who detained them at Dalkeith for some days, till the heat of their resentment was abated ; which prudent precaution prevented a war betwixt the two kingdoms.   He then dismissed them with great ex- pressions of regard ; and, to satisfy Queen Elizabeth,[1]

[1] Her ambassador at Edinburgh refused to lie in a bed of state, which had been provided for him, till this " *oudious fact* " had been enquired into.—MURDIN's *State Papers,* vol. ii. p. 282.

sent Carmichael to York, whence he was soon after honourably dismissed. The field of battle, called the Reidswire, is a part of the Carter Mountain, about ten miles from Jedburgh.—See, for these particulars, GODS CROFT, SPOTTISWOODE, and JOHNSTONE's *History.*

The Editor has adopted the modern spelling of the word Reidswire, to prevent the mistake in pronunciation which might be occasioned by the use of the Scottish *qu* for *w.* The MS. reads *Reidsquhair.* *Swair,* or *Swire,* signifies the descent of a hill; and the epithet *Red* is derived from the colour of the heath, or perhaps, from the Reid-water, which rises at no great distance.

·THE

RAID OF THE REIDSWIRE.

THE seventh of July, the snith to say,
    At the Reidswire the tryst was set;
Our wardens they affixed the day,
    And, as they promised, so they met.
    Alas! that day I'll ne'er forgett!
Was sure sae feard, and then sae faine—
    They came theare justice for to gett,
Will never green[1] to come again.

Carmichael[2] was our warden then,
    He caused the country to conveen;

---

[1] *Green*—Long.

[2] Sir John Carmichael was a favourite of the regent Norton, by whom he was appointed Warden of the Middle Marches, in preference to the Border Chieftains. With the like policy, the regent married Archibald Carmichael, the warden's brother, to the heiress of Edrom, in the Merse, much contrary to the inclination of the lady and her friends. In like manner he compelled another heiress, Jane Sleigh, of Cumlege, to marry Archibald, brother to Auchinleck of Auchinleck, one of his dependents. By such arbitrary practices, Norton meant to strengthen his authority on the Borders; instead of

And the Laird's Wat, that worthie man,[1]

which, he hastened his fall, by giving disgust to his kinsman the Earl of Angus, and his other friends, who had been established in the country for ages.—GODSCROFT, vol. ii. pp. 238, 246.   Sir John Carmichael, the warden, was murdered, 16th June, 1600, by a party of Borderers, at a place called Raesknows, near Lochmaben, whither he was going to hold a court of justice.   Two of the ring-leaders in the slaughter, Thomas Armstrong, called *Ringan's Tam*, and Adam Scott, called the *Pecket*, were tried at Edinburgh at the instance of Carmichael of Edrom.   They were condemned to have their right hands struck off, thereafter to be hanged, and their bodies gibbeted on the Borough Moor ; which sentence was executed 14th November, 1601.   " This *Pecket*," saith Birrel in his *Diary*, " was ane of the most notalrie thieffes that ever raid ;" he calls his name Steill, which appears, from the record, to be a mistake.   Four years afterwards, an Armstrong, called *Sandy of Rowanburn*, and several others of that tribe, were executed for this and other excesses.—*Books of Adjournal of these dates.*

[1] The Chief who led out the sirname of Scott upon this occasion was (saith Satchells) Walter Scott of Ancrum, a natural son of Walter of Buccleuch.   The Laird of Buccleuch was then a minor.   The ballad seems to have been popular in Satchell's days, for he quotes it literally.   He must, however, have been mistaken, in this particular ; for the family of Scott of Ancrum, in all our books of genealogy, deduce their descent from the Scotts of Bal-wearie, in Fife, whom they represent.   The first of this family, settled in Roxburghshire, is stated in *Douglas' Baronage* to have been Patrick Scott, who purchased the lands of Ancrum in the reign of James VI.   He therefore could not be the *Laird's Wat* of the ballad ; indeed, from the list of Border families in 1597, Kerr appears to have been proprietor of Ancrum at the date of the ballad.   It is plainly written in the MS. the *Laird's Wat*, i. e. the Laird's son Wat ; notwithstanding which, it has always hitherto been printed the *Laird Wat*.   If Douglas be accurate in his genealogy, the person meant must be the young laird of Buccleuch, afterwards distinguished for the surprise of Carlisle Castle.—See *Kinmont Willie*.   I am the more confirmed in this opinion, be-

Brought in that sirname weil beseen : [1]
The Armestranges, that aye hae been
A hardy house, but not a hail,[2]
The Elliots' honours to maintaine,
Brought down the lave[3] o' Liddesdale.

Then Tividale came to wi' spied ;
The Sheriffe brought the Douglas down,[4]

cause Kerr of Ancrum was at this time a fugitive, for slaying one
of the Rutherfords, and the tower of Ancrum given in keeping to
the Turnbulls, his hereditary enemies. His mother, however, a
daughter of Home of Wedderburn, contrived to turn out the Turnbulls, and possess herself of the place by surprise.—GODSCROFT,
vol. ii. p. 250.

[1] *Weil beseen*—Well appointed. The word occurs in *Morte
Arthur :* " And when Sir Percival saw this, he hied him thither,
and found the ship covered with silke, more blacker than any beare ;
and therein was a gentlewoman, of great beautie, and she was richly
beseene, that none might be better."

[2] This clan are here mentioned as not being hail, or whole, because they were outlawed or broken men.   Indeed, many of them
had become Englishmen, as the phrase then went. Accordingly we
find, from Patten, that forty of them, under the Laird of Mangertoun, joined Somerset, upon his expedition into Scotland.—PAT-
TEN, *in Dalyell's Fragments*, p. 1. There was an old alliance betwixt the Elliots and Armstrongs, here alluded to. For the enterprise of the Armstrongs, against their native country, when under
English assurance, see MURDIN's *State Papers*, vol. i. p. 43. From
which it appears, that, by command of Sir Ralph Evers, this clan
ravaged almost the whole West Border of Scotland.

[3] *Lave*—Remainder.

[4] Douglas of Cavers, hereditary Sheriff of Teviotdale, descended
from Black Archibald, who carried the standard of his father, the
Earl of Douglas, at the battle of Otterbourne.—*See the Ballad of
that name.*

Wi' Cranstane, Gladstain, good at need,[1]
    Baith Rewle water, and Hawick town.
Beanjeddart bauldly made him boun,
Wi' a' the Trumbills, stronge and stout;
    The Rutherfoords, with grit renown,
Convoy'd the town of Jedbrugh out.[2]

Of other clans I cannot tell,
    Because our warning was not wide—
Be this our folks hae ta'en the fell,
    And planted down palliones,[3] there to bide,
We looked down the other side,
And saw come breasting ower the brae,
    Wi' Sir John Forster for their guyde,[4]
Full fifteen hundred men and mae.

---

[1] Cranstoun of that ilk, ancestor to Lord Cranstoun; and Gladstain of Gladstains.

[2] These were ancient and powerful clans, residing chiefly upon the river Jed. Hence, they naturally convoyed the town of Jedburgh out. Although notorious freebooters, they were specially patronised by Norton, who, by their means, endeavoured to counterpoise the power of Buccleuch and Ferniherst, during the civil wars attached to the Queen's faction. The following fragment of an old ballad is quoted in a letter from an aged gentleman of this name, residing at New York, to a friend in Scotland:

    "Bauld Rutherfurd, he was fou stout,
    Wi' a' his nine sons him round about;
    He led the town o' Jedburgh out,
    All bravely fought that day."

[3] *Palliones*—Tents.

[4] Sir John Forster, or, more properly, Forrester, of Balmbrough Abbey, Warden of the Middle Marches in 1561, was deputy-gover-

It grieved him sair that day, I trow,
　　Wi' Sir George Hearoune of Schipsydehouse ;[1]
Because we were not men enow,
　　They counted us not worth a louse.
　　Sir George was gentle, meek, and douse,
But *he* was hail and het as fire ;
　　And yet, for all his cracking crouse,[2]
He rewd the raid o' the Reidswire.

To deal with proud men is but pain ;
　　For either must ye fight or flee,
Or else no answer make again,
　　But play the beast, and let them be.
　　It was na wonder he was hie,
Had Tindaill, Reedsdaill,[3] at his hand,
　　Wi' Cukdaill, Gladsdaill on the lee,
And Hebsrime,[4] and Northumberland.

nor of Berwick, and governor of Balmborough Castle.　He made a
great figure on the Borders, and is said, on his monument at Balmborough church, to have possessed the office of Warden of the Mid
Marches for thirty-seven years ; indeed, if we can trust his successor, Carey, he retained the situation until he became rather unfit
for its active duties.　His family ended in the unfortunate Thomas
Forster, one of the generals of the Northumbrian insurgents in 1715 ;
and the estate, being forfeited, was purchased by his uncle, Lord
Crewe, and devised for the support of his magnificent charity.

[1] George Heron Miles of Chipchase Castle, probably the same who
was slain at the Reidswire, was Sheriff of Northumberland, 13th
Elizabeth.

[2] *Cracking crouse*—Talking big.

[3] These are districts, or dales, on the English Border.

[4] Mr George Ellis suggests, with great probability, that this is a

Yett was our meeting meek eneugh,
    Begun wi' merriment and mowes,
And at the brae, aboon the heugh,
    The clark sat down to call the rowes.[1]
    And some for kyne, and some for ewes,
Call'd in of Dandrie,[2] Hob, and Jock—
    We saw, come marching ower the knows,
Five hundred Fennicks[3] in a flock,—

With jack and speir, and bows all bent,
    And warlike weapons at their will :
Although we were na weel content,
    Yet, by my troth, we fear'd no ill. ·
    Some gaed to drink, and some stude still,
And some to cards and dice them sped ;
    Till on ane Farnstein they fyled a bill,
And he was fugitive and fled.

mistake, not for Hebburne, as the Editor stated in an earlier edition, but for Hexham, which, with its territory, formed a county independent of Northumberland, with which it is here ranked.

[1] *Rowes*—Rolls.

[2] [Dandrie, Dandy, and Dand, are corruptions of Andrew, familiar in the south of Scotland.]

[3] The Fenwicks; a powerful and numerous Northumberland clan. —The original seat of this ancient family was at Fenwick tower, long since ruinous; but, from the time of Henry IV., their principal mansion was Wallington. Sir John Fenwick, attainted and executed for treason in the reign of William III., represented the chieftain of this clan.

Carmichaell bade them speik out plainlie,
    And cloke no cause for ill nor good ;
The other, answering him as vainlie,
    Began to reckon kin and blood :
He raise,[1] and raxed him where he stood,
And bade him match him with his marrows ;
    Then Tindaill heard them reasun rude,
And they loot off a flight of arrows.[2]

Then was there nought but bow and speir,
    And every man pull'd out a brand ;

[1] *Raise*—Rose.   *Raxed him*—Stretched himself up.   *Marrows*—Equals.

[2] [" I have often thought, a fine subject for a Border painting occurs in the old ballad, called the Raid of the Reidswire, where the Wardens on either side having met on a day of truce, their armed followers, and the various tribes, mingled in a friendly manner on each side, till, from some accidental dispute, words grew high between the Wardens. Mutual insult followed. The English chief addressing the Scottish—

    ' Raise and rax'd him where he stood,
        And bid him match him with his marrows.
    Then Tynedale heard them reason rude,
        And they let fly a flight of arrows.'

The two angry chieftains, especially Forster, drawing himself up in his pride and scorn, would make a good group, backed by the Tynedale men, bending and drawing their bows; on the sides you might have a group busied in their game, whom the alarm had not yet reached; another half disturbed; another, where they were mounting their horses, and taking to their weapons, with the wild character peculiar to the country."—*Letter of Sir Walter Scott. December,* 1811.]

" A Schafton and a Fenwick " thare :
   Gude Symington was slain frae hand.
   The Scotsmen cried on other to stand,
Frae time they saw John Robson slain—
   What should they cry ? the King's command
Could cause no cowards turn again.

Up rose the laird to red the cumber,[1]
   Which would not be for all his boast ;—
What could we doe with sic a number—
   Fyve thousand men into a host ?
   Then Henry Purdie proved his cost,[2]
And very narrowlie had mischief'd him,
   And there we had our warden lost,
Wert not the grit God he relieved him.

Another throw the breiks him bair,
   Whill flatlies to the ground he fell :
Than thought I weel we had lost him there,
   Into my stomack it struck a knell !
   Yet up he raise, the treuth to tell ye,
And laid about him dints full dour ;
   His horsemen they raid sturdily,
And stude about him in the stoure.

Then raise the slogan with ane shout—
   " Fy, Tindaill, to it ! Jedburgh's here !"[3]

[1] *Red the cumber*—Quell the tumult.
[2] *Cost*—Signifies loss or risk.
[3] The gathering word peculiar to a certain name, or set of people,

I trow he was not half sae stout,
But anis his stomach was asteir.[1]

was termed *slogan* or *slughorn,* and was always repeated at an onset, as well as on many other occasions, as appears from the following passage of an old author, whom this custom seems to have offended—for he complains " That, whereas, alweys, both in al tounes of war, and in al campes of armies, quietnes and stilnes without nois is principally in the night, after the watch is set, observed (I need not reason why.) Yet, our northern prikkers, the Borderers, notwithstanding, with great enormitie, (as thought me,) and not unlyke (to be playn) unto a masterless hounde houyling in a hie wey, when he hath lost him he wayted upon, sum hoopying, sum whistelyng, and most with crying, a *Berwyke!* a *Berwyke!* a *Fenwyke!* a *Fenwyke!* a *Bulmer!* a *Bulmer!* or so ootherwise as their captein's names wear, never linnde those troublous and dangerous noyses all the night long. They sayd they did it to fynd out their captein and fellowes ; but if the soldiours of our oother countries and sheres had used the same maner, in that case we shold have oftymes had the state of our campe more lyke the outrage of a dissolute huntyng, than the quiet of a wel ordied army."—PATTEN's *Account of Somerset's Expedition,* p. 76.—*Apud* DALYELL's *Fragments.* Honest Patten proceeds, with great prolixity, to prove, that this was a custom more honoured in the breach than in the observance ; and, like Fluellen, declares, " that such idle pribble-prabbles were contrary to all the good customs and disciplines of war." Nevertheless, the custom of crying the *slogan,* or *ensenzic,* is often alluded to in all our ancient histories and poems. It was usually the name of the clan, or place of rendezvous, or leader. In 1335, the English, led by Thomas of Rosslyne, and William Moubray, assaulted Aberdeen. The former was mortally wounded in the onset ; and, as his followers were pressing forward, shouting " *Rosslyne ! Rosslyne !*" " Cry *Moubray,*" said the expiring chieftian ; " *Rosslyne* is gone ! " The Highland clans had also their appropriate slogans. The Macdonalds cried *Frich,* (heather ;) the Macphersons, *Craig-Ubh ;* the Grants, *Craig-Elachie ;* and the Macfarlanes, *Loch-Sloy.*

[1] *But, &c.*—Till once his anger was set up.

With gun and genzie,[1] bow and speir,
Men might see mony a cracked crown !
But up amang the merchant geir,
They were as busy as we were down.

The swallow taill frae tackles flew,[2]
Five hundredth flain[3] into a flight.
But we had pestelets enew,
And shot among them as we might.
With help of God the game gaed right,
Fra time the foremost of them fell ;
Then ower the know, without goodnight,
They ran with mony a shout and yell.

But after they had turned backs,
Yet Tindail men they turn'd again,
And had not been the merchant packs,[4]

[1] *Genzie*—Engine of war.
[2] The Scots, on this occasion, seem to have had chiefly fire-arms ; the English retaining still their partiality for their ancient weapon, the longbow. It also appears, by a letter from the Duke of Norfolk to Cecil, that the English Borderers were unskilful in fire-arms, or, as he says, " our countrymen be not so commyng with shots as I woolde wishe."—See MURDIN's *State Papers*, vol. i. p. 319.
[3] *Flain*—Arrows ; hitherto absurdly printed *slain*.
[4] The ballad-maker here ascribes the victory to the real cause ; for the English Borderers dispersing to plunder the merchandise, gave the opposite party time to recover from their surprise. It seems to have been usual for travelling merchants to attend Border meetings, although one would have thought the kind of company usually assembled there might have deterred them.

There had been mae of Scotland slain.
But, Jesu! if the folks were fain
To put the bussing on their thies ;
And so they fled, wi' a' their main,
Down ower the brae, like clogged bees.

Sir Francis Russell[1] ta'en was there,
    And hurt, as we hear men rehearse ;
Proud Wallinton[2] was wounded sair,
    Albeit he be a Fennick fierce.
But if ye wald a souldier search,
Among them a' were ta'en that night,
Was nane sae wordie to put in verse,
As Collingwood,[3] that courteous knight.

---

[1] This gentleman was son to the Earl of Bedford, and Warden
of the East Marches.   He was, at this time, chamberlain of Berwick.   He was afterwards killed in a fray of a similar nature, at a
Border meeting between the same Sir John Forster, (father-in-law
to Russell) and Thomas Ker of Fairnihurst, A. D. 1585.

[2] Fenwick of Wallington, a powerful Northumbrian chief.

[3] Sir Cuthbert Collingwood of Esslington, Sheriff of Northumberland, the 10th and 20th of Elizabeth.   [The late gallant Ad-
miral Lord Collingwood was of this family.]   Besides these gentlemen, James Ogle, and many other Northumbrians of note, were
made prisoners.   Sir George Heron, of Chipchase and Ford, was
slain, to the great regret of both parties, being a man highly esteemed by the Scots as well as the English.   When the prisoners
were brought to Morton, at Dalkeith, and among other presents,
received from him some Scottish falcons, one of his train observed,
that the English were nobly treated, since they got live *hawks* for
dead *herons*.—GODSCROFT.

Young Henry Schafton,[1] he is hurt ;
  A souldier shot him wi' a bow ;
Scotland has cause to mak great sturt,
  For laiming of the Laird of Mow.[2]
The Laird's Wat did weel indeed ;
  His friends stood stoutlie by himsell,
With little Gladstain, gude in need,
For Gretein[3] kend na gude be ill.

The Sheriffe wanted not gude will,
  Howbeit he might not fight so fast ;
Beanjeddart, Hundlie, and Hunthill,[4]
  Three, on they laid weel at the last.

[1] The Shaftoes are an ancient family settled at Bavington, in Northumberland, since the time of Edward I. ; of which Sir Cuthbert Shaftoe, Sheriff of Northumberl⁊ ꝺd in 1795, is the present representative.

[2] An ancient family on the Borders. The lands of Mowe are situated upon the river Bowmont, in Roxburghshire. The family is now represented by William ⱱolle, Esq. of ⱱains, who has restored the ancient spelling of the name. The Laird of ⱱowe here mentioned, was the only gentleman of note killed in the skirmish on the Scottish side.

[3] Graden, a family of Kers.

[4] Douglas of Beanjeddart, an ancient branch of the house of Cavers, possessing property near the junction of the Jed and Teviot. *Hundlie.*—Rutherford of Hundlie, or Hundalee, situated on the Jed above Jedburgh. *Hunthill.*—The old tower of Hunthill was situated about a mile above Jedburgh. It was the patrimony of an ancient family of Rutherfords. I suppose the person, here meant, to be the same who is renowned in tradition by the name of the *Cock of Hunthill.* His sons were executed for ⱱarch-treason, or Border-theft, along with the Lairds of Corbet, Greenhead, and Overton, A. D. 1588.—JOHNSTONE's *History,* p. 129.

Except the horsemen of the guard,
If I could put men to availe,
  None stoutlier stood out for their laird,
Nor did the lads of Liddisdail.

But little harness had we there ;
  But auld Badreule[1] had on a jack,
And did right weel, I you declare,
  With all his Trumbills at his back.
Gude Edderstane[2] was not to lack,
Nor Kirktoun, Newton, noble men ![3]

---

[1] Sir Andrew Turnbull of Bedrule, upon Rule Water. This old
laird was so notorious a thief, that the principal gentlemen of the
clans of Hume and Kerr refused to sign a bond of alliance, to
which he, with the Turnbulls and Rutherfords, was a party ; alleging that their proposed allies had stolen Hume of Wedderburn's
cattle. The authority of Norton, however, compelled them to digest the affront. The debate (and a curious one it is) may be seen
at length in GODSCROFT, vol. i. p. 221. The Rutherfords became
more lawless after having been deprived of the countenance of the
court, for slaying the nephew of Forman, Archbishop of St Andrews, who had attempted to carry off the heiress of Rutherford.
This lady was afterwards married to James Stuart of Traquair, son
to James, Earl of Buchan, according to a papal bull, dated 9th November, 1504. By this lady a great estate in Teviotdale fell to
the family of Traquair, which was sold by James, Earl of Traquair, Lord High-Treasurer of Scotland, in consequence of the pecuniary difficulties to which he was reduced, by his loyal exertions
in favour of Charles I.

[2] An ancient family of Rutherfords ; I believe, indeed, the most
ancient now extant. The family is represented by John Rutherford, Esq. of Edgerstane. His seat is about three miles distant
from the field of battle.

[3] *Kirktown.*—The parish of Kirktoun belonged, I believe, about

Thir's all the specials I of speake,
By others that I could not ken.[1]

Who did invent that day of play,
We need not fear to find him soon;
For Sir John Forster, I dare well say,
Made us this noisome afternoon.
Not that I speak preccislie out,
That he supposed it would be perril;
But pride, and breaking out of feuid,
Garr'd Tindaill lads begin the quarrel.[2]

this time, to a branch of the Cavers family; but Kirkton of Stewart-field is mentioned in the list of Border clans in 1597. *Newton.*—This is probably Grinyslaw of Little Newton, mentioned in the said roll of Border clans.

[1] *Thir's*—These are. *By*—Besides.

[2] In addition to what has been said of the ferocity of the Reeds-dale and Tynedale men, may be noticed a by-law of the incor-porated Merchant-adventurers of Newcastle, in 1564, which, al-leging evil repute of these districts for thefts and felonies, enacts, that no apprentices shall be taken " proceeding from such leude and wicked progenitors." This law, though in desuetude, subsisted until 1771.

KINMONT WILLIE.

IN the following rude strains, our forefathers comme-morated one of the last and most gallant achievements performed upon the Border.   The Editor, in place of the extract from Bishop Spottiswoode's History of the Church, is enabled, from a manuscript of the period, the property of Mr Campbell of Shawfield, to give a more minute detail of this celebrated exploit.   The MS. contains many curious articles relating to the High-lands and Borders, arranged in a miscellaneous order. They appear to have been a collection made for the purpose of assisting Archbishop Spottiswoode in com-piling his work.

" *Relation of the Maner of Surprizcing of the Castell of Cair-lell, by the Lord of Buccleugh, in the later End of Q. Eli-zabeth's Reigne.   (Anno 1596.)*

"   THAIR was for the tyme Warden of the West Marches of England, for the Queene, the Lord Scroope;[1]

---

[1] [Thomas, Lord Scroope, of Bolton, was appointed Warden of these Marches in 1596.]

and for the King, the Lord of Buccleugh had the charge of Liddisdail; the deputies of these two officers having met at a day at trewis, as the custome was, (when either the Wardens, in regard of their princes service, or thair ain private distractionnes, could not meitt thameselffis, or the matteris to be redressit was bot ordinarie,) the place of thair meiting was at the Dayholme of Kershoup, quhaire a burne divides England from Scotland, and Liddisdaill from Bewcastle. Thair met for the Lord of Buccleugh, Robert Scott of Hanyug; and for the Lord Scroope, Mr Salkeld, a gentleman of that west wardanrie, that was his deputie for the tyme. Thair was mutuall truce taken, and intimation be sound of trumpett, and proclamation in thair Majesties names, to the trouppes on both sydes, befoir thair meiting, as the custome was: wherefore the meitings war called dayes of trewis, seeing thairthrow pairties on baithe sydes, that otherwise were under deidlie feid and quarrell, did usuallie, in peace and assurance, meit and doe thair busines, one besyde another, and conversed mutuallie and in assurance with such as they had occasion withall; upon the truce taken, the officers or deputies keipt thair meitting, made mutuall redress of such wrongs as had occurred before that tyme, and sunderit in veric good termes, ether partie returning homewards. Be the way it is to be remembered, that the tenor of such trewis as usuallie were taken betuixt the wardaines or thair deputies in the princes names buir, That upon paine of death presently to be execu

ted, all persones whatsoever that came to these meitings, sould be saife fra any proceiding or present occasioun, from the tyme of meiting of the wardens or thair
deputies, till the nixt day at the sun rysing; within
such space it wes presupposed that every persone that
came thair might be returned to thair houses; for other
wayes, where at theiff meitings ther war usuallie manie
pairties that war under feid and quarrall ane with another, the strongest syde might have taken advantage
of the weakness of the other, if the grudge had beine
betuixt the wardanes; or the strongest of the particular pairties of ether syde might, seing the weiknes of
the other there, in his returne homewards towards his
hous, fra the great troupe had sunderit, upon any intelligence, have taken the occasioun of revenge by
putting himselfe in his way. Now this treuce, being
thus wayes parted, and the busines done by the deputies that they met for, there was one called Williame
Armstronge of Kyninmouth, Scottisman, and a Borderer, in companie with the Scottish deputie, whom
against some of the English had quarell, as was alled-
geit, who, being sunderit from that deputie, and ryding
homewards, his way coming down Liddisdaill, the
which was at that pairt dyvidit from England by a river
easilie passable, called Liddell, and the Inglish deputie
haiding his way down the Inglish syde, and within a
myle of the utheris way, those who had the quarrell
against hym, (as afterwards the deputie of England for
his excuse did pretend,) seing him ryding on his ways
bot with three or four in companie, and lyming for na

harme, as that day fell, they brake a chace of more than
200 men out of the English trayne, chases the said Wm.
of Kininmonth more than 3 or 4 myles, comes to him,
and takes him prisoner, brings him back to the deputie,
thinking to doe good service by the seizing of such an
offendar, causit brek the truce, himself caried him away
with him prisoner to the castell of Cairlell. Whereupon, seing the samyne was done to the plaine breache
of the trewes, the Lord of Buccleugh, as the Kingis
officer, did wreat unto Mr Salkeld, the deputie of
England, immediatlie in absence of the Lord Scroop,
for the redress thairof. Mr Salkeld by his anser did
excuise himselfe, and refer the maitter to the Lord
Scroop, warden, who for the tyme was at a hous of his
owin in the countrey. The Lord Scroop thereupon
was written unto in the samyne sence by the Lord of
Buccleugh, to wit, for the setting the prisoner at liber-
tie without condition or bond, seing he was unlawfullie taken, and consequentlie to the tuitch of the king.
It was ansered, that he could do nothing ther anent,
seing it was so hapned, and be reason that the prisoner
was such a malefactor, without the privitie of the
Queue and counsall of England : so as his anser tending to the delay of the matter, the Lord Buccleugh
being loath to informe the Kinge of the maitter least
the samyn might have bred some mistaking betueen
the princes, he made tryell for Mr Robert Bowis, then
resident ambassador for the Queen in Scotland ; who,
upon his desire and informatioun, wrote furiouslie unto

the Lord Scroope for the redress of the maitter, and
that the maitter sould come to no farther hearing. Nothing was done nor anserit till a purpose nevertheless,
nether upon the Kingis his masters awin instance towards the warden, by the ambassador of England first,
and afterwards to the Queen of England by his Majesties selfe. Whereupon the Lord of Buccleugh, being
the Kings officer, and fynding his Majesties honour
tuitched so apparentlie to the world, he did resolve him
selfe to seik the reliefe of the prisoner by the meanes
whereby it was performeit, and that with such foirsight
and regaird as could be, that through any rigorous circumstance of the actioun, in regaird of the place quhairin
he was keipit, the samyne sould breid no greater jarr
betuixt the princes then mearlie that which was to grow
from the simple reliefe of a prisoner unlawfullie taken.
And for such purpose the Lord of Buccleugh, upon
intelligence that the Castle of Cairleill, where the prisoner was keept, was surpriseable, and of the meanes,
by sending some persons of trust to view a postern gaitt,
and to measure the height of the wall very closely, he
did immediately draw togither 200 horse, assured the
place of meeting ane hour before sunset at the toure of
Mortoune, the which is 10 myles from Cairleill, and
upon the water of Sark, in the Debateable Land, quhair
he had preparatioun of ledders for scaleing the castle
wall, and other instruments of iron for breking through
the wall and foirceing of gaites, if neid had beine. The
troupe being assembled at the place, he marcheth for-

wards, and entreth English ground within six miles of Cairleill, and passeth the water of Esk, quhair the Grahames did inhabite, at the falling of the night. Fra he entred English ground, the order was thus : ther was sent some few horsmen before, all the way, to dis-cover, and they were seconded by 40 or 50 horse in case of any encounter ; there was nixt them the led-ders carrying two and two upon a horse, and horses carying the other instruments mentionate befoir ; and, last of all, himselfe with the reste of the troupe. He marched on in this order, and passeth the water of Eden about two hours before day, at the Stoniebank beneath Cairleill brig, the water being at the tyme, through raines that had fallen, weill thick ; he comes to the Sacray, a plaine place under the toune and cas-tell, and halts upon the syde of a litle water or burne that they call Caday. There he makes about 80 men to light from their horses, took the ledders to be set to the wall, and assayes, whilst the sentinels warns the top of the wall above thame, looking over, and crying and speaking ane to another ; but that it hapened to fall to be very dark in the hindnight, and a litle mistie. The ledders proved too short thro' the error of thame quha had bene sent to measure the wall, and could not reach the top of the wall ; and then order was given to make use of the other instruments that were caried, for opening the wall a little, hard by the posterne, the which being set in the way, the Lord of Buccleugh seing the mater was likelie to succeed well, and that no

discoverie was, did retier himselfe for the suretie of
thame that he had set on the castell against the force-
ing of the toun, and so pat himselfe and the horsemen
betwixt the posterne of the castell and the nixt port of
the toune, upon the plaine field, to assure the retreat of
his awin from the castell againe, wha were sent also in
such competent number as was knowne to be able to
master thame that was within, upon their entrie ; quha
did thereupon also correspond upon the first sound of
the trumpet, with a cry and noyse, the more to confirme
his awne that ware gone upon the castell, and to terrifie
both castell and toune by ane imaginatioun of a greater
force.   They enter the castell, the first of thame single,
by the overture that was made, and than brake oppen
immediatelie the posterne with such instruments as was
fitt to mak passage to the greater number.   Thair did
occur to theme, at their firste entrie, allannerlie the
watchmen or sentinells, and some others after upon the
alarm, with the weapons they had. Bot after they were
put back and scattered, the rest that was within doors
heiring the noyse of the trumpet within, and that the
castell was entered, and the noyse of others without,
both the Lord Scroope himselfe and his deputy Salkeld
being thair with the garrisone and his awin retinew,
did keip thamselffis close.   The prisoner was taken out
of the hous quhair he was keiped, the which was knowne
to the Lord of Buccleuch, his sending a woman upon
pretext the day befoir to visite the prisoner, quha re-
porting quhat place he was keiped in, ther lacked not

persones enough thaire that knew all the rewmes thaire,
and so went directlie after the rencounter with the
watchmen, and sum other with them that came to the
alarum to the place, and brought him furth, and so be
the posterne gat away ; some other prisoners were
brought out that were taken in the rancounter, the
which were presentlie returned into the castell againe
by the Lord of Buccleugh, and any uther spoylle or
butting also hinderit, that not so much as any uther
doore that was opin within the castell was entered but
that qubair the prisoner was, the which was broken up ;
nor uther that was shut so much as knocket at, tho'
they that enterit might have taken prisoners the warden and all the prisoners that was there, and made prey
of the haill guids, seing they war maisters of the castell ; such was the reguard of the Lord of Buccleughe,
and the strict order that he gave, being present himselfe, that he walde not have any circumstance to fall
out in that action, in sua farr as it could have bene
eschewed, that could have given the least cause of
offence either to the King his master or to the late
Queen. By which bringing furth of the prisoner the
toun and castell was in a great fear and alarum, and
was a putting of thameselffis in armes; drums war
beatting, belles ringing, and bealles put on the top of
the castell to warne the countrie. The day was brok-
kin, and so the interpryse having so weill succeidit, the
Lord of Buccleugh, after that these [that] went upon
the castell, and the prisoner, were reteired and horsed,

marched close by the Sarkage againe to the river at the
Stainiebank ; where upon the alarum in the castell and
toune, some were assembled in the farre syde in the
passage ; and so having to that tyme reteired himselfe
close and without any noyse from the castell, he causit
sound up his trumpet befoir he tuik the river, it being
both mistie and dark, though the day was brokin, to
the end both to encourage his owne, and to let thame
that war abyding him upon the passage know that he
luikit for and was [ready] to receave any charge that
they sould offer him ; quhairupon they made choyse to
luik to him and give him way, and not adventure upon
so doubtfull ane event with him, wha behoved to reteire
him homewards, and not living thaire, if he could
choyse, after such ane useage of his hoist.   So having
past the river, the day began to grow light, and he did
reteire himselfe in order throw the Grahames of Esk
and Levin, and came back to Scottis ground at about
two hours after sunrysing, and so homewards."

The consequences of the enterprise are thus mentioned by Spottiswoode :—

" This fell out the 13th of April, 1596. The Queen
of England, having notice sent her of what was done,
stormed not a little. One of her chief castles surprised,
a prisoner taken forth of the hands of the warden, and
carried away, so far within England, she esteemed a
great affront. The lieger, [1] Mr Bowes, in a frequent

---

[1] *Lieger*—Ambassador.

convention kept at Edinburgh, the 22d of May, did, as he was charged, in a long oration, aggravate the hein ousness of the fact, concluding that peace could not longer continue betwixt the two realms, unless Baclcuch were delivered in England, to be punished at the Queen's pleasure. Baclcuch compearing, and charged with the fact, made answer,—' That he went not into England with intention to assault any of the Queen's houses, or to do wrong to any of her subjects, but only to relieve a subject of Scotland unlawfully taken, and more un- lawfully detained ; that, in the time of a general assu- rance, in a day of truce, he was taken prisoner against all order, neither did he attempt his relief till redress was refused ; and that he had carried the business in such a moderate manner, as no hostility was committed, nor the least wrong offered to any within the castle ; yet was he content, according to the ancient treaties observed betwixt the two realms, when as mutual in juries were alleged, to be tried by the commissioners that it should please their Majesties to appoint, and submit himself to that which they should decern.'— The convention, esteeming the answer reasonable, did acquaint the ambassador therewith, and offered to send commissioners to the Borders, with all diligence, to treat with such as the Queen should be pleased to ap- point for her part.

" But she, not satisfied with the answer, refused to appoint any commissioners ; whereupon the council of England did renew the complaint in July thereafter ;

and the business being of new agitated, it was resolved
of as before, and that the same should be remitted to
the trial of commissioners ; the King protesting, ' that
he might, with great reason, crave the delivery of Lord
Scroope, for the injury committed by his deputy, it
being less favourable to take a prisoner, than relieve
him that is unlawfully taken ; yet, for the continuing
of peace, he would forbear to do it, and omit nothing,
on his part, that could be desired, either in equity, or
by the laws of friendship.'—The Borders, in the mean-
time, making daily incursions one upon another, filled
all their parts with trouble, the English being conti-
nually put to the worse ; neither were they made quiet,
till, for satisfying the Queen, the Laird of Bacleuch
was first committed in St Andrews, and afterwards
entered in England, where he remained not long "[1]—
SPOTTISWOODE's *History of the Church of Scotland,*
pp. 414, 416, *Ed.* 1677.

Scott of Satchells, in the extraordinary poetical performance, which he has been pleased to entitle *A History of the Name of Scott,* (published 1688,) dwells,
with great pleasure, upon this gallant achievement, at
which, it would seem, his father had been present. He

---

[1] The Bishop is, in this last particular, rather inaccurate. Buccleuch was indeed delivered into England, but this was done in
consequence of the judgment of commissioners of both nations, who
met at Berwick the same year. And his delivery took place, less
on account of the raid of Carlisle, than of a second exploit of the
same nature, to be noticed hereafter.

also mentions, that the Laird of Buccleuch employed
the services of the younger sons and brothers only of
his clan, lest the name should have been weakened by
the landed men incurring forfeiture. But he adds, that
three gentlemen of estate insisted upon attending their
chief, notwithstanding this prohibition. These were,
the Lairds of Harden and Commonside, and Sir Gilbert Elliot of the Stobbs, a relation of the Laird of
Buccleuch, and ancestor to the present Sir William
Elliot, Bart. In many things Satchells agrees with
the ballads current in his time, from which, in all probability, he derived most of his information as to past
events, and from which he sometimes pirates whole
verses, as noticed in the annotations upon the *Raid
of the Reidswire.* In the present instance, he mentions the prisoner's *large spurs,* (alluding to the fetters,)
and some other little incidents noticed in the ballad,
which were, therefore, probably well known in his days.

All contemporary historians unite in extolling the
deed itself as the most daring and well-conducted
achievement of that age. " *Audax facinus, cum mo-
dica manu, in urbe mœnibus et multitudine oppida-
norum munita, et callidæ audaciæ, vix ullo obsisti
modo potuit.*"—JOHNSTONI *Historia, Ed. Amstæl.
p.* 215. Birrel, in his gossiping way, says, the exploit was performed " with shouting and crying, and
sound of trumpet, puttand the said toun and countrie
in sic ane fray, that the like of sic ane wassaladge was
never done since the memory of man, no not in Wal-

lace dayis."—BIRREL's *Diary*, April 6, 1596. This good old citizen of Edinburgh also mentions another incident, which I think proper to insert here, both as relating to the personages mentioned in the following ballad, and as tending to show the light in which the men of the Border were regarded, even at this late period, by their fellow-subjects. The author is talking of the King's return to Edinburgh, after the disgrace which he had sustained there, during the riot excited by the seditious ministers, on December 17, 1596. Proclamation had been made, that the Earl of Mar should keep the West Port, Lord Seaton the Nether-Bow, and Buccleuch, with sundry others, the High Gate. " Upon the morn at this time, and befoir this day, there was ane grate rumour and word among the tounes-men, that the Kinges M. sould send in *Will Kinmonde, the common thieffe*, and so many south-lande men as sould spulyie the toun of Edinburgh. Upon the whilk, the haill merchants tuik their hail gear out of their buiths or chops, and transportit the same to the strongest hous that was in the toune, and remained in the said hous, thair, with thameselfis, thair servants, and luiking for nothing bot that thaye sould have been all spulyeit. Sic lyke the hail craftsmen and commons convenit themselfis, their best guidis, as it wer ten or twelve householdes in ane, whilk wes the strongest bous, and might be best kepit from spuilyeing or burning, with hagbut, pistolet, and other sic armour, as might best defend themselfis. Judge, gentil reader, giff this was playing." The fear of the Borderers being thus before the eyes of the contumacious citizens of Edinburgh, James obtained a quiet hearing for one of his favourite orisons, or harangues, and was finally enabled to prescribe terms to his fanatic metropolis. Good discipline was, however, maintained by the chiefs upon this occasion ; although the fears of the inhabitants were but too well grounded, considering what had happened in Stirling ten years before, when the Earl of Angus, attended by Home, Buccleuch, and other Border chieftains, marched thither to remove the Earl of Arran from the King's councils : the town was miserably pillaged by the Borderers, particularly by a party of Armstrongs, under this very Kinmont Willie, who not only made prey of horses and cattle, but even of the very iron grating of the windows.—JOHNSTONI *Historia*, p. 102, *Ed. Amstæl.*—MOYSE's *Memoirs*, p. 100.

The renown of Kinmont Willie is not surprising, since, in 1587, the apprehending that freebooter, and Robert Maxwell, natural brother to the Lord Maxwell, was the main, but unaccomplished, object of a royal expedition to Dumfries. *Rex Robertum Maxvallium .... et Gulielmum Armstrangum Kinmonthum latrociniis intestinis externisque famosum, conquiri jubet. Missi e ministerio regio qui per aspera loca vitabundos persequuntur, magnoque incommodo afficiunt. At illi latebris aut silvis se eripiunt.*" —JOHNSTONI *Historia*, p. 138. About this time, it is

possible that Kinmont Willie may have held some
connexion with the Maxwells, though afterwards a retainer to Buccleuch, the enemy of that tribe. At
least, the Editor finds, that, in a bond of manrent,
granted by Simon Elliot of Whytheuch, in Liddesdale,
to Lord Maxwell, styled therein Earl of Morton,
dated February 28, 1599, William Armstrong, called
Will of Kinmond, appears as a witness.—SYME'S
MSS. According to Satchells, this freebooter was
descended of Johne Armstrong of Gilnockie. (See
Ballad, p. 392 vol. i.)—*Est in juvencis, est et in
equis, patrum virtus.* In fact, his rapacity made his
very name proverbial. Mas James Melvine, in urging
reasons against subscribing the act of supremacy, in
1584, asks ironically, " Who shall take order with
vice and wickedness ? The court and bishops ? As
well as Martine Elliot, and Will of Kinmont, with
stealing upon the Borders !"—CALDERWOOD, p. 168.

This affair of Kinmont Willie was not the only occasion upon which the undaunted keeper of Liddesdale
gave offence to the haughty Elizabeth. For, even
before this business was settled, certain of the English
Borderers having invaded Liddesdale, and wasted the
country, the Laird of Buccleuch retaliated the injury
by a *raid* into England, in which he not only brought
off much spoil, but apprehended thirty-six of the Tyne
dale thieves, all of whom he put to death.—SPOTTIS
WOODE, p. 450. How highly the Queen of England's
resentment blazed on this occasion, may be judged from

the preface to her letter to Bowes, then her ambassador in Scotland. " I wonder how base-minded that King thinks me, that, with patience, I can digest this dishonourable * * * * * * Let him know, therefore, that I will have satisfaction, or else * * * * * * " These broken words of ire are inserted betwixt the subscription and the address of the letter.—RYMER, vol. xvi. p. 318. Indeed, so deadly was the resentment of the English, on account of the affronts put upon them by this formidable chieftain, that there seems at one time to have been a plan formed (not, as was alleged, without Elizabeth's privity) to assassinate Buccleuch.—RYMER, vol. xvi. p. 107. The matter was at length arranged by the commissioners of both nations in Berwick, by whom it was agreed that delinquents should be delivered up on both sides, and that the chiefs themselves should enter into ward in the opposite countries till these were given up, and pledges granted for the future maintenance of the quiet of the Borders. Buccleuch and Sir Robert Ker of Cessford (ancestor of the Duke of Roxburghe) appear to have struggled hard against complying with this regulation ; so much so, that it required all James's authority to bring to order these two powerful chiefs.—RYMER, vol. xvi. p. 322.—SPOTTISWOODE, p. 448.—CAREY'S *Memoirs*, p. 131, *et sequen.*—When at length they appeared, for the purpose of delivering themselves up to be warded at Berwick, an incident took place, which nearly occasioned a revival of the deadly feud which formerly subsisted between the Scotts and the Kers. Buccleuch had chosen, for his guardian, during his resi- dence in England, Sir William Selby, master of the ordnance at Berwick, and accordingly gave himself into his hands. Sir Robert Ker was about to do the same, when a pistol was discharged by one of his retinue, and the cry of treason was raised. Had not the Earl of Home been present, with a party of Mersemen, to preserve order a dreadful tumult would probably have ensued. As it was, the English commissioners returned in dismay to Berwick, much disposed to wreak their displeasure on Buccleuch ; and he, on his side, mortally offended with Cessford, by whose means, as he con- ceived, he had been placed in circumstances of so much danger. Sir Robert Ker, however, appeased all par- ties, by delivering himself up to ward in England ; on which occasion he magnanimously chose for his guar- dian Sir Robert Carey, Deputy-warden of the East Marches, notwithstanding various causes of animosity which existed betwixt them. The hospitality of Carey equalled the generous confidence of Cessford, and a firm friendship was the consequence.[1]   Buccleuch appears

---

[1] Such traits of generosity illuminate the dark period of which we treat.   Carey's conduct on this occasion almost atones for the cold and unfeeling policy with which he watched the closing mo- ments of his benefactress, Elizabeth, impatient till remorse and sorrow should extort her last sigh, that he might lay the foundation of his future favour with her successor, by carrying him the first tidings of her death.—CAREY's *Memoirs*, p, 172, *et sequen.*   It would appear that Sir Robert Ker was soon afterwards committed

to have remained in England from October, 1597, till February, 1598.—JOHNSTONI *Historia*, p. 231.— SPOTTISWOODE, *ut supra*. According to ancient family tradition, Buccleuch was presented to Elizabeth, who, with her usual rough and peremptory address, demanded of him, " how he dared to undertake an enterprise so desperate and presumptuous ?"—" What is it," answered the undaunted chieftain,—"what is it that a man dares not do ?" Elizabeth, struck with the reply, turned to a lord in waiting ; " With ten thousand such men,"

to the custody of the Archbishop of York ; for there is extant a letter from that prelate to the lord-treasurer, desiring instructions about the mode of keeping this noble hostage. " I understand," saith he, " that the gentleman is wise and valiant, but somewhat haughty here, and resolute. I would pray your lordship, that I may have directions whether he may not go with his keeper in my company, to sermons ; and whether he may not sometimes dine with the council, as the last hostages did ; and, thirdly, whether he may sometimes be brought to sitting to the common-hall, where he may see how careful her Majesty is that the poorest subject in her kingdom may have their right, and that her people seek remedy by law, and not by avenging themselves. Perhaps it may do him good as long as he liveth."—STRYPE's *Annals, ad annum* 1597. It would appear from this letter, that the treatment of the hostages was liberal ; though one can hardly suppress a smile at the zeal of the good bishop for the conversion of the Scottish chieftain to a more Christian mode of thinking than was common among the Borderers of that day. The date is February 25, 1597, which is somewhat difficult to reconcile with those given by the Scottish historians. Another letter follows, stating, that Sir Robert, having been used to open air, prayed for more liberty for his health's sake, " offering his word, which, it is said, he doth chiefly regard, that he would be true prisoner."—STRYPE, *ibid.*

said she, " our brother of Scotland might shake the firmest throne of Europe." Luckily, perhaps, for the murderess of Queen Mary, James's talents did not lie that way.

The articles, settled by the commissioners at Berwick, were highly favourable to the peace of the Border. They may be seen at large in the *Border Laws*, p. 103. By article sixth, all wardens and keepers are discharged from seeking reparation of injuries, in the ancient hostile mode of riding, or causing to ride, in warlike manner against the opposite March; and that under the highest penalty, unless authorized by a warrant under the hand of their Sovereign. The mention of the word *keeper* alludes obviously to the above-mentioned reprisals, made by Buccleuch, in the capacity of keeper of Liddesdale.

This ballad is preserved, by tradition, on the West Borders, but much mangled by reciters; so that some conjectural emendations have been absolutely necessary to render it intelligible. In particular, the *Eden* has been substituted for the *Eske*, p. 56, the latter name being inconsistent with geography.

KINMONT WILLIE.

NEVER BEFORE PUBLISHED.

———————

O HAVE ye na heard o' the fause Sakelde ?[1]
O have ye na heard o' the keen Lord Scroope ?

[1] The Salkeldes, or Sakeldes, were a powerful family in Cumberland, possessing, among other manors, that of Corby, before it came into the possession of the Howards, in the beginning of the seventeenth century. A strange stratagem was practised by an outlaw, called Jock Græme of the Peartree, upon Mr Salkelde, Sheriff of Cumberland; who is probably the person alluded to in the ballad, as the fact is stated to have happened late in Elizabeth's time. The brother of this freebooter was lying in Carlisle jail for execution, when Jock of the Peartree came riding past the gate of Corby Castle. A child of the sheriff was playing before the door, to whom the outlaw gave an apple, saying, "Master, will you ride?" The boy willingly consenting, Grame took him up before him, carried him into Scotland, and would never part with him, till he had his brother safe from the gallows. There is no historical ground for supposing, either that Salkelde, or any one else, lost his life in the raid of Carlisle.

How they hae ta'en bauld Kinmont Willie,[1]
  On Haribee to hang him up?[2]

Had Willie had but twenty men,
  But twenty men as stout as he,
Fause Sakelde had never the Kinmont ta'en,
  Wi' eight score in his cumpanie.

They band his legs beneath the steed,
  They tied his hands behind his back
They guarded him, fivesome on each side,
  And they brought him ower the Liddel-rack.[3]

They led him thro' the Liddel-rack
  And also thro' the Carlisle sands;
They brought him to Carlisle castell,
  To be at my Lord Scroope's commands.

" My hands are tied, but my tongue is free,
  And whae will dare this deed avow?
Or answer by the Border law?
  Or answer to the bauld Buccleuch?"——

[1] In the list of Border clans, 1597, Will of Kinmonth, with
Kyrstie Armestrange, and John Skynbanke, are mentioned as lead
ers of a band of Armstrongs called *Sandies Barnes,* inhabiting the
Debateable Land.
  [2] Haribee is the place of execution at Carlisle.
  [3] The Liddel-rack is a ford on the Liddel.

"Now haud thy tongue, thou rank reiver!
    There's never a Scot shall set thee free:
Before ye cross my castle yate,
    I trow ye shall take farewell o' me."

"Fear na ye that, my lord," quo' Willie:
    "By the faith o' my body, Lord Scroope," he said,
"I never yet lodged in a hostelrie,[1]
    But I paid my lawing[2] before I gaed."—

Now word is gane to the bauld Keeper,
    In Branksome Ha', where that he lay,
That Lord Scroope has ta'en the Kinmont Willie,.
    Between the hours of night and day.

He has ta'en the table wi' his hand,
    He garr'd the red wine sprıng on hie—
"Now Christ's curse on my head," he said,
    "But avenged of Lord Scroope I'll be!

"O is my basnet[3] a widow's curch?[4]
    Or my lance a wand of the willow-tree?
Or my arm a ladye's lilye hand,
    That an English lord should lightly[5] me!

"And have they ta'en him, Kinmont Willie,
    Against the truce of Border tide?

[1] *Hostelrie*—Inn.—[2] *Lawing*—Reckoning.—[3] *Basnet*—Helmet.
—[4] *Curch*—Coif.—[5] *Lightly*—Set light by.

And forgotten that the bauld Buccleuch
   Is Keeper here on the Scottish side?

" And have they e'en ta'en him, Kinmont Willie,
   Withouten either dread or fear?
And forgotten that the bauld Buccleuch
   Can back a steed, or shake a spear?

" O were there war between the lands,
   As well I wot that there is none,
I would slight Carlisle castell high,
   Though it were builded of marble stone.

" I would set that castell in a low,[1]
   And sloken it with English blood!
There's never a man in Cumberland,
   Should ken where Carlisle castell stood.

" But since nae war's between the lands,
   And there is peace, and peace should be;
I'll neither harm English lad or lass,
   And yet the Kinmont freed shall be!"

He has call'd him forty Marchmen bauld,
   I trow they were of his ain name,
Except Sir Gilbert Elliot, call'd
   The Laird of Stobs, I mean the same.

[1] *Low*—Flame.

He has call'd him forty Marchmen bauld,
    Were kinsmen to the bauld Buccleuch ;
With spur on heel, and splent on spauld,[1]
    And gleuves of green, and feathers blue.

There were five and five before them a',
    Wi' hunting-horns and bugles bright :
And five and five came wi' Buccleuch,
    Like warden's men, array'd for fight.

And five and five, like a mason gang,
    That carried the ladders lang and hie ;
And five and five, like broken men ;
    And so they reach'd the Woodhouselee.[2]

And as we cross'd the Bateable Land,
    When to the English side we held,
The first o' men that we met wi',
    Whae sould it be but fause Sakelde ?

" Where be ye gaun, ye hunters keen ?"
    Quo' fause Sakelde ; " come tell to me !"—
" We go to hunt an English stag,
    Has trespass'd on the Scots countrie."

" Where be ye gaun, ye marshal men ?"
    Quo' fause Sakelde ; " come tell me true !"—

[1] *Splent on spauld*—Armour on shoulder.
[2] Woodhouselee ; a house on the Border, belonging to Buccleuch.

" We go to catch a rank reiver,
    Has broken faith wi' the bauld Buccleuch."

" Where are ye gaun, ye mason lads,
    Wi' a' your ladders, lang and hie?"—
" We gang to herry a corbie's nest,
    That wons not far frae Woodhouselee."—

" Where be ye gaun, ye broken men?"
    Quo' fause Sakelde; " come tell to me!"—
Now Dickie of Dryhope led that band,
    And the nevir a word of lear[1] had he.

" Why trespass ye on the English side?
    Row-footed outlaws, stand!" quo' he;
The nevir a word had Dickie to say,
    Sae he thrust the lance through his fause bodie.

Then on we held for Carlisle toun,
    And at Staneshaw-bank the Eden we cross'd;
The water was great and meikle of spait,[2]
    But the nevir a horse nor man we lost.

And when we reach'd the Staneshaw-bank,
    The wind was rising loud and hie;
And there the Laird garr'd leave our steeds,
    For fear that they should stamp and nie.

[1] *Lear*—Lore.—[2] *Spait*—Flood.

And when we left the Staneshaw-bank,
 The wind began full loud to blaw;
But 'twas wind and weet, and fire and sleet,[1]
 When we came beneath the castle wa'.

We crept on knees, and held our breath,
 Till we placed the ladders against the wa';
And sae ready was Buccleuch himsell
 To mount the first before us a'.

He has ta'en the watchman by the throat,
 He flung him down upon the lead—
" Had there not been peace between our lands,
 Upon the other side thou hadst gaed!—

" Now sound out, trumpets!" quo' Buccleuch;
 " Let's waken Lord Scroope right merrilie!"—
Then loud the warden's trumpet blew—
 O wha dare meddle mi' me ?[2]

Then speedilie to wark we gaed,
 And raised the slogan ane and a',
And cut a hole through a sheet of lead,
 And so we wan to the castle ha'

They thought King James and a' his men
 Had won the house wi' bow and spear;

[1] [*Query*—" flyand (flying) sleet ?"]—[2] The name of a Border tune.

It was but twenty Scots and ten,
  That put a thousand in sic a stear [1]

Wi' coulters, and wi' forehammers,
  We garr'd the bars bang merrilie,
Until we came to the inner prison,
  Where Willie o' Kinmont he did lie.

And when we cam to the lower prison,
  Where Willie o' Kinmont he did lie—
" O sleep ye, wake ye, Kinmont Willie,
  Upon the morn that thou's to die?"—

" O I sleep saft,[2] and I wake aft ;
  It's lang since sleeping was fley'd[3] frae me !
Gie my service back to my wife and bairns,
  And a' gude fellows that spier[4] for me."—

Then Red Rowan has hente him up,
  The starkest man in Teviotdale—
" Abide, abide now, Red Rowan,
  Till of my Lord Scroope I take farewell.

" Farewell, farewell, my gude Lord Scroope !
  My gude Lord Scroope, farewell l" he cried—
" I'll pay you for my lodging maill,[5]
  When first we meet on the Border side."—

---

  [1] *Stear*—Stir.—[2] *Saft*—Light.—[3] *Fleyed*—Frightened.—
    [4] *Speir*—Inquire—[5] *Maill*—Rent.

Then shoulder high, with shout and cry,
    We bore him down the ladder lang ;
At every stride Red Rowan made,
    I wot the Kinmont's airns play'd clang [1]

" O mony a time," quo' Kinmont Willie,
    " I have ridden horse baith wild and wood ;
But a rougher beast than Red Rowan
    I ween my legs have ne'er bestrode.

" And mony a time," quo' Kinmont Willie,
    " I've prick'd a horse out oure the furs ;[1]
But since the day I back'd a steed,
    I never wore sic cumbrous spurs !"—[2]

We scarce had won the Staneshaw-bank,
    When a' the Carlisle bells were rung,
And a thousand men on horse and foot,
    Cam wi' the keen Lord Scroope along.

Buccleuch has turn'd to Eden Water,
    Even where it flow'd frae bank to brim,

[1] *Furs*—Furrows.

[2] [In many of the recitals, is a mixture of rough humour, which, like the characterising touches of Hogarth's pencil, gives an animation often attempted in vain by more polished writers. Of this, the ballad of Kinmont Willie affords many examples, especially where he is borne out of prison in irons on the shoulders of Red Rowan, the starkest man in Teviotdale.—STODDART, *Edinburgh Review*, *January*, 1803.]

And he has plunged in wi' a' his band,
    And safely swam them through the stream.

He turu'd him on the other side,
    And at Lord Scroope his glove flung he—
" If ye like na my visit in merry England,
    In fair Scotland come visit me !"

All sore astonish'd stood Lord Scroope,
    He stood as still as rock of stane ;
He scarcely dared to trew his eyes,
    When through the water they had gane.

" He is either himsell a devil frae hell,
    Or else his mother a witch maun be ;
I wadna have ridden that wan water
    For a' the gowd in Christentie."[1]

---

[1] [" A cottage on the road side, between Longtoun and Langholm, is still pointed out as the residence of the smith who was
employed to knock off Kinmont Willie's irons, after his escape.
Tradition preserves the account of the smith's daughter, then a
child, how there was a *sair clatter* at the door about daybreak,
and loud crying for the smith ; but her father not being on the alert,
Buccleuch himself thrust his lance thro' the window, which effectually bestirred him.   On looking out, the woman continued, she
saw, in the grey of the morning, more gentlemen than she had
ever before seen in one place, all on horseback, in armour, and
dripping wet—and that Kinmont Willie, who sat woman-fashion
behind one of them, was the biggest carle she ever saw—and there
was much merriment in the company."—Sir Walter Scott's MS.
Letters. 1826.]

DICK O' THE COW

This ballad, and the two which immediately follow it in the collection, were first published, 1784, in the *Hawick Museum*, a provincial miscellany, to which they were communicated by John Elliot, Esq. of Reidheugh, a gentleman well skilled in the antiquities of the Western Border, and to whose friendly assistance the Editor is indebted for many valuable communications.

These ballads are connected with each other, and appear to have been composed by the same author. The actors seem to have flourished, while Thomas Lord Scroope, of Bolton, was Warden of the West Marches of England, and governor of Carlisle castle ; which offices he acquired upon the death of his father, about 1590, and retained till the union of the crowns.

Dick of the Cow, from the privileged insolence which he assumes, seems to have been Lord Scroope's jester. In the preliminary dissertation, the reader will find the Border custom of assuming *nommes de guerre* particularly noticed. It is exemplified in the following ballad, where one Armstrong is called the *Laird's Jock, (i. e.* the laird's son Jock,) another *Fair Johnie,* a third *Billie Willie,* (brother Willie,) &c.   The *Laird's Jock,* son to the Laird of Mangertoun, appears, as one of the *men of name* in Liddesdale, in the list of the Border Clans, 1597.

Dick of the Cow is erroneously supposed to have been the same with one Ricardus Coldall, de Plumpton, a knight and celebrated warrior, who died in 1462, as appears from his epitaph in the church of Penrith. —NICHOLSON's *History of Westmoreland and Cumberland,* vol. ii. p. 408.

This ballad is very popular in Liddesdale ; and the reciter always adds, at the conclusion, that poor Dickie's cautious removal to Burgh under Stanemore, did not save him from the clutches of the Armstrongs ; for that, having fallen into their power several years after this exploit, he was put to an inhuman death. The ballad was well known in England so early as 1596.   An allusion to it likewise occurs in PARROT's *Laquei Ridiculosi,* or *Springes for Woodcocks;* London, 1613.

> " Owenus wondreth since he came to Wales,
>   What the desciiption of this isle should be,
> That nere had seen but mountains, hills, and dales,
>   Yet would he boast, and stand on pedigree,
> From Rice ap Richard, sprung from *Dick a Cow,*
> Be cod, was right gud gentleman, look ye now !"

Epigr. 76.

DICK O' THE COW.

Now Lid dis-dale has lain lang in,

Fal de ral, lal de ral, lal de ral la; There

Dick o' the Cow.

tether fat, They dow - na stir out o'er the sta', Fal

Bis.

lal de ral de raddy, Fal lal de ral la, Fal

lal de ral   la.

DICK O' THE COW

Now Liddesdale has layen lang in,
    There is na ryding there at a' ;
The horses are a' grown sae lither fat,
    They downa stir out o' the sta'.

Fair Johnie Armstrong to Willie did say—
    " Billie, a riding we will gae ;
England and us have been lang at feid ;
    Ablins we'll light on some bootie."—

Then they are come on to Hatton Ha' ;
    They rade that proper place about,
But the laird he was the wiser man,
    For he had left nae gear without.

For he had left nae gear to steal,
    Except sax sheep upon a lea :
Quo' Johnie—" I'd rather in England die,
    Ere thir sax sheep gae to Liddesdale wi' me.

" But how ca' they the man we last met,
    Billie, as we cam owre the know ?"—

" That same he is an innocent fule,
    And men they call him Dick o' the Cow."—

" That fule has three as good kye o' his ain,
    As there are in a' Cumberland, billie," quo' he :
" Betide me life, betide me death,
    These kye shall go to Liddesdale wi' me."—

Then they have come to the pure fule's house,
    And they hae broken his wa's sae wide ;
They have loosed out Dick o' the Cow's three kye,
    And ta'en three co'erlets frae his wife's bed.

Then on the morn when the day was light,
    The shouts and cries raise loud and hie ·
" O haud thy tongue, my wife," he says,
    And o' thy crying let me be !

" O haud thy tongue, my wife," he says,
    And o' thy crying let me be ;
And aye where thou hast hat ae cow,
    In gude suith I shall bring thee three."—

Now Dickie's gane to the gude Lord Scroope,
    And I wat a dreirie fule was he ;
" Now haud thy tongue, my fule," he says,
    " For I may not stand to jest wi' thee."—

" Shame fa' your jesting, my lord !" quo' Dickie,
    " For nae sic jesting grees wi' me ;

Liddesdale's been in my house last night,
  And they hae awa my three kye frae me.

" But I may nae langer in Cumberland dwell,
  To be your puir fule and your leal,
Unless you gie me leave, my lord,
  To gae to Liddesdale and steal."—

" I gie thee leave, my fule!" he says;
  " Thou speakest against my honour and me,
Unless thou gie me thy trowth and thy hand,
  Thou'lt steal frae nane but whae sta' frae thee."—

" There is my trowth, and my right hand!
  My head shall hang on Hairibee;
I'll near cross Carlisle sands again,
  If I steal frae a man but whae sta' frae me."—

Dickie's ta'en leave o' lord and master;
  I wat a merry fule war he!
He's bought a bridle an a pair o' new spurs,
  And packed them up in his breek thie.[1]

Then Dickie's come on to Pudding-burn house,[2]
  E'en as fast as he might dree;[3]

---

[1] The side pocket of his breeches.
[2] This was a house of strength held by the Armstrongs. The ruins at present form a sheep-fold on the farm of Reidsmoss, belonging to the Duke of Buccleuch.
[3] *Dree*—i. e. Endure.

Then Dickie's come on to Pudding-burn,
 Where there were thirty Armstrangs and three.

" O what's this come o' me now ?" quo' Dickie ;
 " What mickle wae is this ?" quo' he ;
" For here is but ae innocent fule,
 And there are thirty Armstrangs and three !"—

Yet he has come up to the fair ha' board,
 Sae weil he's become his courtesie !
" Weil may ye be, my gude Laird's Jock !
 But the deil bless a' your cumpanie.

" I'm come to plain o' your man, fair Johnie Armstrang,
 And syne o' his billie Willie," quo' he ;
" How they've been in my house last night,
 And they hae ta'en my three kye frae me."—

" Ha !" quo' fair Johnie Armstrang, "we will him hang."
 —" Na," quo' Willie, " we'll him slae."—
Then up and spak another young Armstrang,
 " We'll gae him his batts, and let him gae." 1—

But up and spak the gude Laird's Jock,
 The best falla in a' the cumpanie,
" Sit down thy ways a little while, Dickie,
 And a piece o' thy ain cow's hough I'll gie ye."—

---

1 *Gie him his batts and let him gae*—Dismiss him with a beating.

But Dickie's heart it grew sae grit,
    That the ne'er a bit o't he dought to eat—
Then he was aware of an auld peat-house,
    Where a' the night he thought for to sleep.

Then Dickie was aware of an auld peat-house,
    Where a' the night he thought for to lye—
And a' the prayers the puir fule pray'd,
    Were, "I wish I had amends for my gude three kye!"

It was then the use of Pudding-burn house,
    And the house of Mangerton,[1] all hail,
Them that cam na at the first ca',
    Gat nae mair meat till the neist meal.

The lads, that hungry and weary were,
    Abune the door-head they threw the key;
Dickie he took gude notice o' that,
    Says—" There will be a bootie for me."

Then Dickie has into the stable gane,
    Where there stood thirty horses and three;
He has tied them a' wi' St Mary's knot,
    A' these horses but barely three.[2]

[1] The Laird of Mangerton was chief of the clan Armstrong.

[2] Hamstringing a horse is termed, in the Border dialect, *tying him with St Mary's knot.* Dickie used this cruel expedient to prevent a pursuit. It appears from the narration, that the horses left unhurt, belonged to fair Johnie Armstrang, his brother Willie, and the Laird's Jock—of which Dickie carried off two, and left that

He has tied them a' wi' St Mary's knot,
   A' these horses but barely three;
He's loupen on ane, ta'en another in hand,
   And away as fast as he can hie.

But on the morn, 'when the day grew light,
   The shouts and cries raise loud and hie—
" Ah! whae has done this ?" quo' the gude Laird's Jock,
   " Tell me the truth and the verity l"—

"Whae has done this deed?" quo' the gude Laird's Jock;
   " See that to me ye dinna lie !"—
" Dickie has been in the stable last night,
   And has ta'en my brother's horse and mine frae me."—

" Ye wad ne'er be tauld," quo' the gude Laird's Jock;
   " Have ye not found my tales fu' leil?
Ye ne'er wad out o' England bide,
   Till crooked, and blind, and a' would steal."—

" But lend me thy bay," fair Johnie 'gan say;
   " There's nae horse loose in the stable save he;
And I'll either fetch Dick o' the Cow again,
   Or the day is come that he shall die."—

" To lend thee my bay l" the Laird's Jock 'gan say,
   " He's baith worth gowd and gude monie:

of the Laird's Jock, probably out of gratitude for the protection he
had afforded him on his arrival.

Dick o' the Cow has awa' twa horse :
    I wish na thou may make him three."—

He has ta'en the laird's jack on his back,
    A twa-handed sword to hang by his thie ;
He has ta'en a steil cap on his head,
    And galloped on to follow Dickie.

Dickie was na a mile frae aff the town,
    I wat a mile but barely three,
When he was o'erta'en by fair Johnie Armstrong,
    Hand for hand, on Cannobie lee.[1]

" Abide, abide, thou traitour thiefe !
    The day is come that thou maun die."—
Then Dickie look't ower his left shoulder,
    Said—" Johnie, hast thou nae mae in companie ?

" There is a preacher in our chapell,
    And a' the live-lang day teaches he ·
When day is gane and night is come,
    There's ne'er a word I mark but three.

" The first and second is—Faith and Conscience ;
    The third—Ne'er let a traitour free :
But, Johnie, what faith and conscience was thine,
    When thou took awa my three kye frae me ?

---

[1] A rising-ground on Cannobie, on the borders of Liddesdale.

" And when thou had ta'en awa my three kye,
   Thou thought in thy heart thou wast not weil sped,
Till thou sent thy billie Willie ower the know,
   To tak three coverlets off my wife's bed!"—

Then Johnie let a spear fa' laigh by his thie,
   Thought weel to hae slain the innocent, I trow;
But the powers above were mair than he,
   For he ran but the pure fule's jerkin through.

Together they ran, or ever they blan;[1]
   This was Dickie the fule and he!
Dickie could na win at him wi' the blade o' the sword,
   But fell'd him wi' the plummet under the ee.

Thus Dickie has fell'd fair Johnie Armstrong,
   The prettiest man in the south country—
" Gramercy!" then 'gan Dickie say,
   " I had but twa horse, thou hast made me three!"—

He's ta'en the steil jack aff Johnie's back,
   The twa-handed sword that hung low by his thie;
He's ta'en the steil cap aff his head—
   " Johnie, I'll tell my master I met wi' thee."—

When Johnie wakened out o' his dream,
   I wat a dreirie man was he:

[1] *Blan*—i. e. blew—breathed.

" And is thou gane ? Now, Dickie, than
    The shame and dule is left wi' me.

" And is thou gane ? Now, Dickie, than
    The deil gae in thy companie !
For if I should live these hundred years,
    I ne'er shall fight wi' a fule after thee."—

Then Dickie's come hame to the gude Lord Scroope,
    E'en as fast as he might hie ;
" Now, Dickie, I'll neither eat nor drink,
    Till hie hanged thou shalt be."—

" The shame speed the liars, my lord !" quo' Dickie ;
    " This was na the promise ye made to me !
For I'd ne'er gang to Liddesdale to steal,
    Had I not got my leave frae thee."—

" But what garr'd thee steal the Laird's Jock's horse ?
    And, limmer, what garr'd ye steal him ?" quo' he ;
" For lang thou mightst in Cumberland dwelt,
    Ere the Laird's Jock had stown frae thee."[1]—

---

[1] The commendation of the Laird's Jock's honesty seems but
indifferently founded ; for, in July, 1586, a bill was fouled against
him, Dick of Dryup, and others, by the deputy of Bewcastle, at a
warden-meeting, for 400 head of cattle taken in open foray from
the Drysike in Bewcastle : and in September, 1587, another complaint appears at the instance of one Andrew Rutlege of the Nook,
against the Laird's Jock, and his accomplices, for 50 kine and oxen,

" Indeed I wat ye lied, my lord!
  And e'en sae loud as I hear ye lie!

besides furniture, to the amount of 100 merks sterling.   See Bell's
MSS., as quoted in the *History of Cumberland and Westmoreland.*
In Sir Richard Maitland's poem against the thieves of Liddesdale,
he thus commemorates the Laird's Jock :—

> " They spuilye puir men of their pakis,
> They leif them nocht on bed nor bakis ;
> Baith hen and cok,
> With reil and rok,
> The *Lairdis Jock*
> All with him takis."

Those who plundered Dick had been bred up under an expert
teacher.   Tradition reports that the Laird's Jock survived to extreme old age, when he died in the following extraordinary manner.
A challenge had been given by an Englishman, named Forster, to
any Scottish Borderer, to fight him at a place called Kershope-
foot, exactly upon the Borders.   The Laird's Jock's only son accepted the defiance, and was armed by his father with his own two-
handed sword.   The old champion himself, though bed-ridden, insisted upon being present at the battle.   He was borne to the place
appointed, wrapped, it is said, in blankets, and placed upon a very
high stone to witness the conflict.   In the duel his son fell, treach-
erously slain, as the Scotch tradition affirms.   The old man gave
a loud yell of terror and despair when he saw his son slain and his
noble weapon won by an Englishman, and died as they bore him
home.   A venerable Border poet (though of these latter days) has
composed a poem on this romantic incident.   The stone on which
the Laird's Jock sat to behold the duel, was in existence till wan-
tonly destroyed a year or two since.   It was always called THE
LAIRD'S JOCK'S STONE. 1802. [The reader will find Sir Walter
Scott recurring to the fate of the Laird's Jock, in 1828. See
Waverley Novels, vol. xli, p. 377.]

I wan the horse frae fair Johnie Armstrang,
   Hand to hand, on Cannobie lee.

" There is the jack was on his back ;
   This twa-handed sword hung laigh by his thie,
And there's the steil cap was on his head ;
   I brought a' these tokens to let thee see."—

" If that be true thou to me tells,
   (And I think thou dares na tell a lie,)
I'll gie thee fifteen punds for the horse,
   Weil tauld on thy cloak lap shall be.

" I'll gie thee ane o' my best milk kye,
   To maintain thy wife and children three ;
And that may be as gude, I think,
   As ony twa o' thine wad be."—

" The shame speed the liars, my lord !" quo' Dickie
   " Trow ye aye to make a fule o' me ?
I'll either hae twenty punds for the gude horse,
   Or he's gae to Mortan fair wi' me."—

He's gi'en him twenty punds for the gude horse,
   A' in goud and gude monie ;
He's gi'en him ane o' his best milk kye,
   To maintain his wife and children three.

Then Dickie's come down thro' Carlisle toun,
   E'en as fast as he could drie :

The first o' men that he met wi',
  Was my Lord's brother, Bailiff Glozenburrie.

" Weil be ye met, my gude Ralph Scroope !"—
  " Welcome, my brother's fule !" quo' he ·
" Where didst thou get fair Johnie Armstrang's horse?"
  —" Where did I get him, but steal him," quo' he.

" But wilt thou sell me the bonny horse ?
  And, billie, wilt thou sell him to me ?" quo' he :—
" Ay ; if thou'lt tell me the monie on my cloak lap :
  For there's never ae penny I'll trust thee."—

" I'll gie thee ten punds for the gude horse,
  Weil tauld on thy cloak lap they shall be ;
And I'll gie thee ane o' the best milk kye,
  To maintain thy wife and children three."—

" The shame speed the liars, my lord !" quo' Dickie
  " Trow ye aye to make a fule o' me !
I'll either hae twenty punds for the gude horse,
  Or he's gae to Mortan fair wi' me."—

He's gi'en him twenty punds for the gude horse,
  Baith in goud and gude monie ;
He's gi'en him ane o' his milk kye,
  To maintain his wife and children three.

Then Dickie lap a loup fu' hie,
  And I wat a loud laugh laughed he—

" I wish the neck o' the third horse was broken,
  If ony of the twa were better than he !"—

Then Dickie's come hame to his wife again ;
  Judge ye how the puir fule had sped !
He has gi'en her twa score English punds,
  For the three auld coverlets ta'en aff her bed.

" And tak thee these twa as gude kye,
  I trow, as a' thy three might be ;
And yet here is a white-footed nagie,
  I trow he'll carry baith thee and me.

" But I may nae langer in Cumberland bide ,
  The Armstrangs they would hang me hie."—
So Dickie's ta'en leave at lord and master,
  And at Burgh under Stanmuir there dwells he.

JOCK O' THE SIDE.

THE subject of this ballad being a common event in those troublesome and disorderly times, became a favourite theme of the ballad-makers. There are, in this collection, no fewer than three poems on the rescue of prisoners, the incidents in which nearly resemble each other ; though the poetical description is so different, that the Editor did not think himself at liberty to reject any one of them, as borrowed from the others. As however, there are several verses, which, in recitation, are common to all these three songs, the Editor, to prevent unnecessary and disagreeable repetition, has used the freedom of appropriating them to that in which they seem to have the best poetic effect.

The reality of this story rests solely upon the foundation of tradition. Jock o' the Side seems to have been nephew to the Laird of Mangertoun, cousin to the Laird's Jock, one of his deliverers, and probably brother to Christie of the Syde, mentioned in the list of Bor der clans, 1597. Like the Laird's Jock, he also is commemorated by Sir Richard Maitland.—See the *In troduction*.

" He is weil kend, Johne of the Syde,
A greater thief did never ryde ;
He nevir tyris,
For to brek byris,
Our muir and myris
Ouir gude ane guide," &c.

Jock o' the Side appears to have assisted the Earl of
Westmoreland in his escape after his unfortunate insurrection with the Earl of Northumberland, in the twelfth
year of Elizabeth. " The two rebellious rebels went
into Liddesdale in Scotland, yesternight, where Martin
Ellwood [Elliot] and others, that have given pledges to
the regent of Scotland, did raise their forces against them ;
being conducted by black Ormeston, an outlaw of Scotland, that was a principal murtherer of the King of Scots,
[Darnley] where the fight was offered, and both parties
alighted from their horses ; and, in the end, Ellwood
said to Ormeston, he would be sorry to enter deadly
feud with him by bloodshed ; but he would charge him
and the rest before the regent for keeping of the rebels ;
and if he did not put them out of the country, the next
day, he would doe his worst again them ; whereupon
the two Earls were driven to leave Liddesdale, and to
fly to one of the Armstrongs, a Scot upon the batable
[debateable] land on the Borders between Liddesdale
and England. The same day the Liddesdale men
stole the horses of the Countess of Northumberland, and
of her two women, and ten others of their company ;
so as, the earls being gone, the lady of Northumberland was left there on foot, at John of the Side's house,

a cottage not to be compared to many a dog-kennel in England.   At their departing from her, they went not above fifty horse, and the Earl of Westmoreland, to be the more unknown, changed his coat of plate and sword with John of the Side, and departed like a Scottish Borderer."—*Advertisements from Hexham,* 22d December, 1569, in the Cabala, p. 160.

JOCK O' THE SIDE.

Now Liddesdale has ridden a raid,
  But I wat they had better hae staid at hame;
For Michael o' Winfield he is dead,
  And Jock o' the Side is prisoner ta'en.

For Mangerton house Lady Downie has gane,
  Her coats she has kilted up to her knee;
And down the water wi' speed she rins,
  While tears in spaits[1] fa' fast frae her ee.

Then up and spoke her gude auld lord—
  " What news, what news, sister Downie, to me?"—
" Bad news, bad news, my Lord Mangerton;
  Michael is killed, and they hae ta'en my son Johnie."

—" Ne'er fear, sister Downie," quo' Mangerton;
  " I have yokes of onsen, eighty and three;
My barns, my byres, and my faulds, a' weil fill'd,
  I'll part wi' them a' ere Johnie shall die.

[1] *Spaits*—Torrents.

" Three men I'll send to set him free,
    A' harneist wi' the best o' steil ;
The English louns may hear, and drie
    The weight o' their braid-swords to feel.

" The Laird's Jock ane, the Laird's Wat twa,
    O Hobbie Noble, thou ane maun be !
Thy coat is blue, thou hast been true,
    Since England banished thee, to me."—

Now Hobbie was an English man,
    In Bewcastle-dale was bred and born ;
But his misdeeds they were sae great,
    They banished him ne'er to return.

Lord Mangerton them orders gave,
    " Your horses the wrang way maun be shod ;
Like gentlemen ye mauna seem,
    But look like corn-caugers[1] ga'en the road.

" Your armour gude ye mauna shaw,
    Nor yet appear like men o' weir ;
As country lads be a' array'd,
    Wi branks and brecham[2] on each mare."—

Sae now their horses are the wrang way shod,
    And Hobbie has mounted his grey sae fine ;

[1] *Caugers*—Carriers.—[2] *Branks and Brecham*—Halter and cart-collar.

Jock his lively bay, Wat's on his white horse behind,
 And on they rode for the water of Tyne.

At the Cholerford[1] they a' light down,
 And there, wi' the help of the light o' the moon,
A tree they cut, wi' fifteen nogs on each side,
 To climb up the wa' of Newcastle toun.

But when they cam to Newcastle toun,
 And were alighted at the wa',
They fand thair tree three ells ower laigh,
 They fand their stick baith short and sma'.

Then up spake the Laird's ain Jock ;
 " There's naething for't ; the gates we maun force."—
But when they cam the gate until,
 A proud porter withstood baith men and horse.

His neck in twa the Armstrangs wrang ;
 Wi' fute or hand he ne'er play'd pa !
His life and his keys at anes they hae ta'en,
 And cast the body ahint the wa'.

Now sune they reach Newcastle jail,
 And to the prisoner thus they call ;
" Sleeps thou, wakes thou, Jock o' the Side,
 Or art thou weary of thy thrall ?"

[1] *Cholerford* is a ford on the Tyne, above Hexham.

Jock answers thus, wi' dolefu' tone ;
   " Aft, aft I wake—I seldom sleep ·
But whae's this kens my name sae weel,
   And thus to mese[1] my waes does seek ?"—

Then out and spak the gude Laird's Jock,
   " Now fear ye na, my billie," quo' he ;
" For here are the Laird's Jock, the Laird's Wat,
   And Hobbie Noble, come to set thee free."—

" Now haud thy tongue, my gude Laird's Jock,
   For ever, alas ! this canna be ;
For if a' Liddesdale were here the night,
   The morn's the day that I maun die.

" Full fifteen stane o' Spanish iron,
   They hae laid a' right sair on me ;
Wi' locks and keys I am fast bound
   Into this dungeon dark and dreirie."—

" Fear ye na' that," quo' the Laird's Jock ;
   " A faint heart ne'er wan a fair ladie ;
Work thou within, we'll work without,
   And I'll be sworn we'll set thee free."—

The first strong door that they cam at,
   They loosed it without a key ;

[1] *Mese*—Soothe.

The next chain'd door that they cam at,
   They garr'd it a' to flinders flee.

The prisoner now upon his back
   The Laird's Jock has gotten up fu' hie ;
And down the stairs, him, airns and a',
   Wi' nae sma' speed and joy brings he.

" Now, Jock, my man," quo' Hobbie Noble,
   " Some o' his weight ye may lay on me."—
" I wat weel no !" quo' the Laird's ain Jock,
   " I count him lighter than a flee."—

Sae out at the gates they a' are gane,
   The prisoner's set on horseback hie ;
And now wi' speed they've ta'en the gate,
   While ilk ane jokes fu' wantonlie ·

" O Jock ! sae winsomely ye ride,
   Wi' baith your feet upon ae side ;
Sae weel ye're harneist, and sae trig,
   In troth ye sit like ony bride !"—

The night, tho' wat, they did na mind,
   But hied them on fu' merrilie,
Until they cam to Cholerford brae,
   Where the water ran like mountains hie.

But when they cam to Cholerford,
   There they met 'with an auld man ;

Says—" Honest man, will the water ride?
   Tell us in haste, if that ye can."—

" I wat weel no," quo' the gude auld man ;
   " I hae lived here thretty years and three,
And I ne'er yet saw the Tyne sae big,
   Nor running anes sae like a sea."—

Then out and spoke the Laird's saft Wat,
   The greatest coward in the cumpanie
" Now halt, now halt! we need na try't
   The day is come we a' maun die !"—

" Puir faint-hearted thief!" cried the Laird's ain Jock,
   " There'll nae man die but him that's fie ;[1]
I'll guide ye a' right safely thro';
   Lift ye the pris'ner on ahint me."—

Wi' that the water they hae ta'en,
   By ane's and twa's they a' swam thro';
" Here are we a' safe," quo' the Laird's Jock,
   " And, puir faint Wat, what think ye now ?"—

They scarce the other brae had won,
   When twenty men they saw pursue ;
Frae Newcastle toun they had been sent,
   A' English lads baith stout and true.

---

[1] *Fie*—Predestined.

But when the land-sergeant[1] the water saw,
   "It winna ride, my lads," says he;
Then cried aloud—"The prisoner take,
   But leave the fetters, I pray, to me."—

"I wat weel no," quo' the Laird's ain Jock,
   "I'll keep them a'; shoon to my mare they'll be:
My gude bay mare—for I am sure,
   She has bought them a' right dear frae thee."—

Sae now they are on to Liddesdale,
   E'en as fast as they could them hie;
The prisoner is brought to's ain fire-side,
   And there o's airns they mak him free.

"Now, Jock, my billie," quo' a' the three,
   "The day is comed thou was to die;
But thou's as weel at thy ain ingle-side,
   Now sitting, I think, 'twixt thee and me."

[1] The land-sergeant (mentioned also in Hobbie Noble) was an officer under the warden, to whom was committed the apprehending of delinquents, and the care of the public peace.

THE

DEATH OF FEATHERSTONHAUGH.

THIS old Northumbrian ballad was originally printed
in the Notes to *Marmion*, but it is here inserted in its
proper place.   It was taken down from the recitation
of a woman eighty years of age, mother of one of the
miners in Alston-Moor, by the agent of the lead mines
there, who communicated it to my friend and corre-
pondent, R. Surtees, Esq. of Mainsforth.   She had not,
she said, heard it for many years ; but, when she was
a girl, it used to be sung at merry-makings, " till the
roof rung again."   To preserve this curious, though
rude rhyme, it is here inserted.   The ludicrous turn
given to the slaughter, marks that wild and disorderly
state of society, in which a murder was not merely a
casual circumstance, but, in some cases, an exceedingly
good jest.   The structure of the ballad resembles the
" Fray of Suport," having the same irregular stanza
and wild chorus.   1810.[1]

[1] [One of the house of Thirlwall, mentioned in this ballad, and
in the notes to it, figures in Sir Walter Scott's last novel — *Castle
Dangerous.*—ED.]

THE

DEATH OF FEATHERSTONHAUGH.

Hoot awa', lads, hoot awa',
Ha' ye heard how the Ridleys, and Thirlwalls, and a',
Ha' set upon Albany[1] Featherstonhaugh,
And taken his life at the Deadmanshaugh?
There was Willimoteswick,
And Hardriding Dick,
And Hughie of Hawdon, and Will of the Wa'.[2]
I canno tell a', I canno tell a',
And mony a mair that the deil may knaw.

---

[1] Pronounced *Awbony*.

[2] In explanation of this ancient ditty, Mr Surtees has furnished me with the following local memorandum : Willimoteswick, now more commonly called Ridley Hall, is situated at the confluence of the Allon and Tyne, and was the chief seat of the ancient family of Ridley. Hardriding Dick is not an epithet referring to horsemanship, but means Richard Ridley of Hardriding, the seat of another family of that name, which, in the time of Charles I., was sold on account of expenses incurred by the loyalty of the proprietor, the immediate ancestor of Sir Matthew Ridley. Will of the Wa' seems to be William Ridley of Walltown, so called from its

The auld man went down, but Nicol, his son,
Ran away afore the fight was begun;
    And he run, and he run,
    And afore they were done,
There was many a Featherston gat sic a stun,
As never was seen since the world begun.

I canno tell a', I canno tell a';
Some gat a skelp,[1] and some gat a claw;
But they garr'd the Featherstons haud their jaw,[2]
    Nicol, and Alick, and a'.

situation on the great Roman Wall.   Thirlwall Castle, whence the
clan of Thirlwalls derived their name, is situated on the small river
of Tippell, near the western boundary of Northumberland.   It is
near the wall, and takes its name from the rampart having been
thirled, i. e. pierced, or breached, in its vicinity.   Featherston
Castle lies south of the Tyne, towards Alston-Moor.   Albany
Featherstonhaugh, the chief of that ancient family, made a figure in
the reign of Edward VI.   A feud did certainly exist between the
Ridleys and Featherstones, productive of such consequences as the
ballad narrates.   " 24 *Oct.* 22*do Henrici* 8*vi Inquisitio capt. apud
Hautwhistle, sup. visum corpus Alexandri Featherston, Gen.
apud Grensilhaugh, felonice interfecti,* 21 *Oct.* per Nicolaum
Ridley de Unthanke, Gen. *Hugon Ridle, Nicolaum Ridle, et
alios ejusdem nominis.*"   Nor were the Featherstones without their
revenge; for 36to Henrici 8vi, we have — " *Utlagatio Nicolui
Featherston, ac Thomæ Nyxon, &c. pro homicidio Willmi. Ridle
de Morale.*"

[1] *Skelp*—signifies slap, or rather is the same word which was
originally spelled *schlap.*

[2] *Haud their jaw*—Hold their jaw; a vulgar expression still in use.

Some gat a hurt, and some gat nane ;
Some had harness, and some gat sta'en.[1]

Ane gat a twist o' the craig ;[2]
Ane gat a bunch[3] o' the wame ;[4]
Symy Haw gat lamed of a leg,
And syne ran wallowing[5] hame.

Hoot, hoot, the auld man's slain outright '
Lay him now wi' his face down :—he's a sorrowful sight.
    Janet, thou donot,[6]
    I'll lay my best bonnet,
Thou gets a new gude-man afore it be night.

Hoo away, lads, hoo away,
We's a' be hangid if we stay.
    Tak' up the dead man, and lay him anent the bigging :
Here's the Bailey o' Haltwhistle,[7]
Wi' his great bull's pizzle,
    That supp'd up the broo', and syne——in the piggin.

---

[1] *Gat sta'en*—Got stolen, or were plundered ; a very likely termination of the fray.

[2] *Craig*—Neck.—[3] *Bunch*—Punch.—[4] *Wame*—Belly.—[5] *Wallowing*—Bellowing.

[6] *Donot*—Silly slut. [Do-nought.] The Border bard calls her so, because she was weeping for her husband ; a loss which he seems to think might be soon repaired.

[7] *Bailey o' Haltwhistle*—The Bailiff of Haltwhistle seems to have arrived when the fray was over. This supporter of social order is treated with characteristic irreverence by the moss-trooping poet.

[8] An iron-pot with two ears.

HOBBIE NOBLE.

WE have seen the hero of this ballad act a distinguished part in the deliverance of Jock o' the Side, and
are now to learn the ungrateful return which the Armstrongs made him for his faithful services.[1]   Halbert,
or Hobbie Noble, appears to have been one of those
numerous English outlaws, who, being forced to flv
their own country, had established themselves on the
Scottish Borders.   As Hobbie continued his depredations upon the English, they bribed some of his hosts,

---

[1] The original editor of the *Reliques of Ancient Poetry* has
noticed the perfidy of this clan in another instance ; the delivery of
the banished Earl of Northumberland into the hands of the Scottish regent, by Hector of Harelaw, an Armstrong, with whom he
had taken refuge.—*Percy*, vol. i. p. 283.—This Hector of Harelaw seems to have been an Englishman, or under English assurance ; for he is one of those, against whom bills were exhibited by
the Scottish commissioners, to the Lord Bishop of Carlisle.—*Introduction to the History of Westmoreland and Cumberland*, p.
81.   In the list of Borderers, 1597, Hector of Harelaw, with the
Griefs and Cuts of Harelaw, also figures as an inhabitant of the
Debateable Land. It would appear, from a spirited invective in the
Maitland MS. against the regent, and those who delivered up the
unfortunate earl to Elizabeth, that Hector had been guilty of this

the Armstrongs, to decoy him into England under
pretence of a predatory expedition.   He was there delivered, by his treacherous companions, into the hands
of the officers of justice, by whom he was conducted to
Carlisle, and executed next morning.   The Laird of
Mangertoun, with whom Hobbie was in high favour,
is said to have taken a severe revenge upon the traitors
who betrayed him.   The principal contriver of the
scheme, called here Sim o' the Maynes, fled into England from the resentment of his chief; but experienced
there the common fate of a traitor, being himself executed at Carlisle, about two months after Hobbie's
death.   Such is, at least, the tradition of Liddesdale.
Sim o' the Maynes appears among the Armstrongs of
Whitauch, in Liddesdale, in the list of Clans so often
alluded to.

treachery, to redeem the pledge which had been exacted from him
for his peaceable demeanour.   The poet says, that the perfidy of
Morton and Lochlevin was worse than even that of—

> " the traitour Eckie of Harelaw,
> That says he sould him to redeem his pledge ;
> Your deed is war, as all the world does know—
> You nothing can but covatice allege."
>   PINKERTON'S *Maitland Poems,* vol. i. p. 290.

Eckie is the contraction of Hector among the vulgar.
These little memoranda may serve still farther to illustrate the
beautiful ballads, upon that subject, published in the *Reliques.*

HOBBIE NOBLE.

FOUL fa' the breast first Treason bred in!
    That Liddesdale may safely say ;
For in it there was baith meat and drink,
    And corn unto our geldings gay.

And we were a' stout-hearted men,
    As England she might often say ;
But now we may turn our backs and flee,
    Since brave Noble is sold away.

Now Hobbie was an English man,
    And born into Bewcastle dale ;
But his misdeeds they were so great,
    They banish'd him to Liddesdale.

At Kershope foot the tryste was set,
    Kershope of the lilye lee ; [1]

---

[1] Kershope-burn, where Hobbie met his treacherous companions, falls into the Liddel, from the English side, at a place called Turnersholm, where, according to tradition, tourneys and games of chivalry were often solemnized.

And there was traitour Sim o' the Mains,[1]
    And with him a private companie.

Then Hobbie has graithed[2] his body fair,
    Baith wi' the iron and wi' the steel;
And he has ta'en out his fringed grey,
    And there, brave Hobbie, he rade him weel.

Then Hobbie is down the water gane,
    E'en as fast as he could hie;
Tho' a' should hae bursten and broken their hearts,
    Frae that riding-tryst he wad na be.

" Well be ye met, my feres[3] five!
    And now, what is your will wi' me?"—
Then they cried a', wi' ae consent,
    " Thou'rt welcome here, brave Noble, to me.

" Wilt thou with us into England ride,
    And thy safe warrand we will be?
If we get a horse worth a hundred pound,
    Upon his back thou sune sall be."—

" I dare not by day into England ride;
    The Land-Sergeant has me at feid:

---

[1] The Mains was anciently a Border-keep, near Castletown, on the north side of the Liddel, but is now totally demolished.
[2] *Graithed*—Clad.—[3] *Feres*—Companions.

And I know not what evil may betide,
   For Peter of Whitfield, his brother, is dead.

" And Anton Shiel he loves not me,
   For I gat twa drifts o' his sheep ;
The great Earl of Whitfield[1] loves me not,
   For nae gear frae me he e'er could keep.

" But will ye stay till the day gae down,
   Until the night come o'er the grund,
And I'll be a guide worth ony twa
   That may in Liddesdale be found ?

" Though the night be black as pick and tar,
   I'll guide ye o'er yon hill sae hie ;
And bring ye a' in safety back,
   If ye'll be true and follow me."—

He has guided them o'er moss and muir
   O'er hill and hope, and mony a down ;
Until they came to the Foulbogshiel,
   And there, brave Noble, he lighted down.

[1] Whitfield is explained by Mr Ellis of Otterbourne to be a large
and rather wild manorial district in the extreme southwest part of
Northumberland ; the proprietor of which might be naturally called
the Lord, though not *Earl* of Whitfield. I suspect, however, that
the reciters may have corrupted the *great* Ralph Whitfield into
Earl of Whitfield. Sir Matthew Whitfield of Whitfield was Sheriff of Northumberland in 1433, and the estate continued in the
family from the reign of Richard II. till about fifty years since.

But word is gane to the Land-Sergeant,
    In Askerton[1] where that he lay—
" The deer, that ye hae hunted sae lang,
    Is seen into the Waste this day."—

" The Hobbie Noble is that deer !
    I wat he carries the style fu' hie ;
Aft has he driven our bluidhounds back,[2]
    And set ourselves at little lee.

" Gar warn the bows of Hartlie-burn,
    See they sharp their arrows on the wa' !

[1] Askerton is an old castle, now ruinous, situated in the wilds of Cumberland, about seventeen miles north-east of Carlisle, amidst that mountainous and desolate tract of country bordering upon Liddesdale, emphatically termed the Waste of Bewcastle.

> " The russet bloodhound, wont, near Annand's stream,
> To trace the sly thief with avenging foot,
> Close as an evil conscience still at hand."

Our ancient statutes inform us, that the blood-hound, or sluith-hound (so called from its quality of tracing the slot, or track, of men and animals) was early used in the pursuit and detection of marauders. *Nullus perturbet aut impediat canem trassantem, aut homines trassantes cum ipso, ad sequendum latrones.—Regium Majestatem*, lib. 4tus, cap. 32. And, so late as 1616, there was an order from the king's commissioners of the northern counties, that a certain number of slough-hounds should be maintained in every district of Cumberland, bordering upon Scotland. They were of great value, being sometimes sold for a hundred crowns.— *Exposition of Bleau's Atlas, voce Nithsdale.* The breed of this sagacious animal, which could trace the human footstep with the most unerring accuracy, is now nearly extinct.

Warn Willeva and Speir Edom,[1]
   And see the morn they meet me a'.

" Gar meet me on the Rodric-haugh,[2]
   And see it be by break o' day ;
And we will on to Conscouthart-green,
   For there, I think, we'll get our prey."—

Then Hobbie Noble has dreimit a dreim,
   In the Foulbogshiel where that he lay ;
He dreimit his horse was aneath him shot,
   And he himself got hard away.

The cocks 'goud[3] craw, the day 'goud daw,
   And I wot sae even fell down the rain ;

---

[1] Willeva and Speir Edom are small districts in Bewcastledale, through which also the Hartlie-burn takes its course.

[2] Conscouthart-Green, and Rodric-haugh, and the Foulbogshiel, are the names of places in the same wilds, through which the Scottish plunderers generally made their raids upon England ; as appears from the following passage in a letter from William, Lord Dacre, to Cardinal Wolsey, 18th July, 1528; *Appendix to* PINKERTON'S *Scotland*, v. 12, No. XIX. " Like it also your grace, seeing the disordour within Scotlaund, that all the mysguyded men, Borderers of the same, inhabiting within Eskdale, Ewsdale, Walghopedale, Liddesdale, and a part of Tividale, foranempt Bewcastelldale, and a part of the Middle Marches of this the King's Bordours, entres not this West and Middle Marches, to do any attemptate to the King our said soveraine's subjects : but thaye come thorow Bewcastelldale, and retornes, for the most parte, the same waye agayne."

[3] *Goud—i. e.* begoud—*began.*

Had Hobbie na wakened at that time
    In the Foulbogshiel, he had been ta'en or slain.

" Awake, awake, my feres five '
    I trow here makes a fu' ill day ;
Yet the worst cloak o' this company,
    I hope shall cross the Waste this day."—

Now Hobbie thought the gates were clear ;
    But, ever alas ! it was na sae :
They were beset by cruel men and keen,
    That away brave Hobbie might na gae.

" Yet follow me, my feres five,
    And see ye keep of me gude ray ;
And the worst cloak o' this company
    Even yet may cross the Waste this day."—

But the Land-Sergeant's men cam Hobbie before,
    The traitor Sim cam Hobbie behin',
So had Noble been wight as Wallace was,
    Away, alas ! he might na win.

Then Hobbie had but a laddie's sword ;
    But he did mair than a laddie's deed ;
For that sword had clear'd Conscouthart-green,
    Had it not broke o'er Jerswigham's head.

Then they hae ta'en brave Hobbie Noble,
    Wi's ain bowstring they band him sae

But his gentle heart was ne'er sae sair,
   As when his ain five bound him on the brae.

They hae ta'en him on for west Carlisle;
   They ask'd him, if he kend the way?
Though much he thought, yet little he said;
   He knew the gate as weel as they.

They hae ta'en him up the Ricker-gate;[1]
   The wives they cast their windows wide;
And every wife to another can say,
   " That's the man loosed Jock o' the Side!"—

" Fy on ye, women! why ca' ye me man?
   For it's nae man that I'm used like;
I am but like a forfoughen[2] hound,
   Has been fighting in a dirty syke."[3]

They hae had him up through Carlisle town,
   And set him by the chimney fire;
They gave brave Noble a loaf to eat,
   And that was little his desire.

They gave him a wheaten loaf to eat,
   And after that a can of beer;
And they a' cried, with one consent,
   " Eat, brave Noble, and make gude cheir.

[1] A street in Carlisle.—[2] *Forfoughen*—Quite fatigued.
—[3] *Syke*—Ditch.

" Confess my lord's horse, Hobbie," they said,
  " And to-morrow in Carlisle thou's na dee."—
" How can I confess them," Hobbie says,
  " When I never saw them with my ee?"—

Then Hobbie has sworn a fu' great aith,
  By the day that he was gotten and born,
He never had onything o' my lord's,
  That either eat him grass or corn.

" Now fare thee weel, sweet Mangerton [1]
  For I think again I'll ne'er thee see ·
I wad hae betray'd nae lad alive,
  For a' the gowd o' Christentie.

" And fare thee weel, sweet Liddesdale!
  Baith the hie land and the law;
Keep ye weel frae the traitor Mains!
  For goud and gear he'll sell ye a'.

[1] Of the Castle of Mangertoun, so often mentioned in these ballads, there are very few vestiges. It was situated on the banks of the Liddell, below Castletoun. In the wall of a neighbouring mill, which has been entirely built from the ruins of the tower, there is a remarkable stone, bearing the arms of the Lairds of Mangertoun, and a long broadsword, with the figures 1583; probably the date of building, or repairing, the castle. On each side of the shield are the letters S. A. and E. E., standing probably for Symon Armstrong and Elizabeth Elliott. Such is the only memorial of the Lairds of Mangertoun, except those rude ballads, which the Editor now offers to the public.

" Yet wad I rather be ca'd Hobbie Noble,
   In Carlisle, where he suffers for his fau't,
Than I'd be ca'd the traitor Mains,
   That eats and drinks o' the meal and maut."

ROOKHOPE RYDE.

THIS is a Bishopric Border song, composed in 1569, taken down from the chanting of George Collingwood the elder, late of Boltsburn, in the neighbourhood of Ryhope, who was interred at Stanhope, the 16th December, 1785.

Rookhope is the name of a valley about five miles in length; at the termination of which, Rookhope burn empties itself into the river Wear: the dale lies in the north part of the parish of Stanhope, in Weardale. Rookhope-head is the top of the vale. The ballad derives some additional interest, from the date of the event being so precisely ascertained to be the 6th December, 1572, when the Tynedale robbers, taking advantage of the public confusion occasioned by the rebellion of Westmoreland and Northumberland, and which particularly affected the bishopric of Durham, determined to make this foray into Weardale.

The late eminent antiquary, Joseph Ritson, took down this ballad from the mouth of the reciter, and printed it as part of an intended collection of Border

Ballads, which was never published. His nephew, Mr Frank, was so good as to favour me with the copy from which it is here given. To the illustrations of Mr Ritson, I have been enabled to add those of my friend Mr Surtees, of Mainsforth.

ROOKHOPE RYDE.

ROOKHOPE stands in a pleasant place,
  If the false thieves wad let it be,
But away they steal our goods apace,
  And ever an ill death may they dee!

And so is the men of Thirlwall[1] and Willie-haver,[2]
  And all their companies thereabout,

[1] Thirlwall, or Thirlitwall, is said by Fordun, the Scottish historian, to be a name given to the Picts' or Roman wall, from its having been thirled, or perforated, in ancient times, by the Scots and Picts. Wyntown also, who most probably copied Fordun, calls it Thirlwall. Thirlwall castle, though in a very ruinous condition, is still standing by the site of this famous wall, upon the river Tippal. It gave name to the ancient family, De Thirlwall. [Sir John Thirlwall, of this family, is mentioned in Sir Walter Scott's last novel as English Governor of Douglas Castle in the time of Robert Bruce.—ED.]

[2] Willie-haver, or Willeva, is a small district or township in the parish of Lanercost, near Bewcastledale, in Cumberland, mentioned in the preceding ballad of *Hobbie Noble* :—

" Warn Willeva, and Spear Edom,
  And see the morn they meet them a'."

That is minded to do mischief,
 And at their stealing stands not out.

But yet we will not slander them all,
 For there is of them good enow ;
It is a sore consumed tree
 That on it bears not one fresh bough.

Lord God ! is not this a pitiful case,
 That men dare not drive their goods to the fell,
But limmer thieves drives them away,
 That fears neither heaven nor hell ?

Lord, send us peace into the realm,
 That every man may live on his own !
I trust to God, if it be his will,
 That Weardale men may never be overthrown.

For great troubles they've had in hand,
 With Borderers pricking hither and thither,
But the greatest fray that e'er they had,
 Was with the men of Thirlwall and Willie-haver.

They gather'd together so royally,
 The stoutest men and the best in gear ;
And he that rade not on a horse,
 I wat he rade on a weel-fed mear.

So in the morning, before they came out,
 So weel I wot they broke their fast ;

In the forenoon they came into a bye fell,
    Where some of them did eat their last.[1]

When they had eaten aye and done,
    They say'd some captains here needs must be:
Then they choosed forth Harry Corbyl,
    And " Symon Fell," and Martin Ridley.

Then o'er the moss, where as they came,
    With many a brank and whew,
One of them could to another say,
    " I think this day we are men enew.

" For Weardale-men have a journey ta'en,
    They are so far out o'er yon fell,
That some of them's with the two earls,[2]
    And others fast in Bernard castell.

[1] This would be about eleven o'clock, the usual dinner-hour in that period.

[2] The two Earls were Thomas Percy, Earl of Northumberland, and Charles Nevil, Earl of Westmoreland, who, on the 15th of November, 1569, at the head of their tenantry and others, took arms for the purpose of liberating Mary, Queen of Scots, and restoring the old religion. They besieged Barnard castle, which was, for eleven days, stoutly defended by Sir George Bowes, who, afterward, being appointed the Queen's marshal, hanged the poor constables and peasantry by dozens in a day, to the amount of 800. The Earl of Northumberland, betrayed by the Scots, with whom he had taken refuge, was beheaded at York, on the 22d of August, 1572; and the Earl of Westmoreland, deprived of the ancient and

" There we shall get gear enough,
    For there is nane but women at hame;
The sorrowful fend that they can make,
    Is loudly[1] cries as they were slain."

Then in at Rookhope-head they came,
    And there they thought tul a' had their prey,
But they were spy'd coming over the Dry-rig,
    Soon upon Saint Nicolas' day.[2]

Then in at Rookhope-head they came,
    They ran the forest but a mile;
They gather'd together in four hours
    Six hundred sheep within a while.

And horses I trow they gat,
    But either ane or twa,
And they gat them all but ane
    That belang'd to great Rowley.

That Rowley was the first man that did them spy,
    With that he raised a mighty cry;

noble patrimony of the Nevils, and reduced to beggary, escaped
over sea, into Flanders, and died in misery and disgrace, being the
last of his family.   See two ballads on this subject, in Percy's Collection, (i. 271, 281,) and consider whether they be genuine.
RITSON.

[1] This is still the phraseology of Westmoreland : a *poorly* man, a
softly day, and the like.—[2] The 6th of December.

The cry it came down Rookhope burn,
    And spread through Weardale hasteyly.

Then word came to the bailiff's house
    At the East-gate,[1] where he did dwell;[2]
He was walk'd out to the Smale-burns,
    Which stands above the Hanging-well.[3]

His wife was wae when she heard tell,
    So weel she wist her husband wanted gear;

[1] Now a straggling village so called; originally, it would seem, the gate-house, or ranger's lodge, at the east entrance of Stanhope-park. At some distance from this place is West-gate, so called for a similar reason.—RITSON.

[2] The mention of the bailiff's house at the East-gate is (were such a proof wanting) strongly indicative of the authenticity of the ballad. The family of Emerson of East-gath, a fief, if I may so call it, held under the bishop, long exercised the office of bailiff of Wolsingham, the chief town and borough of Weardale, and of Forster, &c., under successive prelates; and the present bishop's game-keeper and ranger within Weardale, may be said to claim his office by maternal descent, being Emerson Muschamp, (another ancient name,) and, though somewhat shorn of his beams, the lineal heir of the old bailiffs of Weardale. " Rob. Emerson Parcarius de Stanhopp. 13 Aug. 7 Rob. Nevill Epi.—Cuthb. Emerson de Eastgat sub Forestar. Parci de Stanhopp. I Wolsey.—Lease of the East-gate to Mr George Emerson for 30 years, 10l. p. ann. 4 Ed. C. Bp. Tunstall.—Rob. Emerson de Eastgat. sede vacante p. depriv. Tunstall parear. Dne Regine.—Geo. et Ric. Emerson Ballivi de Wolsingham. 12 Sept. 1616, sieut Geo. Rolli vel. Rollands Emerson olim tenuere."—SURTEES.

[3] A place in the neighbourhood of East-gate, known at present, as well as the Dry-rig, or Smale-burns; being the property of Mr Robert Richardson, by inheritance, since before 1583.—RITSON.

She gar'd saddle him his horse in haste,
   And neither forget sword, jack,[1] nor spear.

The bailiff got wit before his gear came,
   That such news was in the land,
He was sore troubled in his heart,
   That on no earth that he could stand.

His brother was hurt three days before,
   With limmer thieves that did him prick ;
Nineteen bloody wounds lay him upon,
   What ferly was't that he lay sick ?

But yet the bailiff shrinked nought,
   But fast after them he did hye,
And so did all his neighbours near,
   That went to bear him company

But when the bailiff was gathered,
   And all his company,
They were numbered to never a man
   But forty under fifty.

The thieves was numbered a hundred men,
   I wat they were not of the worst ;

---

[1] A jacket, or short coat, plated or institched with small pieces
of iron, and usually worn by the peasantry of the Border in their
journeys from place to place, as well as in their occasional skirmishes
with the moss-troopers, who were most probably equipped with the
same sort of harness.—RITSON.

That could be choosed out of Thirlwall and Willie-
    haver,
    " I trow they were the very first."[1]

But all that was in Rookhope-head,
    And all that was i' Nuketon-cleugh,
Where Weardale-men o'ertook the thieves,
    And there they gave them fighting eneugh.

So sore they made them fain to flee,
    As many was a' out of hand,
And, for tul have been at home again,
    They would have been in iron bands.

And for the space of long seven years
    As sore they mighten a' had their lives,
But there was never one of them
    That ever thought to have seen their wives.

About the time the fray began,
    I trow it lasted but an hour,
Till many a man lay weaponless,
    And was sore wounded in that stour.

Also before that hour was done,
    Four of the thieves were slain,

---

[1] The reciter, from his advanced age, could not recollect the original line thus imperfectly supplied.—RITSON.

Besides all those that wounded were,
   And eleven prisoners there was ta'en.

George Carrick, and his brother Edie,
   Them two, I wot they were both slain ;
Harry Corbyl, and Lennie Carrick,
   Bore them company in their pain.

One of our Weardale-men was slain,
   Rowland Emerson his name hight ;
I trust to God his soul is well,
   Because he fought unto the right.

But thus they say'd, " We'll not depart
   While we have one :—Speed back again ! "—
And when they came amongst the dead men,
   There they found George Carrick slain.

And when they found George Carrick slain,
   I wot it went well near their heart ;
Lord, let them never make a better end,
   That comes to play them sicken a part.

I trust to God, no more they shall,
   Except it be one for a great chance ;
For God will punish all those
   With a great heavy pestilence.

Thir limmer thieves, they have good hearts,
   They nevir think to be o'erthrown ;

Three banners against Weardale-men they bare,
    As if the world had been all their own.

Thir Weardale-men, they have good hearts,
    They are as stiff as any tree;
For, if they'd every one been slain,
    Never a foot back man would flee.

And such a storm amongst them fell,
    As I think you never heard the like;
For he that bears his head so high,
    He oft-tymes falls into the dyke.

And now I do entreat you all,
    As many as are present here,
To pray for the singer of this song,
    For he sings to make blythe your cheer.

BARTHRAM'S DIRGE.

THE following beautiful fragment was taken down by Mr Surtees, from the recitation of Anne Douglas, an old woman, who weeded in his garden. It is imperfect, and the words within brackets were inserted by my correspondent, to supply such stanzas as the chantress's memory left defective. The hero of the ditty, if the reciter be correct, was shot to death by nine brothers, whose sister he had seduced, but was afterwards buried at her request, near their usual place of meeting; which may account for his being laid, not in holy ground, but beside the burn. The name of Barthram, or Bertram, would argue a Northumbrian origin, and there is, or was, a Headless Cross, among many so named, near Elsdon in Northumberland. But the mention of the Nine-Stane Burn, and Nine-Stane Rig, seems to refer to those places in the vicinity of Hermitage Castle,[1] which is countenanced by the mentioning our Lady's Chapel. Perhaps the hero may have been an Englishman, and the lady a native of Scotland,

---

[1] See the Ballad of Lord Soulis, *post.*

which renders the catastrophe even more probable. The style of the ballad is rather Scottish than Northumbrian. They certainly did bury in former days near the Nine-Stane Burn; for the Editor remembers finding a small monumental cross, with initials lying among the heather. It was so small, that, with the assistance of another gentleman, he easily placed it upright.

BARTHRAM'S DIRGE.

THEY shot him dead at the Nine-Stone Rig,
   Beside the Headless Cross,
And they left him lying in his blood,
   Upon the moor and moss.

*   *   *

They made a bier of the broken bough,
   The sauch and the aspin gray,
And they bore him to the Lady Chapel,
   And waked him there all day.

A lady came to that lonely bower,
   And threw her robes aside,
She tore her ling [long] yellow hair,
   And knelt at Barthram's side.

She bathed him in the Lady-Well
    His wounds so deep and sair,
And she plaited a garland for his breast,
    And a garland for his hair.

They rowed him in a lily-sheet,
    And bare him to his earth,
[And the Gray Friars sung the dead man's mass,
    As they pass'd the Chapel Garth.]

They buried him at [the mirk] midnight,
    [When the dew fell cold and still,
When the aspin gray forgot to play,
    And the mist clung to the hill.]

They dug his grave but a bare foot deep,
    By the edge of the Ninestone Burn,
And they covered him [o'er with the heather-flower,]
    The moss and the [Lady] fern.

A Gray Friar staid upon the grave,
    And sang till the morning tide,
And a friar shall sing for Barthram's soul,
    While the Headless Cross shall bide.[1]

[1] Mr Surtees observes, on this passage, that in the return made
by the commissioners, on the dissolution of Newminster Abbey,
there is an item of a Chauntery, for one priest to sing daily *ad cru-
cem lapideam.* Probably many of these crosses had the like expi-
atory solemnities for persons slain there.

ARCHIE OF CA'FIELD.

IT may perhaps be thought, that, from the near resemblance which this ballad bears to Kinmont Willie, and Jock o' the Side, the Editor might have dispensed with inserting it in this collection. But although the incidents in these three ballads are almost the same, yet there is considerable variety in the language; and each contains minute particulars, highly characteristic of Border manners, which it is the object of this publication to illustrate. Ca'field, or Calfield, is a place in Wauchopdale, belonging of old to the Armstrongs. In the account betwixt the English and Scottish Marches, Jock and Geordie of Ca'field, there called Calf-hill, are repeatedly marked as delinquents.—*History of Westmoreland and Cumberland,* vol. i. Introduction, p. 33.

The Editor has been enabled to add several stanzas to this ballad, since publication of the first edition. They were obtained from recitation; and, as they contrast the brutal indifference of the elder brother with the zeal and spirit of his associates, they add considerably to the dramatic effect of the whole.

ARCHIE OF CA'FIELD.

As I was a-walking mine alane,
    It was by the dawning of the day,
I heard twa brithers make their mane,
    And I listen'd weel to what they did say.

The youngest to the eldest said,
    " Blythe and merrie how can we be?
There were three brithren of us born,
    And ane of us is condemn'd to die."—

" An ye wad be merrie, an ye wad be sad,
    What the better wad billy[1] Archie be?
Unless I had thirty men to mysell,
    And a' to ride in my cumpanie.

" Ten to hald the horses' heads,
    And other ten the watch to be,
And ten to break up the strong prison,
    Where billy Archie he does lie."—

[1] *Billy*—Brother.

Then up and spak him mettled John Hall,[1]
    (The luve of Teviotdale aye was he,)
" An I had eleven men to mysell,
    It's aye the twalt man I wad be."—

Then up bespak him coarse Ca'field,
    (I wot and little gude worth was he,)
" Thirty men is few anew,
    And a' to ride in our companie."—

There was horsing, horsing in haste,
    And there was marching on the lee ;
Until they cam to Murraywhate,
    And they lighted there right speedilie.

" A smith ! a smith ! " Dickie he cries,
    " A smith, a smith, right speedilie,
To turn back the caukers of our horses' shoon !
    For it's unkensome[2] we wad be."—

" There lives a smith on the water-side,
    Will shoe my little black mare for me ;
And I've a crown in my pocket,
    And every groat of it I wad gie."—

---

[1] Mettled John Hall, from the laigh Teviotdale, is perhaps John
Hall of Newbigging, mentioned in the list of Border clans, as one
of the chief men of name residing on the Middle Marches in 1597.
  [2] *Unkensome*—Unknown.

" The night is mirk, and it's very mirk,
    And by candle-light I canna weel see;
The night is mirk, and it's very pit mirk,
    And there will never a nail ca' right for me."—

" Shame fa' you and your trade baith,
    Canna beet[1] a good fellow by your mystery [2]
But leeze me on thee, my little black mare,
    Thou's worth thy weight in gold to me."—

There was horsing, horsing in haste,
    And there was marching upon the lee;
Until they cam to Dumfries port,
    And they lighted there right speedilie.

" There's five of us will hold the horse,
    And other five will watchmen be:
But wha's the man among ye a',
    Will gae to the Tolbooth door wi' me?"—

O up then spak him mettled John Hall,
    (Frae the Laigh Teviotdale was he,)
" If it should cost my life this very night,
    I'll gae to the Tolbooth door wi' thee."—

" Be of gude cheir, now, Archie, lad!
    Be of gude cheir, now, dear billie!

---

[1] *Beet*—Abet, aid.—[2] *Mystery*—Trade. See Shakspeare.

Work thou within, and we without,
   And the morn thou'se dine at Ca'field wi' me."——

O Jockie Hall stepp'd to the door,
   And he bended low back his knee,
And he made the bolts, the door hang on,
   Loup frae the wa' right wantonlie.

He took the prisoner on his back,
   And down the Tolbooth stair cam he:
The black mare stood ready at the door,
   I wot a foot ne'er stirred she.

They laid the links out owre her neck,
   And that was her gold twist to be ;[1]
And they cam doun thro' Dumfries toun,
   And wow but they cam speedilie.

The live-lang night these twelve men rade,
   And aye till they were right wearie,
Until they cam to the Murraywhate,
   And they lighted there right speedilie.

" A smith! a smith!" then Dickie he cries,
   " A smith, a smith, right speedilie.
To file the irons frae my dear brither!
   For forward, forward we wad be."——

[1] The *Gold Twist* means the small gilded chains drawn across
the chest of a war-horse, as a part of his caparison.

They hadna filed a shackle of iron,
    A shackle of iron but barely thrie,
When out and spak young Simon brave,
    " O dinna you see what I do see ?

" Lo ! yonder comes Lieutenant Gordon,
    Wi' a hundred men in his companie ;
This night will be our lyke-wake night,
    The morn the day we a' maun die."—

O there was mounting, mounting in haste,
    And there was marching upon the lee ;
Until they cam to Annan water,
    And it was flowing like the sea.

" My mare is young and very skeigh,[1]
    And in o' the weil[2] she will drown me ;
But ye'll take mine, and I'll take thine,
    And sune through the water we sall be."—

Then up and spak him, coarse Ca'field,
    (I wot and little gude worth was he,)
" We had better lose ane than lose a' the lave ;
    We'll lose the prisoner, we'll gae free."—

" Shame fa' you and your lands baith !
    Wad ye e'en[3] your lands to your born billy ?

[1] *Skeigh*—Shy.—[2] *Weil*—Eddy.—[3] *E'en*—Even; put into comparison.

But hey ! bear up, my bonnie black mare,
   And yet thro' the water we sall be."—

Now they did swim that wan water,
   And wow but they swam bonnilie !
Until they cam to the other side,
   And they wrang their cloathes right drunkily.

" Come thro', come thro', Lieutenant Gordon !
   Come thro' and drink some wine wi' me !
For there is an ale-house here hard by,
   And it shall not cost thee ae penny."—

" Throw me my irons," quo' Lieutenant Gordon ;
   " I wot they cost me dear eneugh."—
" The shame a ma," quo' mettled John Ha',
   " They'll be gude shackles to my pleugh."—

" Come thro', come thro', Lieutenant Gordon !
   Come thro' and drink some wine wi' me !
Yestreen I was your prisoner,
   But now this morning am I free."

ARMSTRONG'S GOODNIGHT.[1]

The following verses are said to have been composed by one of the ARMSTRONGS, *executed for the murder of Sir* JOHN CARMICHAEL *of Edrom, Warden of the Middle Marches. (See Notes on the Raid of the Reidswire—ante.) The tune is popular in Scotland ; but whether these are the original words, will admit of a doubt.*

THIS night is my departing night,
    For here nae langer must I stay ;
There's neither friend nor foe o' mine,
    But wishes me away.

What I have done thro' lack of wit,
    I never, never can recall ;
I hope ye're a' my friends as yet ;
    Goodnight and joy be with you all ![2]
    *   *   *   *   *

[1] [" The music of the most accomplished singer," says Goldsmith, in his Essays, " is dissonance, to what I felt when an old dairy-maid sang me into tears with *Johnie Armstrong's Last Goodnight.*"—ED.]

[2] [Mr Buchan gives what he considers a better copy of these verses, in his Ancient Ballads, vol. ii. p. 129. But those stanzas are hardly entitled to disturb the impression of the beautiful fragment in the text.—ED.]

THE FRAY OF SUPORT.

AN ANCIENT BORDER GATHERING SONG.

FROM TRADITION.

—————

Of all the Border ditties, which have fallen into the Editor's hands, this is by far the most uncouth and savage. It is usually chanted in a sort of wild recitative, except the burden, which swells into a long and varied howl, not unlike to a view hollo'. The words, and the very great irregularity of the stanza (if it deserves the name) sufficiently point out its intention and origin. An English woman, residing in Suport, near the foot of the Kers-hope, having been plundered in the night by a band of the Scottish moss-troopers, is supposed to convoke her servants and friends for the pursuit, or *Hot Trod;* upbraiding them, at the same time, in homely phrase, for their negligence and security. The *Hot Trod* was followed by the persons who had lost goods, with blood-hounds and horns, to raise the country to help. They also used to carry a burning wisp of straw at a spear head, and to raise a cry, similar to the Indian war-whoop. It appears, from articles made by the Wardens of the English Marches, September

12th, in 6th of Edward VI., that all, on this cry being raised, were obliged to follow the fray, or chase, under pain of death. With these explanations, the general purport of the ballad may be easily discovered, though particular passages have become inexplicable, probably through corruptions introduced by reciters. The present text is collected from four copies, which differed widely from each other.

THE FRAY OF SUPORT.

SLEEP'RY Sim of the Lamb-hill,
And snoring Jock of Suport-mill,
Ye are baith right het and fou';—
But my wae wakens na you.
Last night I saw a sorry sight—
Nought left me o' four-and-twenty gude onsen and ky,
My weel-ridden gelding, and a white quey,
But a toom byre[1] and a wide,
And the twelve nogs[2] on ilka side.
   Fy, lads! shout a' a' a' a' a',
   My gear's a' gane.

Weel may ye ken,
Last night I was right scarce o' men:
But Toppet Hob o' the Mains had guesten'd in my
  house by chance;
I set him to wear the fore-door wi' the speir, while I
  kept the back-door wi' the lance;

---

[1] *Toom byre*—Empty cowhouse.—[2] *Nogs*—Stakes.

But they hae run him thro' the thick o' the thie, and
    broke his knee-pan,
And the mergh[1] o' his shin-bane has run down on his
    spur-leather whang:
He's lame while he lives, and where'er he may gang.
        Fy, lads! shout a' a' a' a' a',
        My gear's a' gane.

But Peenye, my gude son, is out at the Hagbut-head,
His een glittering for anger like a fiery gleed;[2]
Crying—"Mak sure the nooks
Of Maky's-muir crooks;
For the wily Scot takes by nooks, hooks, and crooks.
Gin we meet a' together in a head the morn,
We'll be merry men."
        Fy, lads! shout a' a' a' a' a',
        My gear's a' gane.

There's doughty Cuddy in the Heugh-head,
Thou was aye gude at a need:
With thy brock-skin bag[3] at thy belt,
Aye ready to mak a puir man help.
Thou maun awa' out to the Cauf-craigs,
(Where anes ye lost your ain twa naigs,)
And there toom thy brock-skin bag.
        Fy, lads! shout a' a' a' a' a',
        My gear's a' ta'en.

[1] *Mergh*— Marrow.—[2] *Fiery gleed*—a bar of iron *glowing* on the
anvil.—[3] The badger-skin pouch was used for carrying ammunition.

Doughty Dan o' the Houlet Hirst,
Thou was aye gude at a birst :
Gude wi' a bow, and better wi' a speir,
The bauldest March-man that e'er follow'd gear ;
Come thou here.
      Fy, lads ! shout a' a' a' a' a',
      My gear's a' gane.

Rise, ye carle coopers, frae making o' kirns and tubs,
In the Nicol forest woods.[1]
Your craft hasna left the value of an oak rod,
But if you had ony fear o' God,
Last night ye hadna slept sae sound,
And let my gear be a' ta'en.
      Fy, lads ! shout a' a' a' a' a',
      My gear's a' ta'en.

Ah ! lads, we'll fang them a' in a net,
For I hae a' the fords o' Liddel set ;[2]
The Dunkin and the Door-loup,
The Willie-ford, and the Water-slack,
The Black-rack and the Trout-dub of Liddel ;
There stands John Forster, wi' five men at his back,
Wi bufft coat and cap of steil ;

---

[1] A wood in Cumberland, in which Suport is situated.
[2] Watching fords was a ready mode of intercepting the marauders; the names of the most noted fords upon the Liddel are recited in this verse.

Boo! ca' at them e'en, Jock;
That ford's sicker,[1] I wat weil.
    Fy, lads! shout a' a' a' a' a',
    My gear's a' ta'en.

Hoo! hoo! gar raise the Reid Souter, and Ringan's
    Wat,
Wi' a broad elshin[2] and a wicker;
I wat weil they'll mak a ford sicker.
Sae, whether they be Elliots or Armstrangs,
Or rough-riding Scots, or rude Johnstones,
Or whether they be frae the Tarras or Ewsdale,
They maun turn and fight, or try the deeps o' Liddel.
    Fy, lads! shout a' a' a' a' a'.
    My gear's a' ta'en.

" Ah! but they will play ye anither jigg,
For they will out at the big rig,
And thro' at Fargy Grame's gap." [3]
But I hae another wile for that:
For I hae little Will, and Stalwart Wat,
And lang Aicky, in the Souter Moor,
Wi' his sleuth-dog sits in his watch right sure;[4]

---

[1] *Sicker*—Secure.—[2] *Elshin*—A shoemaker's awl.

[3] Fergus Grame of Sowport, as one of the chief men of that clan, became security to Lord Scroope for the good behaviour of his friends and dependents, 8th January, 1662.—*Introduction to History of Westmoreland and Cumberland*, p. 111.

[4] See Note A, p. 131.

Shou'd the dog gie a bark,
He'll be out in his sark,[1]
And die or won.
      Fy, lads! shout a' a' a' a' a',
      My gear's a' ta'en.

Ha! boys!—I see a party appearing—wha's yon?
Methinks it's the Captain of Bewcastle,[2] and Jephtha's
    John,
Coming down by the foul steps of Catlowdie's loan :[3]
They'll make a' sicker, come which way they will.
      Ha, lads! shout a' a' a' a' a',
      My gear's a' ta'en

Captain Musgrave,[4] and a' his band,
Are coming down by the Siller-strand
And the Muckle toun-bell o' Carlisle is rung :
My gear was a' weel won,
And before it's carried o'er the Border, mony a man's
    gae down.
      Fy, lads! shout a' a' a' a' a',
      My gear's a' gane.

[1] *Sark*—Shirt.
[2] According to the late Glenriddel's notes on this ballad, the
office of Captain of Bewcastle was held by the chief of the Nixons.
[3] Catlowdie is a small village in Cumberland, near the junction
of the Esk and Liddel.
[4] This was probably the famous Captain Jack Musgrave, who
had charge of the watch along the Cryssop, or Kershope, as appears from the order of the watches appointed by Lord Wharton,
when Deputy-Warden-General, in the 6th Edward VI.

APPENDIX.

Note A.

Wi' his sleuth-dog sits in his watch right sure.—P. 129, bottom.

THE sentinels, who, by the March laws, were planted upon the Border each night, had usually sleuth-dogs, or blood-hounds, along with them.—See NICHOLSON's *Border Laws*, and LORD WHARTON's *Regulations in the 6th of Edward VI.*

Of the blood-hound we have said something in the notes on *Hobbie Noble;* but we may, in addition, refer to the following poetical description of the qualities and uses of that singular animal :—

—— " Upon the banks
Of Tweed, slow winding thro' the vale, the seat
Of war and rapine once, ere Britons knew
The sweets of peace, or Anna's dread commands
To lasting leagues the haughty rivals awed,
There dwelt a pilfering race ; well train'd and skill'd
In all the mysteries of theft, the spoil
Their only substance, feuds and war their sport.
Not more expert in every fraudful art
The arch felon was of old, who by the tail
Drew back his lowing prize : in vain his wiles,
In vain the shelter of the covering rock,
In vain the sooty cloud and ruddy flames,
That issued from his mouth ; for soon he paid
His forfeit life ; a debt how justly due
To wrong'd Alcides, and avenging Heaven !
" Veil'd in the shades of night they ford the stream ;

Then, prowling far and near, whate'er they seize
Becomes their prey; nor flocks nor herds are safe,
Nor stalls protect the steer, nor strong barr'd doors
Secure the favourite horse. Soon as the morn
Reveals his wrongs, with ghastly visage wan
The plunder'd owner stands, and from his lips
A thousand thronging curses burst their way.
He calls his stout allies, and in a line
His faithful hounds he leads; then, with a voice
That utters loud his rage, attentive cheers.
Soon the sagacious brute, his curling tail
Flourish'd in air, low bending, plies around
His busy nose, the steaming vapour snuffs
Inquisitive, nor leaves one turf untried :
Till, conscious of the recent stains, his heart
Beats quick, his snuffling nose, his active tail,
Attest his joy ; then, with deep-opening mouth
That makes the welkin tremble, he proclaims
The audacious felon ! foot by foot he marks
His winding way, while all the listening crowd
Applaud his reasonings. O'er the watery ford,
Dry sandy heaths and stony barren hills,
O'er beaten tracks, with men and beast distain'd,
Unerring he pursues; till, at the cot
Arrived, and seizing by his guilty throat
The caitiff vile, redeems the captive prey ;
So exquisitely delicate his sense ! "

                          SOMERVILLE'S *Chase.*

LORD MAXWELL'S GOODNIGHT.

NEVER BEFORE PUBLISHED.

———

THIS beautiful ballad is published from a copy in Glenriddel's MSS., with some slight variations from tradition. It alludes to one of the most remarkable feuds upon the West Marches.

A. D. 1585, John Lord Maxwell, or, as he styled himself, Earl of Morton, having quarrelled with the Earl of Arran, reigning favourite of James VI., and fallen, of course, under the displeasure of the court, was denounced rebel. A commission was also given to the Laird of Johnstone, then Warden of the West Marches, to pursue and apprehend the ancient rival and enemy of his house. Two bands of mercenaries, commanded by Captains Cranstoun and Lammie, who were sent from Edinburgh to support Johnstone, were attacked and cut to pieces at Crawford-muir, by Robert Maxwell, natural brother to the chieftain;[1] who, fol-

———

[1] It is devoutly to be wished, that this Lammie (who was killed in the skirmish) may have been the same miscreant, who, in the

lowing up his advantage, burned Johnstone's Castle of
Lochwood, observing, with savage glee, that he would
give Lady Johnstone light enough by which "to set her
hood." In a subsequent conflict, Johnstone himself
was defeated, and made prisoner, and is said to have
died of grief at the disgrace which he sustained.—See
SPOTTISWOODE and JOHNSTONE'S *Histories*, and
MOYSE'S *Memoirs, ad annum* 1585.

By one of the revolutions, common in those days,
Maxwell was soon after restored to the King's favour
in his turn, and obtained the wardenry of the West
Marches. A bond of alliance was subscribed by him,
and by Sir James Johnstone, and for some time the
two clans lived in harmony. In the year 1593, however, the hereditary feud was revived, on the following
occasion : A band of marauders, of the clan Johnstone,
drove a prey of cattle from the lands belonging to the
Lairds of Crichton, Sanquhar, and Drumlanrig ; and
defeated, with slaughter, the pursuers, who attempted
to rescue their property.—[*See the Lads of Wamphray, post,* p. 148.] The injured parties, being appre-
hensive that Maxwell would not cordially embrace their
cause, on account of his late reconciliation with the

day of Queen Mary's distress, "hes ensign being of quhyt taffitae,
had painted one it ye cruell murther of King Henry, and layed
down before her Majestie, at qubat time she presented herself as
prisoner to ye lordis."—BIRREL'S *Diary, June* 15, 1567. It
would be some satisfaction to know, that the grey hairs of this worthy personage did not go down to the grave in peace.

Johnstones, endeavoured to overcome his reluctance, by offering to enter into bonds of manrent, and so to become his followers and liegemen; he, on the other hand, granting to them a bond of maintenance, or protection, by which he bound himself, in usual form, to maintain their quarrel against all mortals, saving his loyalty. Thus, the most powerful and respectable families in Dumfries-shire, became, for a time, the vassals of Lord Maxwell. This secret alliance was discovered to Sir James Johnstone by the Laird of Cummertrees, one of his own clan, though a retainer to Maxwell. Cummertrees even contrived to possess himself of the bonds of manrent, which he delivered to his chief. The petty warfare betwixt the rival barons was instantly renewed. Buccleuch, a near relation of Johnstone, came to his assistance with his clan, " the most renowned freebooters, [says a historian,] the fiercest and bravest warriors among the Border tribes."[1] With Buccleuch also came the Elliots, Armstrongs, and Græmes. Thus reinforced, Johnstone surprised and cut to pieces a party of the Maxwells, stationed at Lochmaben. On the other hand, Lord Maxwell, armed with the royal authority, and numbering among his followers all the barons of Nithsdale, displayed his banner as the King's lieutenant, and invaded Annandale at the head of 2000 men. In those days, however, the royal auspices seem

---

[1] " *Inter accolas latrociniis famosos, Scotos Buccleuchi clientes— fortissimos tribulium et ferocissimos.*"—JOHNSTONI *Historia*, Ed. *Amstæl.* p. 182.

to have carried as little good fortune as effective strength
with them. A desperate conflict, still renowned in tradition, took place at the Dryffe Sands, not far from
Lockerby, in which Johnstone, although inferior in
numbers, partly by his own conduct, partly by the valour of his allies, gained a decisive victory. Lord Maxwell, a tall man, and heavily armed, was struck from
his horse in the flight, and cruelly slain, after the hand,
which he stretched out for quarter, had been severed
from his body. Many of his followers were slain in the
battle, and many cruelly wounded, especially by slashes
in the face, which wound was thence termed a *"Lockerby lick."* The Barons of Lag, Closeburn, and Drumlanrig, escaped by the fleetness of their horses ; a circumstance alluded to in the following ballad.

This fatal battle was followed by a long feud, attended
with all the circumstances of horror proper to a barba-
rous age. Johnstone, in his diffuse manner, describes it
thus : *" Ab eo die ultro citroque in Annandia et
Nithia magnis utriusque regionis jacturis certatum.
Cædes, incendia, rapinæ, et nefanda facinora ; liberi
in maternis gremiis trucidati, mariti in conspectu
conjugum suarum; incensæ villæ; lamentabiles ubi-
que querimoniæ, et horribiles armorum fremitus."*
—JOHNSTONI *Historia, Ed. Amstæl.* p. 182.

John, Lord Maxwell, with whose *Goodnight* the
reader is here presented, was son to him who fell at
the battle of Dryffe Sands, and is said to have early
avowed the deepest revenge for his father's death.

Such, indeed, was the fiery and untameable spirit of the man, that neither the threats nor entreaties of the King himself could make him lay aside his vindictive purpose; although Johnstone, the object of his resentment, had not only reconciled himself to the court, but even obtained the wardenry of the Middle Marches, in room of Sir John Carmichael, murdered by the Armstrongs. Lord Maxwell was therefore prohibited to approach the Border counties; and having, in contempt of that mandate, excited new disturbances, he was confined in the castle of Edinburgh. From this fortress, however, he contrived to make his escape; and, having repaired to Dumfries-shire, he sought an amicable interview with Johnstone, under a pretence of a wish to accommodate their differences. Sir Robert Maxwell, of Orchardstane, (mentioned in the Ballad, verse 1,) who was married to a sister of Sir James Johnstone, persuaded his brother-in-law to accede to Maxwell's proposal. The following relation of what followed is taken from an article in Shawfield's MS., mentioned in the introduction to the ballad called *Kinmont Willie*:—

" The simple truth and cause of the treasonable murther of umquhile Sir James Johnstoun of Dunskellie, knight, was as efter followes. To wit, John Lord Maxwell having dealt and useit his best means with some nobilemen and baronnes within the cuntrey, and likeways with sundrie of the name of Maxwell, being refuised of them all to be partakers of so foull ane

deed ; till at last he unhappily persuaded one Charles
Maxwell, one of the brether of Kirkhouse, to be with
him, and having made him assuired to be pairtner in
that treasonable plot : therefore, taking advantage of
the weakness and unabilitie of umquhill Sir Robert
Maxwell of Orchyardtoun, knight, presuming that he
had power of the said Sir James, being brother-in-law
to him, to bring him to anye part he pleased ; Maxwell, pretending he had special busines to do with Sir
James, hearing he was going from the court of England, so gave out by reasoun he was the king's rebell
for the time, for breaking weird out of the castle of
Edinburgh, that he had no other houpes to obtaine the
King's favour but be his meanes.   So upon this pretence, the said Sir James was moved to meet him at
Auchnamhill, near by Arthorstane, without the house
of Bent, upon the 6th Aprile, 1608, with one man onlie
with him as was with the uther, therselves two onlie
and the forsaid Sir Robert Maxwell with them, and
their servantes being a little off.   The forsaid Charles
falls out with opprobrious and malicious speeches to
Sir James his servant, William Johnstoune of Gun-
menlie, and before he was aware shott him with ane
pistoll.   Sir James hearing the shott and his man's
words, turning about to see what was past, immediatelie Maxwell shott him behind his back with ane pistoll
chairgit with two poysonit bulletts, at which shott the
said Sir James fell from his horse.   Maxwell not being
content therewith, raid about him ane lang tyme, and

persued him farder, vowing to use him more cruelly and treacherouslie than he had done, for which it is known sufficiently what followed."—" A fact," saith Spottiswoode, " detested by all honest men, and the gentleman's misfortune severely lamented, for he was a man full of wisdom and courage."—SPOTTISWOODE, *Edition* 1677, pp. 467, 504. JOHNSTONI *Historia*, *Ed. Amstæl.* pp. 254, 283, 449.

Lord Maxwell, the murderer, made his escape to France; but having ventured to return to Scotland, he was apprehended lurking in the wilds of Caithness, and brought to trial at Edinburgh. The royal authority was now much strengthened by the union of the crowns, and James employed it in stanching the feuds of the nobility, with a firmness which was no attribute of his general character. But in the best actions of that monarch, there seems to have been an unfortunate tincture of that meanness, so visible on the present occasion. Lord Maxwell was indicted for the murder of Johnstone; but this was combined with a charge of *fire-raising*, which, according to the ancient Scottish law, if perpetrated by a landed man, constituted a species of treason, and inferred forfeiture. Thus the noble purpose of public justice was sullied by being united with that of enriching some needy favourite. John, Lord Maxwell, was condemned, and beheaded, 21st May, 1613. Sir Gideon Murray, treasurer-depute, had a great share of his forfeiture; but the attainder was afterwards reversed, and the honours and estate

were conferred upon the brother of the deceased.
—LAING's *History of Scotland,* vol. i. p. 62.—JOHN-
STONI *Historia,* p. 493.

The lady mentioned in the ballad, was sister to the
Marquis of Hamilton, and, according to Johnstone
the historian, had little reason to regret being separated
from her husband, whose harsh treatment finally occasioned her death. But Johnstone appears not to be
altogether untinctured with the prejudices of his clan,
and is probably, in this instance, guilty of exaggeration ;
as the active share taken by the Marquis of Hamilton
in favour of Maxwell, is a circumstance inconsistent
with such a report.

Thus was finally ended, by a salutary example of severity, the " foul debate" betwixt the Maxwells and
Johnstones, in the course of which each family lost two
chieftains ; one dying of a broken heart, one in the field
of battle, one by assassination, and one by the sword of
the executioner.

It seems reasonable to believe, that the following
ballad must have been written before the death of Lord
Maxwell, in 1613 ; otherwise there would have been
some allusion to that event. It must therefore have
been composed betwixt 1608 and that period.

THE LORD MAXWELL'S GOOD NIGHT.

A - dieu Madame, my mother dear, But and my sisters three, O; A - - dieu! fair Robert of

Orchardstane, My heart is wae for thee, O.

Lord Maxwell.

LORD MAXWELL'S GOODNIGHT.[1]

"ADIEU, madame, my mother dear,
  But and my sisters three !
Adieu, fair Robert of Orchardstane !
  My heart is wae for thee.
Adieu, the lily and the rose,
  The primrose fair to see ;
Adieu, my ladye, and only joy !
  For I may not stay with thee.

" Though I hae slain the Lord Johnstone,
  What care I for their feid ?
My noble mind their wrath disdains,—
  He was my father's deid.
Both night and day I labour'd oft
  Of him avenged to be ;
But now I've got what lang I sought,
  And I may not stay with thee.

" Adieu ! Drumlanrig, false wert aye,
  And Closeburn in a band ![2]

The Laird of Lag, frae my father that fled,
    When the Johnston struck aff his hand.
They were three brethren in a band—
    Joy may they never see!
Their treacherous art, and cowardly heart,
    Has twined my love and me.

" Adieu! Dumfries, my proper place,
    But and Carlaverock fair!
Adieu! my castle of the Thrieve [1]
    Wi' a' my buildings there:
Adieu! Lochmaben's gate sae fair,
    The Langholm-holm, where birks there be;
Adieu! my ladye, and only joy,
    For, trust me, I may not stay wi' thee.

" Adieu! fair Eskdale up and down,
    Where my puir friends do dwell;
The bangisters [2] will ding them down,
    And will them sair compell.
But I'll avenge their feid mysell,
    When I come o'er the sea;
Adieu! my ladye, and only joy,
    For I may not stay wi' thee."—

" Lord of the land!"—that ladye said,
    " O wad ye go wi' me,
Unto my brother's stately tower,
    Where safest ye may be!

[1] See Note B, p. 146.—[2] *Bangisters*—The prevailing party.

There Hamiltons, and Douglas baith,
   Shall rise to succour thee."—
" Thanks for thy kindness, fair my dame,
   But I may not stay wi' thee."—

Then he tuik aff a gay gold ring,
   Thereat hang signets three ;
" Hae, tak thee that, mine ain dear thing,
   And still hae mind o' me :
But if thou take another lord,
   Ere I come ower the sea—
His life is but a three days' lease,
   Though I may not stay wi' thee."—

The wind was fair, the ship was clear,
   That good lord went away ;
And most part of his friends were there,[1]
   To give him a fair convey.
They drank the wine, they didna spair,
   Even in that gude lord's sight—
Sae now he's o'er the floods sae gray,[2]
   And Lord Maxwell has ta'en his Goodnight.

[1] The ancestor of the present Mr Maxwell of Broomholm is particularly mentioned in Glenriddel's MS. as having attended his chieftain in his distress, and as having received a grant of lands, in reward of this manifestation of attachment.

[2] This seems to have been a favourite epithet in old romances. Thus in *Hornchilde*, and *Maiden Rimuild*,

     " Thai sayled ower the *flode so gray,*
     In Ingloud arrived were thay,
     Ther him levest ware."

APPENDIX.

Note A.

Adieu! Drumlanrig, &c.—P. 141, v. 3.

The reader will perceive, from the Introduction, what connexion the bond, subscribed by Douglas of Drumlanrig, Kirkpatrick of Closeburn, and Grierson of Lagg, had with the death of Lord Maxwell's father. For the satisfaction of those who may be curious as to the form of these bonds, I have transcribed a letter of manrent,[*] from a MS. collection of upwards of twenty deeds of that nature, copied from the originals by the late John Syme, Esq., writer to the signet; for the use of which, with many other favours of a similar nature, I am indebted to Dr Robert Anderson of Edinburgh. The bond is granted by Thomas Kirkpatrick of Closeburn, to Robert Lord Maxwell, father of him who was slain at the battle of the Dryffe Sands.

BOND OF MANRENT.

" Be it kend till all men be thir present lettres, me, Thomas Kirkpatrick of Closburn, to be bundin and oblist, and be the tenor heirof, bindis and oblissis me, be the faith and treuth of my body,

---

[*] The proper spelling is *manred.* Thus, in the romance of *Florice and Blanchefloure*—

> " He wil falle to thi fot,
> And bicom thi man gif he mot;
> His *manred* thou schalt afonge,
> And the trewthe of his honde."

in manrent and service to ane nobil and mychty loid, Robert Lord Maxwell, induring all the dayis of my lyfe; and byndis and oblissis me, as said is, to be leil and trew man and servant to the said Robert Lord Maxwell, my master, and sall nowthir heir nor se his skaith, but sall lat the samyn at my utir power, an warn him therof. And I sall conceill it that the said lord schawis to me, and sall gif him agane the best leill and true counsale that I can, quhen he only askis at me; and that I sall ryde with my kyn, freyndis, servandis, and allies, that wil do for me, or to gang with the said lord; and to do him æfauld, trew, and thankful service, and take æfauld plane part with the said lord, my maister, in all and sindry his actionis, cansis, quarrellis, leful and honest, movit, or to be movit, be him, or aganis him, baith in peace and weir, contrair or aganis all thae that leiffes or de may (my allegeance to owr soveran ladye the quenis grace, her tutor and governor, allanerly except.) And thir my lettres of manrent, for all the dayis of my life foresaid to indure, all dissimulations, fraud, or gyle, secludit and away put. In witness," &c. The deed is signed at Edinburgh, 3d February, 1542.

In the collection, from which this extract is made, there are bonds of a similar nature granted to Lord Maxwell, by Douglas of Drumlanrig, ancestor to the Dukes of Queensberry; by Crichton Lord Sanquhar, ancestor of the Earls of Dumfries, and many of his kindred; by Stuart of Castlemilk; by Stuart of Garlies, ancestor of the Earls of Galloway; by Murray of Cockpool, ancestor of the Murrays, Lords Annandale; by Grierson of Lagg, Gordon of Lochmaben, and many other of the most ancient and respectable barons in the south-west of Scotland, binding themselves, in the most submissive terms, to become the liegemen and the vassals of the house of Maxwell; a circumstance which must highly excite our idea of the power of that family. Nay, even the rival chieftain, Johnstone of Johnstone, seems at one time to have come under a similar obligation to Maxwell, by a bond, dated 11th February, 1528, in which reference is made to the counter-obligation of the patron, in these words: " Forasmeikle as the said lord has oblist him to supple, maintene, and defend me, in the peciabill brouking and joysing of all my landis, rentis, &c., and to take my æfald, leill, and trew part, in all my good actionis, causis, and quarles, leiful and honest, aganes all deedlie, his alledgeance to our soveraigne lord the king allanerly excepted, as at mair length is contained in his lettres of maintenance maid to me therupon; therefore," &c. he proceeds to bind himself as liegeman to the Maxwell.

I cannot dismiss the subject without observing, that, in the dangerous times of Queen Mary, when most of these bonds are dated, many barons, for the sake of maintaining unanimity and good order, may have chosen to enrol themselves among the clients of Lord Maxwell, then Warden of the Border, from which, at a less turbulent period, personal considerations would have deterred them.

NOTE B.

Adieu! my castle of the Thrieve, &c.—P. 142, v. 2.

THIS fortress is situated in the stewartry of Kirkcudbright, upon an island several acres in extent, formed by the river Dee. The walls are very thick and strong, and bear the marks of great antiquity. It was a royal castle; but the keeping of it, agreeable to the feudal practice, was granted by charter, or sometimes by a more temporary and precarious right, to different powerful families, together with lands for their good service in maintaining and defending the place. This office of heritable keeper remained with the Nithesdale family (chief of the Maxwells) till their forfeiture, 1715. The garrison seems to have been victualled upon feudal principles; for each parish in the stewartry was burdened with the yearly payment of a *lardner mart cow*, i. e. a cow fit for being killed and salted at Martinmas, for winter provisions. The right of levying these cattle was retained by the Nithesdale family, when they sold the castle and estate, in 1704, and they did not cease to exercise it till their attainder.—FOUNTAINHALL's *Decisions*, vol. i. p. 688.

This same castle of the Thrieve was, A. D. 1451-2, the scene of an outrageous and cruel insult upon the royal authority. The fortress was then held by William VIII. Earl of Douglas, who, in fact, possessed a more unlimited authority over the southern districts of Scotland, than the reigning monarch. The Earl had, on some pretence, seized and imprisoned a baron, called Maclellan, tutor of Bombie, whom he threatened to bring to trial, by his power of hereditary jurisdiction. The uncle of this gentleman, Sir Patrick Gray of Foulis, who commanded the body-guard of James II., obtained from that prince a warrant, requiring from Earl Douglas the body of the prisoner. When Gray appeared, the earl instantly suspected his errand. " You have not dined," said he, without suffering him to open his commission : " it is ill talking between a full man and a fasting." While Gray was at meat, the unfortunate prisoner was, by Douglas's command, led forth to the courtyard and beheaded. When the repast was finished, the King's letter was presented and opened. " Sir Patrick," says Douglas, leading Gray to the court, " right glad had I been to honour the King's messenger ; but you have come too late. Yonder lies your sister's son, without the head : you are welcome to his dead body." Gray, having mounted his horse, turned to the Earl, and expressed his wrath in a deadly oath, that he would requite the injury with Douglas's heart's blood.—" To horse ! " cried the haughty baron ; and the messenger of his prince was pursued till within a few miles of Edinburgh.[1] Gray, however, had an opportunity of keeping his vow ; for, being upon guard in the King's antechamber at Stirling, when James, incensed at the insolence of the Earl, struck him with his dagger, Sir Patrick rushed in, and dispatched him with a poleaxe. The castle of Thrieve was the last of the fortresses which held out for the house of Douglas, after their grand rebellion in 1553. James II. writes an account of the exile of this potent family, to Charles VII. of France, 8th July, 1555 ; and adds, that all their castles had been yielded to him, " *Excepto duntaxat castro de Trefe, per nostros fideles impræsentiarum obsesso ; quod, domino concedente, in brevi obtinere speramus.*"—PINKERTON's *History, Appendix,* vol. i. p. 486.—See PITSCOTTIE's *History,* GODSCROFT, &c.

[1] [This incident, no doubt, suggested the scene between Archibald Bell-the-Cat and Lord Marmion. See *Marmion.* Canto V. xiv.—ED]

THE LADS OF WAMPHRAY.

THE reader will find, prefixed to the foregoing ballad, an account of the noted feud betwixt the families of Maxwell and Johnstone. The following song celebrates the skirmish, in 1593, betwixt the Johnstones and Crichtons, which led to the revival of the ancient quarrel betwixt Johnstone and Maxwell, and finally to the battle of Dryffe Sands, in which the latter lost his life. Wamphray is the name of a parish in Annandale. Lethenhall was the abode of Johnstone of Wamphray, and continued to be so till of late years. William Johnstone of Wamphray, called the *Galliard*, was a noted freebooter. A place, near the head of Teviotdale, retains the name of the *Galliard's Faulds*, (folds,) being a valley, where he used to secrete and divide his spoil, with his Liddesdale and Eskdale associates. His *nom de guerre* seems to have been derived from the dance called *The Galliard*. The word is still used in Scotland, to express an active, gay, dissipated character.[1] Willie of the Kirkhill, nephew to the Galliard, and his.

[1] Cleveland applies the phrase in a very different manner, in treating of the assembly of Divines at Westminster, 1644 :—

avenger, was also a noted Border robber. Previous to the battle of Dryffe Sands, so often mentioned, tradition reports, that Maxwell had offered a ten-pound-land to any of his party, who should bring him the head or hand of the Laird of Johnstone. This being reported to his antagonist, he answered, he had not a ten-pound-land to offer, but would give a five-merk-land to the man who should that day cut off the head or hand of Lord Maxwell. Willie of the Kirkhill, mounted upon a young grey horse, rushed upon the enemy, and earned the reward, by striking down their unfortunate chieftain, and cutting off his right hand.

From a pedigree in the appeal case of Sir James Johnstone of Westeraw, claiming the honours and titles of Annandale, it appears that the Johnstones of Wam phray were descended from James, sixth son of the sixth baron of Johnstone. The male line became extinct in 1657.

> " And Selden is a *Galliard* by himself,
> And wel might be ; there's more divines in him,
> Than in all this their Jewish Sanhedrim."

Skelton, in his railing poem against James **IV.**, terms him *Sir Slyr Galyard.*

THE LADS OF WAMPHRAY.

Twixt Girth-head[1] and the Langwood end,
Lived the Galliard, and the Galliard's men;
But and the lads of Leverhay,
That drove the Crichton's gear away.

It is the lads of Lethenha',
The greatest rogues amang them a':
But and the lads of Stefenbiggin,
They broke the house in at the rigging.

The lads of Fingland, and Helbeck-hill,
They were never for good, but aye for ill;
'Twixt the Staywood-bush and Langside-hill,
They steal'd the broked cow and the branded bull.

It is the lads of the Girth-head,
The deil's in them for pride and greed;
For the Galliard, and the gay Galliard's men,
They ne'er saw a horse but they made it their ain.

[1] Leverhay, Stefenbiggin, Girth-head, &c., are all situated in the parish of Wamphray.

The Galliard to Nithsdale is gane,
To steal Sim Crichton's winsome dun,
The Galliard is unto the stable gane,
But instead of the dun, the blind he has ta'en.

" Now Simmy, Simmy of the Side,
Come out and see a Johnstone ride!
Here's the bonniest horse in a' Nithside,
And a gentle Johnstone aboon his hide."—

Simmy Crichton's mounted then,
And Crichtons has raised mony a ane;
The Galliard trow'd his horse had been wight,
But the Crichtons beat him out o' sight.

As soon as the Galliard the Crichton saw,
Behind the saugh-bush he did draw;
And there the Crichtons the Galliard hae ta'en,
And nane wi' him but Willie alane.

" O Simmy, Simmy, now let me gang,
And I'll never mair do a Crichton wrang!
O Simmy, Simmy, now let me be,
And a peck o' gowd I'll give to thee!

" O Simmy, Simmy, now let me gang,
And my wife shall heap it with her hand."—
But the Crichtons wadna let the Galliard be,
But they hang'd him hie upon a tree.

O think then Willie he was right wae,
When he saw his uncle guided sae ;
" But if ever I live Wamphray to see,
My uncle's death avenged shall be !"—

Back to Wamphray he is gane,
And riders has raised mony a ane ;
Saying—" My lads, if ye'll be true,
Ye shall a' be clad in the noble blue."—

Back to Nithsdale they have gane,
And awa' the Crichtons' nowt[1] hae ta'en ;
But when they cam to the Wellpath-head,[2]
The Crichtons bade them 'light and lead.

And when they cam to the Biddes-burn,[3]
The Crichtons bade them stand and turn ;
And when they cam to the Biddes-strand,
The Crichtons they were hard at hand.

But when they cam to the Biddes-law,[4]
The Johnstones bade them stand and draw ;
" We've done nae ill, we'll thole[5] nae wrang,
But back to Wamphray we will gang."—

---

[1] *Nowt*—Cattle.—[2] The Wellpath is a pass by which the Johnstones were retreating to their fastnesses in Annandale.

[3] The Biddes-burn, where the skirmish took place betwixt the
Johnstones and their pursuers, is a rivulet which takes its course
among the mountains on the confines of Nithesdale and Annandale.

[4] *Law*—A conical hill.—[5] *Thole*—Endure.

And out spoke Willie of the Kirkhill
" Of fighting, lads, ye'se hae your fill."—
And from his horse Willie he lap,
And a burnish'd brand in his hand he gat.

Out through the Crichtons Willie he ran,
And dang them down baith horse and man;
O but the Johnstones were wondrous rude,
When the Biddes-burn ran three days blood!

" Now, sirs, we have done a noble deed;
We have revenged the Galliard's bleid,
For every finger of the Galliard's hand,
I vow this day I've kill'd a man."—

As they cam in at Evan-head,
At Ricklaw-holm they spread abread;[1]
" Drive on, my lads! it will be late;
We'll hae a pint at Wamphray gate.[2]

" For where'er I gang, or e'er I ride,
The lads of Wamphray are on my side;
And of a' the lads that I do ken,
A Wamphray lad's the king of men."

[1] Ricklaw-holm is a place upon the Evan water, which falls into
the Annan, below Moffat.
[2] Wamphray-gate was in those days an alehouse.

LESLY'S MARCH.

" But, O my country! how shall memory trace
Thy glories, lost in either Charles's days,
When through thy fields destructive rapine spread,
Nor sparing infants' tears, nor hoary head!
In those dread days, the unprotected swain
Mourn'd, in the mountains, o'er his wasted plain;
Nor longer vocal, with the shepherd's lay,
Were Yarrow's banks, or groves of Endermay."
                    LANGHORNE—*Genius and Valour.*

SUCH are the verses, in which a modern bard has painted the desolate state of Scotland, during a period highly unfavourable to poetical composition. Yet the civil and religious wars of the seventeenth century have afforded some subjects for traditionary poetry, and the reader is now to be presented with the ballads of that disastrous era. Some prefatory history may not be un-acceptable.

That the Reformation was a good and a glorious work, few will be such slavish bigots as to deny. But the enemy came, by night, and sowed tares among the wheat; or rather, the foul and rank soil, upon which the seed was thrown, pushed forth, together with the rising crop, a plentiful proportion of pestilential weeds. The morals of the reformed clergy were severe; their learning was usually respectable, sometimes profound; and their eloquence, though often coarse, was vehement, animated, and popular. But they never could forget, that their rise had been achieved by the degradation, if not the fall, of the Crown; and hence, a body of men, who, in most countries, have been attached to monarchy, were in Scotland, for nearly two centuries, sometimes the avowed enemies, always the ambitious rivals, of their prince. The disciples of Calvin could scarcely avoid a tendency to democracy, and the republican form of church government was sometimes hinted at, as no unfit model for the state; at least, the kirkmen laboured to impress upon their followers and hearers the fundamental principle, that the church should be solely governed by those, unto whom God had given the spiritual sceptre. The elder Melvine, in a conference with James VI., seized the monarch by the sleeve, and addressing him as *God's sillie vassal,* told him, " There are two kings, and two kingdomes. There is Christ, and his kingdome, the kirke; whose subject King James the Sixth is, and of whose kingdome he is not a king, nor a head, nor a lord, but a member; and they whom Christ hath called and commanded to watch ower his kirke, and govern his spiritual kingdome, have sufficient authoritie and power from him so to do; which no Christian king, nor prince, should control or discharge, but fortifie and assist; otherwise they are not faithful

subjects to Christ."—CALDERWOOD, p. 329. The dele-
gated theocracy, thus sternly claimed, was exercised
with equal rigour. The offences in the King's house-
hold fell under their unceremonious jurisdiction, and he
was formally reminded of his occasional neglect to say
grace before and after meat—his repairing to hear the
word more rarely than was fitting—his profane banning
and swearing, and keeping of evil company—and, finally,
of his queen's carding, dancing, night-walking, and such-
like profane pastimes.—CALDERWOOD, p. 313. A
curse, direct or implied, was formally denounced against
every man, horse, and spear, that should assist the King
in his quarrel with the Earl of Gowrie; and from the
pulpit, the favourites of the listening sovereign were
likened to Haman, his wife to Herodias, and he himself
to Ahab, to Herod, and to Jeroboam.

These effusions of zeal could not be very agreeable
to the temper of James; and accordingly, by a course
of slow, and often crooked and cunning policy, he laboured to arrange the church government upon a less
turbulent and menacing footing. His eyes were naturally turned towards the English hierarchy, which had
been modelled, by the despotic Henry VIII., into such
a form, as to connect indissolubly the interest of the
church with that of the regal power.[1] The Reformation, in England, had originated in the arbitrary will of

[1] Of this the Covenanters were so sensible, as to trace (what
they called) the Antichristian hierarchy, with its idolatry, superstition, and human inventions, " to the prelacy of England, the foun-

the prince; in Scotland, and in all other countries of Europe, it had commenced among insurgents of the lower ranks. Hence, the deep and essential difference which separated the Huguenots, the Lutherans, the Scottish Presbyterians, and, in fine, all the other reformed churches, from that of England. But James, with a timidity which sometimes supplies the place of prudence, contented himself with gradually imposing upon the Scottish nation a limited and moderate system of Episcopacy, which, while it gave to a proportion of the churchmen a seat in the council of the nation, induced them to look up to the sovereign, as the power to whose influence they owed their elevation. In other respects, James spared the prejudices of his subjects; no ceremonial ritual was imposed upon their consciences; the leading pastors were reconciled by the prospect of preferment;[1] the dress and train of the bishops were plain and decent; the system of tithes was placed upon a moderate and unoppressive footing;[2] and, perhaps, on the whole, the Scottish hierarchy con-

tain whence all these Babylonish streams issue unto us."—See their manifesto on entering England, in 1640.

[1] Many of the preachers, who had been loudest in the cause of presbytery, were induced to accept of bishoprics. Such was, for example, William Cooper, who was created Bishop of Galloway. This recreant Mass John was a hypochondriac, and conceived his lower extremities to be composed of glass; hence, on his court advancement, the following epigram was composed:

" *Aureus, heu! fragilem confregit malleus urnam.*"

[2] This part of the system was perfected in the reign of Charles I.

tained as few objectionable points as any system of church government in Europe.   Had it subsisted to the present day, although its doctrines could not have been more pure, nor its morals more exemplary, than those of the present Kirk of Scotland, yet its degrees of promotion might have afforded greater encouragement to learning, and objects of laudable ambition to those who might dedicate themselves to its service. But the precipitate bigotry of the unfortunate Charles I. was a blow to Episcopacy in Scotland, from which it never perfectly recovered.

It has frequently happened, that the virtues of the individual, at least their excesses, (if, indeed, there can be an excess in virtue,) have been fatal to the prince. Never was this more fully exemplified than in the history of Charles I.   His zeal for religion, his family affection, the spirit with which he defended his supposed rights, while they do honour to the man, were the fatal shelves upon which the monarchy was wrecked.   Impatient to accomplish the total revolution, which his father's cautious timidity had left incomplete, Charles endeavoured at once to introduce into Scotland the church government, and to renew, in England, the temporal domination, of his predecessor, Henry VIII. The furious temper of the Scottish nation first took fire ; and the brandished footstool of a prostitute[1] gave the signal for civil dissension, which ceased not till the

---

[1] " *Out, false loon ! wilt thou say the mass at my lug* [*ear*] *?*" was the well-known exclamation of Margaret Geddes, as she discharged

church was buried under the ruins of the constitution; till the nation had stooped to a military despotism; and the monarch to the block of the executioner.

The consequence of Charles's hasty and arbitrary measures was soon evident. The united nobility, gentry, and clergy of Scotland, entered into the SOLEMN LEAGUE AND COVENANT, by which memorable deed, they subscribed and swore a national renunciation of the hierarchy. The walls of the prelatic Jericho (to use the language of the times) were thus levelled with the ground, and the curse of Hiel, the Bethelite, de nounced against those who should rebuild them. While the clergy thundered, from the pulpits, against the prelatists and malignants, (by which names were distinguished the scattered and heartless adherents of Charles,) the nobility and gentry, in arms, hurried to oppose the march of the English army, which now advanced towards their Borders. At the head of their defensive forces they placed Alexander Lesly, who, with many of his best officers, had been trained to war under the great Gustavus Adolphus. They soon assembled an army of 26,000 men, whose camp, upon Dunse-Law, is thus described by an eyewitness. Mr Baillie acknowledges, that "it was an agreeable feast to

1640.

---

her missile tripod against the Bishop of Edinburgh, who, in obedience to the orders of the privy-council, was endeavouring to rehearse the common prayer. Upon a seat more elevated, the said Margaret had shortly before done penance before the congregation, for the sin of fornication; such, at least, is the Tory edition.

his eyes to survey the place ; it is a round hill, about a
Scots mile in circle, rising, with very little declivity,
to the height of a bow-shot, and the head somewhat
plain, and near a quarter of a mile in length and breadth ;
on the top it was garnished with near forty field-pieces,
pointed towards the east and south. The colonels,
who were mostly noblemen, as Rothes, Cassilis, Egling-
ton, Dalhousie, Lindsay, Lowdon, Boyd, Sinclair, Bal-
carras, Flemyng, Kirkcudbright, Erskine, Montgomery, Yester, &c., lay in large tents at the head of
their respective regiments ; their captains, who generally were barons, or chief gentlemen, lay around them :
next to these were the lieutenants, who were general
ly old veterans, and had served in that, or a higher
station, over sea ; and the common soldiers lay out-
most, all in huts of timber, covered with divot, or
straw. Every company, which, according to the first
plan, did consist of two hundred men, had their colours
flying at the captain's tent door, with the Scots arms
upon them, and this motto, in golden letters, ' FOR
CHRIST'S CROWN AND COVENANT.' "

Against this army, so well arrayed and disciplined,
and whose natural hardihood was edged and exalted by
a high opinion of their sacred cause, Charles marched at
the head of a large force, but divided by the emulation
of the commanders, and enervated by disuse of arms. A
faintness of spirit pervaded the royal army, and the
King stooped to a treaty with his Scottish subjects.
This treaty was soon broken ; and, in the following year,

Dunse-law again presented the same edifying spec-
tacle of a Presbyterian army. But the Scots were not
contented with remaining there. They passed the
Tweed; and the English troops, in a skirmish at Newcastle, showed either more disaffection, or cowardice,
than had at any former period disgraced their national
character. This war was concluded by the treaty of
Rippon; in consequence of which, and of Charles's con-
cessions, made during his subsequent visit to his native
country, the Scottish parliament congratulated him on
departing " a contented king from a contented people."
If such content ever existed, it was of short duration.

The storm, which had been soothed to temporary
rest in Scotland, burst forth in England with treble
violence. The popular clamour accused Charles, or his
ministers, of fetching into Britain the religion of Rome,
and the policy of Constantinople. The Scots felt most
keenly the first, and the English the second, of these
aggressions. Accordingly, when the civil war of England broke forth, the Scots nation, for a time, regarded
it in neutrality, though not with indifference. But,
when the success of a Prelatic monarch, against a Presbyterian parliament, was paving the way for rebuilding
the system of hierarchy, they could no longer remain
inactive. Bribed by the delusive promise of Sir Henry
Vane, and Marshall, the parliamentary commissioners,
that the Church of England should be " *reformed,
according to the word of God*," which, they fondly
believed, amounted to an adoption of presbytery, they

agreed to send succours to their brethren of England. Alexander Lesly, who ought to have ranked among the *contented* subjects, having been raised by the King to the honours of Earl of Leven, was, nevertheless, readily induced to accept the command of this second army.   Doubtless, where insurrection is not only pardoned, but rewarded, a monarch has little right to expeet gratitude for benefits, which all the world, as well as the receiver, must attribute to fear.   Yet something is due to decency; and the best apology for Lesly, is his zeal for propagating Presbyterianism in England, the bait which had caught the whole parliament of Scotland.   But, although the Earl of Leven was commander-in-chief, David Lesly, a yet more renowned and active soldier than himself, was major-general of the cavalry, and, in truth, bore away the laurels of the expedition.

The words of the following march, which was played in the van of this Presbyterian crusade, were first published by Allan Ramsay in his *Evergreen;* and they breathe the very spirit we might expect.   Mr Ritson, in his collection of Scottish songs, has favoured the public with the music—which seems to have been adapted to the bagpipes.

The hatred of the old Presbyterians to the organ was apparently invincible.   It is here vilified with the name of a *" chest-full of whistles,"* as the Episcopal Chapel at Glasgow was, by the vulgar, opprobriously termed the *Whistling Kirk.*   Yet, such is the revolution of sentiment upon this, as upon more important points, that reports have lately been current, of a plan to introduce this noble instrument into presbyterian congregations.[1]

The share which Lesly's army bore in the action of Marston Moor, has been exalted, or depressed, as writers were attached to the English or Scottish nations, to the Presbyterian or Independent factions. Mr Laing concludes with laudable impartiality, that the victory was equally due to " Cromwell's iron brigade of disciplined Independents, and to three regiments of Lesly's horse."—Vol. i. p. 244.

[1] [An attempt to introduce the organ into one of the churches of Glasgow was made since the above was written—and, as might have been expected, from the choice of the West of Scotland for such an experiment, wholly failed. The Presbytery forthwith silenced the instrument.—ED.]

LESLY'S MARCH.

MARCH! march!
Why the devil do ye na march?
Stand to your arms, my lads,
Fight in good order ;
Front about, ye musketeers all,
Till ye come to the English Border ;
    Stand till't, and fight like men,
    True gospel to maintain.
The parliament's blythe to see us a' coming.
    When to the kirk we come,
    We'll purge it ilka room,
Frae popish relics, and a' sic innovation,
    That a' the world may see,
    There's nane in the right but we,
Of the auld Scottish nation.
Jenny shall wear the hood,
Jocky the sark[1] of God ;
And the kist-fou of whistles,
That mak sic a cleiro,

---

[1] *Sark*—shirt.   The surplice.

Our pipers braw
Shall hae them a',
Whate'er come on it:
Busk up your plaids, my lads l
Cock up your bonnets !

Da Capo.

THE

BATTLE OF PHILIPHAUGH.

THIS ballad is so immediately connected with the former, that it enables me to continue my sketch of his torical transactions from the march of Lesly.

In the insurrection of 1640, all Scotland, south from the Grampians, was actively and zealously engaged. But, after the treaty of Rippon, the first fury of the revolutionary torrent may be said to have foamed off its force, and many of the nobility began to look round with horror, upon the rocks and shelves amongst which it had hurried them. Numbers regarded the defence of Scotland as a just and necessary warfare, who did not see the same reason for interfering in the affairs of England. The visit of King Charles to the metropolis of his fathers, in all probability, produced its effect on his nobles. Some were allied to the house of Stuart by blood; all regarded it as the source of their honours, and venerated the ancient hereditary royal line of Scotland. Many, also, had failed in obtaining the private objects of ambition, or selfish policy, which had induced them to rise up against the crown. Amongst these late penitents, the well-known Marquis of Montrose was distinguished—as the first who endeavoured to recede from the paths of "rude rebellion." Moved by the enthusiasm of patriotism, or perhaps of religion, but yet more by ambition, the sin of noble minds, Montrose had engaged, eagerly and deeply, upon the side of the Covenanters. He had been active in pressing the town of Aberdeen to take the covenant, and his success against the Gordons, at the bridge of Dee, left that royal burgh no other means of safety from pillage. At the head of his own battalion, he waded through the Tweed, in 1640, and totally routed the vanguard of the King's cavalry. But, in 1643, moved with resentment against the Covenanters, who preferred, to his prompt and ardent character, the caution of the wily and politic Earl of Argyle—or seeing, perhaps, that the final views of that party were inconsistent with the interests of monarchy and of the constitution—Montrose espoused the falling cause of royalty, and raised the Highland clans, whom he united to a small body of Irish, commanded by Alexander Macdonald, still renowned in the north, under the title of *Colkitto*. With these tumultuary and uncertain forces, he rushed forth, like a torrent from the mountains, and commenced a rapid and brilliant career of victory. At Tippermoor, where he first met the Covenanters, their defeat was so effectual, as to appal the presbyterian courage, even after the lapse of eighty years.[1] A second army was defeated under the walls of

[1] Upon the breaking out of the insurrection, in the year 1715, the Earl of Rothes, sheriff and lord-lieutenant of the county of

Aberdeen; and the pillage of the ill-fated town was doomed to expiate the principles which Montrose himself had formerly imposed upon them. Argyleshire next experienced his arms; the domains of his rival were treated with more than military severity; and Argyle himself, advancing to Inverlochy for the defence of his country, was totally and disgracefully routed by Montrose.[1] Pressed betwixt two armies, well appointed, and commanded by the most experienced generals of the Covenant, Montrose displayed more military skill in the astonishingly rapid marches, by which he avoided

Fife, issued out an order for " all the fencible men of the countie to meet him at a place called Cashmoor. The gentlemen took no notice of his orders, nor did the commons, except those whom the ministers forced to go to the place of rendezvouse, to the number of fifteen hundred men, being all that their utmost dilligence could perform. But those of that countie having been taught by their experience that it is not good meddling with edge tools, especiallie in the hands of Highlandmen, were very averse from taking armes. No sooner they reflected on the name of the place of rendezvouse, Cashmoor, than Tippermoor was called to mind; a place not far from thence, where Montrose had routed them, when under the command of my great-grand-uncle, the Earl of Wemyss, then general of God's armie. In a word, the unlucky choice of a place, called *Moor*, appeared ominous; and that, with the flying report of the Highlandmen having made themselves masters of Perth, made them throw down their armes, and run, notwithstanding the trouble that Rothes and the ministers gave themselves to stop them."—MS. Memoirs of John Master of Sinclair, vol. i. p. 130.—[This gentleman commanded a party of Fifeshire cavaliers at Sheriffmoor, and died in 1750, leaving these *Memoirs*, which are written with very considerable talent.—Ed.]

[1] [See the Legend of Montrose. Waverley Novels, vol. xv.—Ed.]

*f*ighting to disadvantage, than even in the field of victory. By one of those hurried marches, from the banks
of Loch Katrine to the heart of Inverness-shire, he
was enabled to attack, and totally to defeat, the Covenanters at Auldearn, though he brought into the field
hardly one-half of their force. Baillie, a veteran officer,
was next routed by him, at the village of Alford, in
Strathbogie. Encouraged by these repeated and splendid successes, Montrose now descended into the heart
of Scotland, and fought a bloody and decisive battle
near Kilsyth, where four thousand Covenanters fell
under the Highland claymore.

This victory opened the whole of Scotland to Montrose. He occupied the capital, and marched forward to
the Border; not merely to complete the subjection of
the southern provinces, but with the flattering hope of
pouring his victorious army into England, and bringing
to the support of Charles the sword of his paternal tribes.

Half a century before Montrose's career, the state of
the Borders was such as might have enabled him easily
to have accomplished his daring plan. The Marquis
of Douglas, the Earls of Home, Roxburgh, Traquair,
and Annandale, were all descended of mighty Border
chiefs, whose ancestors could, each of them, have led
into the field a body of their own vassals, equal in numbers, and superior in discipline, to the army of Montrose.[1] But the military spirit of the Borderers, and

---

[1] [In this passage, Sir Walter Scott must have had in remem-
brance John Home's sorrowful account of the Earl of Home's ap-

their attachment to their chiefs, had been much broken
since the union of the Crowns. The disarming acts of
James had been carried rigorously into execution, and
the smaller proprietors, no longer feeling the necessity
of protection from their chiefs in war, had aspired to
independence, and embraced the tenets of the Covenant.
Without imputing, with Wishart, absolute treachery to
the Border nobles, it may be allowed, that they looked
with envy upon Montrose, and with dread and aversion
upon his rapacious and disorderly forces. Hence, had it
been in their power, it might not have altogether suited
their inclinations, to have brought the strength of the
Border lances to the support of the northern clans. The
once formidable name of Douglas still sufficed to raise
some bands, by whom Montrose was joined in his march
down the Gala.   With these reinforcements, and with
the remnant of his Highlanders, (for a great number
had returned home with Colkitto, to deposit their plunder, and provide for their families,) Montrose, after
traversing the Border, finally encamped upon the field
of Philiphaugh.

  The river Ettrick, immediately after its junction with
the Yarrow, and previous to its falling into the Tweed,
makes a large sweep to the southward, and winds almost beneath the lofty bank, on which the town of Selkirk stands : leaving, upon the northern side, a large
and level plain, extending in an easterly direction, from

pearance, with only a couple of menial servants, at the head-quarters
of the royal army, in the campaign of 1745.—ED.]

a hill, covered with natural copsewood, called the Hare head-wood, to the high ground which forms the banks of the Tweed, near Sunderland hall. This plain is called Philiphaugh:[1] it is about a mile and a half in length, and a quarter of a mile broad; and being defended, to the northward, by the hills which separate Tweed from Yarrow, by the river Ettrick in front, and by the high grounds, already mentioned, on each flank, it forms, at once, a convenient and a secure field of encampment. On each flank Montrose threw up some trenches, which are still visible; and here he posted his infantry, amounting to about twelve or fifteen hundred men. He himself took up his quarters in the burgh of Selkirk, and, with him, the cavalry, in number hardly one thousand, but respectable, as being chiefly composed of gentlemen and their immediate retainers. In this manner, by a fatal and unaccountable error, the river Ettrick was thrown betwixt the cavalry and infantry, which were to depend upon each other for intelligence and mutual support. This might be over looked by Montrose, in the conviction, that there was no armed enemy of Charles in the realm of Scotland; for he is said to have employed the night in writing and dispatching this agreeable intelligence to the King. Such an enemy, however, was already within four miles of his camp.

[1] The Scottish language is rich in words expressive of local situation. The single word *haugh* conveys to a Scotsman almost all that I have endeavoured to explain in the text, by circumlocutory description.

Recalled by the danger of the cause of the Covenant, General David Lesly came down from England, at the head of those iron squadrons, whose force had been proved in the fatal battle of Long Marston Moor. His army consisted of from five to six thousand men, chiefly cavalry. Lesly's first plan seems to have been, to occupy the midland counties, so as to intercept the return of Montrose's Highlanders, and to force him to an unequal combat. Accordingly, he marched along the eastern coast, from Berwick to Tranent; but there he suddenly altered his direction, and, crossing through Mid-Lothian, turned again to the southward, and following the course of Gala Water, arrived at Melrose, the evening before the engagement. How it is possible that Montrose should have received no notice whatever of the march of so considerable an army, seems almost inconceivable, and proves, that the country was strongly disaffected to his cause or person. Still more extraordinary does it appear, that, even with the advantage of a thick mist, Lesly should have, the next morning, advanced from Melrose, forded the Ettrick, and come close upon Montrose's encampment, without being descried by a single scout. Such, however, was the case, and it was attended with all the consequences of the most complete surprisal.

The first intimation that Montrose received of the march of Lesly, was the noise of the conflict, or, rather, that which attended the unresisted slaughter of his infantry, who never formed a line of battle; the right wing alone, supported by the thickets of Hare-head-wood, and by the intrenchments, which are there still visible, stood firm for some time. But Lesly had detached two thousand men, who, crossing the Ettrick still higher up than his main body, assaulted the rear of Montrose's right wing. At this moment, the Marquis himself arrived, and beheld his army dispersed, for the first time, in irretrievable rout. He had thrown himself upon a horse the instant he heard the firing, and, followed by such of his disorderly cavalry as had gathered upon the alarm, he galloped from Selkirk, crossed the Ettrick, and made a bold and desperate attempt to retrieve the fortune of the day. But all was in vain; and, after cutting his way, almost singly, through a body of Lesly's troopers, the gallant Montrose graced by his example the retreat of the fugitives. That retreat he continued up Yarrow, and over Minchmoor; nor did he stop till he arrived at Traquair, sixteen miles from the field of battle. Upon Philiphaugh he lost, in one defeat, the fruit of six splendid victories; nor was he again able effectually to make head, in Scotland, against the covenanted cause. The number slain in the field did not exceed three or four hundred; for the fugitives found refuge in the mountains, which had often been the retreat of vanquished armies, and were impervious to the pursuer's cavalry. Lesly abused his victory, and dishonoured his arms, by slaughtering, in cold blood, many of the prisoners whom he had taken; and the courtyard of Newark Castle is said to have been the spot, upon which they were shot by his command.

Many others are said, by Wishart, to have been preci-
pitated from a high bridge over the Tweed.   This, as
Mr Laing remarks, is impossible; because there was
not then a bridge over the Tweed betwixt Peebles and
Berwick.   But there is an old bridge over the Ettrick,
only four miles from Philiphaugh—and another over
the Yarrow, both of which lay in the very line of flight
and pursuit; and either might have been the scene of
the massacre.   But if this is doubtful, it is too certain,
that several of the royalists were executed by the Covenanters, as traitors to the King and Parliament.[1]

I have reviewed, at some length, the details of this
memorable engagement, which, at the same time, terminated the career of a hero, likened, by no mean judge
of mankind,[2] to those of antiquity, and decided the fate
of his country.   It is farther remarkable, as the last
field which was fought in Ettrick forest, the scene of so
many bloody actions.[3]   The unaccountable neglect of

---

[1] A covenanted minister, present at the execution of these gentlemen, observed, " This wark gaes bonnilie on !" an amiable exclamation, equivalent to the modern ça ira, so often used on similar
occasions.—WISHART's *Memoirs of Montrose.*

[2] Cardinal du Retz.

[3] [I have often heard Sir Walter Scott tell the story of one of
Lesly's officers who had his quarters the night before the battle at
the farm-house of Toftfield, included in the estate of Abbotsford.
This gentleman having been courteously treated by his hosts, before
he mounted his horse in the morning drew the goodwife aside, and
intrusted his purse to her keeping. " You have been kind to me,"
he said, " and being a brotherless and childless man, in case I fall
this day, I would as soon you should be my heir as any other per-

patrols, and the imprudent separation betwixt the horse
and foot, seem to have been the immediate cause of
Montrose's defeat. But the ardent and impetuous character of this great warrior, corresponding with that of
the troops which he commanded, was better calculated
for attack than defence; for surprising others, rather
than for providing against surprise himself. Thus, he
suffered loss by a sudden attack upon part of his forces,
stationed at Aberdeen;[1] and, had he not extricated himself with the most singular ability, he must have lost
his whole army, when surprised by Baillie, during the

son." He returned in the evening, but only to die in his old quarters, and the farmer's family were said to have risen some steps in the
world, in consequence of his bequest.—ED.]

[1] Colonel Hurry, with a party of horse, surprised the town, while
Montrose's Highlanders and cavaliers were " dispersed through the
town, drinking carelessly in their lodgings ; and, hearing the horses'
feet, and great noise, were astonished, never dreaming of their enemy.
However, Donald Farquharson happened to come to the causey,
where he was cruelly slain, anent the Court de Guard ; a brave
gentleman, and one of the noblest captains amongst all the Highlanders of Scotland. Two or three others were killed, and some
(taken prisoners) had to Edinburgh, and cast into irons in the tolbooth. Great lamentation was made for this gallant, being still the
King's man for life and death."—SPALDING, vol. ii. p. 281. The
journalist, to whom all matters were of equal importance, proceeds
to inform us, that Hurry took the Marquis of Huntly's best horse,
and, in his retreat through Montrose, seized upon the Marquis's
second son. He also expresses his regret, that " the said Donald
Farquharson's body was found in the street, stripped naked ; for
they tirr'd from off his body a rich stand of apparel, but put on the
same day."—Ibid.

plunder of Dundee.   Nor has it escaped an ingenious
modern historian, that his final defeat at Dunbeath so
nearly resembles in its circumstances the surprise at
Philiphaugh, as to throw some shade on his military
talents.—LAING's *History.*

The following ballad, which is preserved by tradition
in Selkirkshire, coincides accurately with historical fact.
This, indeed, constitutes its sole merit.   The Cove
nanters were not, I dare say, addicted more than their
successors, to " the profane and unprofitable art of poem
making." [1]   Still, however, they could not refrain from
some strains of exultation over the defeat of the *trucu-
lent tyrant,* James Graham.   For, gentle reader, Montrose, who, with resources which seemed as none, gained six victories, and reconquered a kingdom ; who, a
poet, a scholar, a cavalier, and a general, could have
graced alike a court, and governed a camp, this Montrose was numbered, by his covenanted countrymen,
among " the troubles of Israel, the firebrands of hell,
the Corahs, the Balaams, the Doegs, the Rabshakehs,
the Hamans, the Tobias, and Sanballats of the time." [2]

[1] So little was the spirit of illiberal fanaticism decayed in some
parts of Scotland, that only thirty yeais ago, when Wilson, the ingenious author of a poem called " *Clyde*," now republished, was
inducted into the office of schoolmaster at Greenock, he was obliged
formally, and in writing, to abjure the " *profane and unprofitable
art of poem-making.*"   It is proper to add, that such an incident is
now as unlikely to happen in Greenock as in London.   1803.

[2] [See Notes to the Legend of Montrose.   Waverley Novels,
vol. XV.—ED.]

THE

BATTLE OF PHILIPHAUGH.

ON Philiphaugh a fray began,
    At Hairhead-wood it ended;
The Scots out o'er the Græmes they ran,
    Sae merrily they bended.

Sir David frae the Border came,
    Wi' heart an' hand came he;
Wi' him three thousand bonny Scots,
    To bear him company.

Wi' him three thousand valiant men,
    A noble sight to see!
A cloud o' mist them weel conceal'd,
    As close as e'er might be.

When they came to the Shaw burn,[1]
    Said he, " Sae weel we frame,

---

[1] A small stream, that joins the Ettrick, near Selkirk, on the south side of the river.

I think it is convenient
    That we should sing a psalm."—[1]

When they came to the Lingly burn,[2]
    As daylight did appear,
They spy'd an aged father,
    And he did draw them near.

" Come hither, aged father!"
    Sir David he did cry,
" And tell me where Montrose lies,
    With all his great army."—

" But, first, you must come tell to me,
    If friends or foes you be ;
I fear you are Montrose's men,
    Come frae the north country."—

" No, we are nane o' Montrose's men,
    Nor e'er intend to be ;
I am Sir David Lesly,
    That's speaking unto thee."—

" If you're Sir David Lesly,
    As I think weel ye be,

---

[1] Various reading : " That we should take a dram."

[2] A brook, which falls into the Ettrick, from the north, a little above the Shaw burn.

I am sorry ye hae brought so few
    Into vour company.

" There's fifteen thousand armed men,
    Encamped on yon lee ;
Ye'll never be a bite to them,
    For aught that I can see.

" But halve your men in equal parts,
    Your purpose to fulfill ;
Let ae half keep the water side,
    The rest gae round the hill.

" Your nether party fire must,
    Then beat a flying drum ;
And then they'll think the day's their ain,
    And frae the trench they'll come ;

" Then, those that are behind them, maun
    Gie shot, baith grit and sma' ;
And so, between your armies twa,
    Ye may make them to fa'. "—

" O were ye ever a soldier ? "—
    Sir David Lesly said ;
" O yes ; I was at Solway Flow,
    Where we were all betray'd.[1]

[1] The traditional commentary upon this ballad states this man's

" Again I was at curst Dunbar,
    And was a pris'ner ta'en :
And many weary night and day,
    In prison I hae lien."—

" If ye will lead these men aright,
    Rewarded shall ye be ;
But, if that ye a traitor prove,
    I'll hang thee on a tree."—

" Sir, I will not a traitor prove ;
    Montrose has plunder'd me ;
I'll do my best to banish him
    Away frae this country."—

He halved his men in equal parts,
    His purpose to fulfill ;
The one part kept the water side,
    The other gaed round the hill.

The nether party fired brisk
    Then turn'd and seem'd to rin ;

name to have been Brydone, ancestor to several families in the parish of Ettrick, particularly those occupying the farms of Midge-
hope and Redford Green.   It is a strange anachronism, to make
this aged father state himself to have been at the battle of *Solway
Flow*, which was fought a hundred years before Philiphaugh ; and
a still stranger, to mention that of Dunbar, which did not take place
till five years after Montrose's defeat.

And then they a' came frae the trench,
    And cry'd, " The day's our ain !"——

The rest then ran into the trench
    And loosed their cannons a' ·
And thus, between his armies twa,
    He made them fast to fa'.

Now, let us a' for Lesly pray,
    And his brave company !
For they hae vanquish'd great Montrose,
    Our cruel enemy.[1]

[1] A tradition, annexed to a copy of this ballad, transmitted to me by Mr James Hogg, bears, that the Earl of Traquair, on the day of the battle, was advancing with a large sum of money, for the payment of Montrose's forces, attended by a blacksmith, one of his retainers. As they crossed Minchmoor, they were alarmed by firing, which the Earl conceived to be Montrose exercising his forces, but which his attendant, from the constancy and irregularity of the noise, affirmed to be the tumult of an engagement. As they came below Broadmeadows, upon Yarrow, they met their fugitive friends, hotly pursued by the parliamentary troopers. The Earl, of course, turned, and fled also ; but his horse, jaded with the weight of dollars which he carried, refused to take the hill ; so that the Earl was fain to exchange with his attendant, leaving him with the breathless horse, and bag of silver, to shift for himself ; which he is supposed to have done very effectually. Some of the dragoons, attracted by the appearance of the horse and trappings, gave chase to the smith, who fled up the Yarrow ; but finding himself, as he said, encumbered with the treasure, and unwilling that it should be taken, he flung it into a well, or pond, near the Tin-

nies, above Hangingshaw. Many wells were afterwards searched in vain ; but it is the general belief, that the smith, if he ever hid the money, knew too well how to anticipate the scrutiny. There is, however, a pond, which some peasants began to drain, not long ago, in hopes of finding the golden prize, but were prevented, as they pretended, by supernatural interference. 1803.

THE

GALLANT GRAHAMS.

THE preceding ballad was a song of triumph over the defeat of Montrose at Philiphaugh; the verses which follow, are a lamentation for his final discomfiture and cruel death. The present edition of " *The Gallant Grahams*" is given from tradition, enlarged and corrected by an ancient printed edition, entitled, " *The gallant Grahams of Scotland,*" to the tune of " *I will away, and I will not tarry,*" of which Mr Ritson favoured me with an accurate copy.

The conclusion of Montrose's melancholy history is too well known. The Scottish army, which sold King Charles I. to his Parliament, had, we may charitably hope, no idea that they were bartering his blood; although they must have been aware, that they were consigning him to perpetual bondage.[1] At least the sentiments of the kingdom at large differed widely from those of the military merchants, and the danger of King

[1] As Salmasius quaintly, but truly, expresses it, *Presbyteriani ligaverunt, Independentes trucidaverunt.*

Charles drew into England a well-appointed Scottish
army, under the command of the Duke of Hamilton.
But he met with Cromwell, and to meet with Cromwell was inevitable defeat. The death of Charles, and
the triumph of the Independents, excited still more
highly the hatred and the fears of the Scottish nation.
The outwitted Presbyterians, who saw, too late, that
their own hands had been employed in the hateful task
of erecting the power of a sect yet more fierce and fanatical than themselves, deputed a commission to the
Hague, to treat with Charles II., whom, upon certain
conditions, they now wished to restore to the throne
of his fathers. At the court of the exiled monarch,
Montrose also offered to his acceptance a splendid plan
of victory and conquest, and pressed for his permission
to enter Scotland; and there, collecting the remains
of the royalists, to claim the crown for his master,
with the sword in his hand. An able statesman might
perhaps have reconciled these jarring projects; a good
man would certainly have made a decided choice betwixt them. Charles was neither the one nor the other;
and, while he treated with the Presbyterians, with a view
of accepting the crown from their hands, he scrupled not
to authorize Montrose, the mortal enemy of the sect,
to pursue his separate and inconsistent plan of conquest.

Montrose arrived in the Orkneys with six hundred
Germans, was furnished with some recruits from those
islands, and was joined by several royalists, as he tra-
versed the wilds of Caithness and Sutherland; but,

advancing into Ross-shire, he was surprised, and totally defeated, by Colonel Strachan, an officer of the Scottish Parliament, who had distinguished himself in the civil wars, and who afterwards became a decided Cromwellian. Montrose, after a fruitless resistance, at length fled from the field of defeat, and concealed himself in the grounds of Macleod of Assaint, to whose fidelity he intrusted his life, and by whom he was delivered up to Lesly, his most bitter enemy.

He was tried for what was termed treason against the Estates of the Kingdom; and, despite the commission of Charles for his proceedings, he was condemned to die by a Parliament who acknowledged Charles to be their king, and whom, on that account only, Montrose acknowledged to be a Parliament.

" The clergy," says a late animated historian, " whose vocation it was to persecute the repose of his last moments, sought, by the terrors of his sentence, to extort repentance; but his behaviour, firm and dignified to the end, repelled their insulting advances with scorn and disdain. He was prouder, he replied, to have his head affixed to the prison-walls, than to have his picture placed in the King's bedchamber : 'and, far from being troubled that my limbs are to be sent to your principal cities, I wish I had flesh enough to be dispersed through Christendom, to attest my dying attachment to my King.' It was the calm employment of his mind, that night, to reduce this extravagant sentiment to verse. He appeared next day on the scaffold, in a rich habit, with

the same serene and undaunted countenance, and ad
dressed the people, to vindicate his dying unabsolved
by the church, rather than to justify an invasion of the
kingdom, during a treaty with the estates. The insults
of his enemies were not yet exhausted. The history
of his exploits was attached to his neck by the public
executioner; but he smiled at their inventive malice;
declared that he wore it with more pride than he had
done the garter; and when his devotions were finished,
demanding if any more indignities remained to be practised, submitted calmly to an unmerited fate."—LAING'S
History of Scotland, vol. i. p. 404.

Such was the death of James Graham, the great
Marquis of Montrose, over whom some lowly bard has
poured forth the following elegiac verses. To say that
they are far unworthy of the subject, is no great re-
proach; for a nobler poet might have failed in the at
tempt. Indifferent as the ballad is, we may regret its
being still more degraded by many apparent corruptions.
There seems an attempt to trace Montrose's career,
from his first raising the royal standard, to his second
expedition and death; but it is interrupted and imperfect. From the concluding stanza, I presume the song
was composed upon the arrival of Charles in Scotland,
which so speedily followed the execution of Montrose,
that the King entered the city while the head of his
most faithful and most successful adherent was still
blackening in the sun.

THE GALLANT GRAHAMS.

Now, fare thee well, sweet Ennerdale [1]
    Baith kith and countrie I bid adieu;
For I maun away, and I may not stay,
    To some uncouth land which I never knew.

To wear the blue I think it best,
    Of all the colours that I see;
And I'll wear it for the gallant Grahams,
    That are banished from their countrie.

I have no gold, I have no land,
    I have no pearl nor precious stane;
But I wald sell my silken snood,
    To see the gallant Grahams come hame.

In Wallace days, when they began,
    Sir John the Graham [2] did bear the gree

[1] A corruption of Endrickdale. The principal and most ancient possessions of the Montrose family lie along the water of Endrick, in Dumbartonshire.

[2] The faithful friend and adherent of the immortal Wallace, slain at the battle of Falkirk.

Through all the lands of Scotland wide ·
   He was a lord of the south countrie.

And so was seen full many a time ;
   For the summer flowers did never spring,
But every Graham, in armour bright,
   Would then appear before the king.

They were all drest in armour sheen,
   Upon the pleasant banks of Tay ;
Before a king they might be seen,
   These gallant Grahams in their array.

At the Goukhead our camp we set,
   Our leaguer down there for to lay ;
And, in the bonny summer light,
   We rode our white horse and our gray.

Our false commander sold our king
   Unto his deadly enemie,
Who was the traitor, Cromwell,[1] then ;
   So I care not what they do with me.

They have betray'd our noble prince,
   And banish'd him from his royal crown ;
But the gallant Grahams have ta'en in hand
   For to command those traitors down.

[1] See Note A, p. 195.

In Glen-Prosen[1] we rendezvous'd,
    March'd to Glenshie by night and day,
And took the town of Aberdeen,
    And met the Campbells in their array.

Five thousand men, in armour strong,
    Did meet the gallant Grahams that day
At Inverlochie, where war began,
    And scarce two thousand men were they.

Gallant Montrose, that chieftain bold,
    Courageous in the best degree,
Did for the king fight well that day;—
    The Lord preserve his majestic!

Nathaniel Gordon,[2] stout and bold,
    Did for King Charles wear the blue;
But the cavaliers they all were sold,
    And brave Harthill,[3] a cavalier too.

[1] Glen-Prosen is in Angus-shire.

[2] Of the family of Gicht in Aberdeenshire. See Note B, at the end of the ballad, p. 196.

[3] Leith, of Harthill, was a determined loyalist, and hated the Covenanters, not without reason. His father, a haughty, high-spirited baron, and chief of a clan, happened, in 1639, to sit down in the desk of Provost Lesly, in the high kirk of Aberdeen. He was disgracefully thrust out by the officers, and, using some threatening language to the provost, was imprisoned, hke a felon, for many months, till he became furious, and nearly mad. Having got free of the shackles with which he was loaded, he used his li-

And Newton-Gordon,[1] burd-alone,
And Dalgatie,[2] both stout and keen,

berty by coming to the tolbooth window, where he uttered the most violent and horrible threats against Provost Lesly, and the other covenanting magistrates, by whom he had been so severely treated. Under pretence of this new offence, he was sent to Edinburgh, and lay long in prison there; for, so fierce was his temper, that no one would give surety for his keeping the peace with his enemies, if set at liberty. At length he was delivered by Montrose, when he made himself master of Edinburgh.—SPALDING, vol. i. pp. 201, 266. His house of Harthill was dismantled, and miserably pillaged by Forbes of Craigievar, who expelled his wife and children with the most relentless inhumanity.—Ibid. vol. ii. p. 225. Meanwhile, young Harthill was the companion and associate of Nathaniel Gordon, whom he accompanied at plundering the fair of Elgin, and at most of Montrose's engagements. He retaliated severely on the Covenanters, by ravaging and burning their lands.—Ibid. vol. ii. p. 301. His fate has escaped my notice.

[1] Newton, for obvious reasons, was a common appellation of an estate, or barony, where a new edifice had been erected. Hence, for distinction's sake, it was anciently compounded with the name of the proprietor; as, Newton-Edmonstone, Newton-Don, Newton-Gordon, &c. Of Gordon of New-town, I only observe, that he was, like all his clan, a steady loyalist, and a follower of Montrose.

[2] Sir Francis Hay, of Dalgatie, a steady cavalier, and a gentleman of great gallantry and accomplishments. He was a faithful follower of Montrose, and was taken prisoner with him at his last fatal battle. He was condemned to death with his illustrious general. Being a Roman Catholic, he refused the assistance of the Presbyterian clergy, and was not permitted, even on the scaffold, to receive ghostly comfort, in the only form in which his religion taught him to consider it as effectual. He kissed the axe, avowed his fidelity to his sovereign, and died like a soldier.—MONTROSE'S Memoirs, p. 322.—[The Dugald Dalgetty of the Legend of Montrose, owes his surname at least to this gentleman.—ED.]

And gallant Veitch[1] upon the field,
A braver face was never seen.

[1] I presume this gentleman to have been David Veitch, brother
to Veitch of Dawick, who, with many other of the Peebles-shire
gentry, was taken at Philiphaugh. The following curious accident
took place, some years afterwards, in consequence of his loyal zeal :
—" In the year 1653, when the loyal party did arise in arms
against the English, in the North and West Highlands, some noblemen and loyal gentlemen, with others, were forward to repair to
them with such forces as they could make ; which the English with
marvelouse diligence, night and day, did bestir themselves to im-
pede ; making their troops of horse and dragoons to pursue the
loyal party in all places, that they might not come to such a considerable number as was designed. It happened one night, that one
Captain Masoun, commander of a troop of dragoons, that came
from Carlisle, in England, marching through the town of Sanquhar
in the night, was encountered by one Captain Palmer, commanding
a troop of horse, that came from Ayr, marching eastward ; and,
meeting at the tolhouse, or tolbooth, one David Veitch, brother to
the Laird of Dawick, in Tweeddale, and one of the loyal party,
being prisoner in irons by the English, did arise, and came to the
window at their meeting, and cryed out, that they should *fight va-
liantly for King Charles.* Wherethrough, they, taking each other
for the loyal party, did begin a brisk fight, which continued for a
while, till the dragoons, having spent their shot, and finding the
horsemen to be too strong for them, did give ground ; but yet retired in some order towards the castle of Sanquhar, being hotly
pursued by the troop, through the whole town, above a quarter of a
mile, till they came to the castle ; where both parties did, to their
mutual grief, become sensible of their mistake. In this skirmish
there were several killed on both sides, and Captain Palmer himself dangerously wounded, with many more wounded in each troop,
who did peaceably dwell together afterward for a time, until their
wounds were cured, in Sanquhar castle."—*Account of Presbytery
of Penpont, in Macfarlane's MSS.*

Now, fare ye weel, Sweet Ennerdale!
    Countrie and kin I quit ye free;
Cheer up your hearts, brave cavaliers,
    For the Grahams are gone to High Germany.

Now brave Montrose he went to France,
    And to Germany, to gather fame;
And bold Aboyne is to the sea,
    Young Huntly is his noble name.[1]

Montrose again, that chieftain bold,
    Back unto Scotland fair he came,
For to redeem fair Scotland's land,
    The pleasant, gallant, worthy Graham!

At the water of Carron he did begin,
    And fought the battle to the end;
Where there were kill'd, for our noble king,
    Two thousand of our Danish men.[2]

Gilbert Menzies, of high degree,
    By whom the king's banner was borne;

[1] James, Earl of Aboyne, who fled to France, and there died
heart-broken. It is said his death was accelerated by the news of
King Charles's execution. He became representative of the Gordon family, or *Young Huntly*, as the ballad expresses it, in couse-
quenco of the death of his elder brother, George, who fell in the
battle of Alford.—*History of Gordon Family.*

[2] Montrose's foreign auxiliaries, who, by the way, did not exceed
600 in all.

For a brave cavalier was he,
    But now to glory he is gone.[1]

Then woe to Strachan, and Hacket[2] baith!
    And, Leslie, ill death may thou die!
For ye have betray'd the gallant Grahams,
    Who aye were true to majestic.

And the Laird of Assaint has seized Montrose,
    And had him into Edinburgh town;
And frae his body taken the head
    And quarter'd him upon a trone.

And Huntly's[3] gone the self-same way,
    And our noble king is also gone;

---

[1] Gilbert Menzies, younger of Pitfoddells, carried the royal ban
ner in Montrose's last battle. It bore the headless corpse of
Charles I., with this motto, " *Judge and revenge my cause, O
Lord!* " Menzies proved himself worthy of this noble trust, and,
obstinately refusing quarter, died in defence of his charge.—MON-
TROSE's *Memoirs.*

[2] Sir Charles Hacket, an officer in the service of the Estates.

[3] George Gordon, second Marquis of Huntly, one of the very
few nobles in Scotland who had uniformly adhered to the King
from the very beginning of the troubles, was beheaded by the sentence of the Parliament of Scotland (so calling themselves) upon
the 22d March, 1649, one month and twenty-two days after the
martyrdom of his master. He has been much blamed for not cordially co-operating with Montrose; and Bishop Wishart, in the
zeal of partiality for his hero, accuses Huntly of direct treachery.
But he is a true believer, who seals with his blood his creed, reli-

He suffer'd death for our nation,
    Our mourning tears can ne'er be done.

But our brave young king is now come home
    King Charles the Second in degree;
The Lord send peace into his time,
    And God preserve his majestie!

gious or political; and there are many reasons, short of this foul charge, which may have dictated the backward conduct of Huntly towards Montrose. He could not forget that, when he first stood out for the King, Montrose, then the soldier of the Covenant, had actually made him prisoner; and we cannot suppose Huntly to have been so sensible of Montrose's superior military talents, as not to think himself, as equal in rank, superior in power, and more uniform in loyalty, entitled to equally high marks of royal trust and favour. This much is certain, that the gallant clan of Gordon contributed greatly to Montrose's success; for the gentlemen of that name, with the brave and loyal Ogilvies, composed the principal part of his cavalry.

APPENDIX.

NOTE A.

Who was the traitor, Cromwell, then.—P. 188, v. 5.

THIS extraordinary character, to whom, in crimes and in success, our days only have produced a parallel, was no favourite in Scotland. There occurs the following invective against him in a MS. in the Advocates' Library. The humour consists in the dialect of a Highlander, speaking English, and confusing *Cromwell* with *Gramach,* ugly :—

> " Te commonwelt, tat Gramagh ting
> Gar brek hem's word, gar de hem's king ;
> Gar pay hem's sesse, or take hem's (geers)
> We'l no de at, del cowe de leers ;
> We'l bide a file amang te crowes, [*i.e.* in the woods,]
> We'l scor te sword, and whiske te bowes ;
> And fen her nen sel se te re, [the king,]
> Te del may care for *Gromaghee.*"

The following tradition, concerning Cromwell, is preserved by an uncommonly direct line of traditional evidence; being related (as I am informed) by the grandson of an eyewitness. When Cromwell, in 1650, entered Glasgow, he attended divine service in the High Church ; but the Presbyterian divine who officiated, poured forth, with more zeal than prudence, the vial of his indignation upon the person, principles, and cause, of the Independent General. One of Cromwell's officers rose, and whispered his commander ; who seemed to give him a short and stern answer, and the sermon was concluded without interruption. Among the crowd, who were assembled to gaze at the General, as he came out of the church, was a shoemaker, the son of one of James the Sixth's Scottish footmen. This man had been born and bred in England, but, after his father's death, had settled in Glasgow. Cromwell eyed him among the crowd, and immediately called him by his name—the man fled; but, at Cromwell's command, one of his retinue followed him, and brought him to the General's lodgings. A number of the inhabitants remained at the door, waiting the end of this extraordinary scene. The shoemaker soon came out, in high spirits, and, showing some gold, declared, he was going to drink Cromwell's health. Many attended him to hear the particulars of his interview: among others the grandfather of the narrator. The shoemaker said that he had been a playfellow of Cromwell, when they were both boys, their parents residing in the same street; that he had fled, when the General first called to him, thinking he might owe him some ill will, on account of his father being in the service of the royal family. He added, that Cromwell had been so very kind and familiar with him, that he ventured to ask him, what the officer had said to him in the church. " He proposed," said Cromwell, " to pull forth the minister by the ears; and I answered, that the preacher was one fool and he another." In the course of the day, Cromwell held an interview with the minister, and contrived to satisfy his scruples so effectually, that the evening discourse, by the same man, was tuned to the praise and glory of the victor of Naseby.

Note B.

Nathaniel Gordon, stout and bold,
Did for King Charles wear the blue.—P. 189, v. 4.

This gentleman was of the ancient family of Gordon of Gight. He had served, as a soldier, upon the continent, and acquired great military skill. When his chief, the Marquis of Huntly, took up arms in 1640, Nathaniel Gordon, then called Major Gordon, joined him, and was of essential service during that short insurrection. But, being checked for making prize of a Danish fishing buss, he left the service of the Marquis, in some disgust. In 1645, he assisted at a sharp and dexterous *camisade*, (as it was then called,) when the Barons of Haddo, of Gight, of Drum, and other gentlemen, with only sixty men under their standard, galloped through the old town of Aberdeen, and, entering the burgh itself, about seven in the morning, made prisoners and carried off four of the covenanting magistrates, and effected a safe retreat, though the town was then under the domination of the opposite party. After the death of the Baron of Haddo, and the severe treatment of Sir George Gordon of Gight, his cousin-german, Major Nathaniel Gordon, seems to have taken arms in despair of finding mercy at the Covenanters' hands. On the 24th of July, 1645, he came down, with a band of horsemen, upon the town of Elgin, while St James's fair was held, and pillaged the merchants of 14,000 merks of money and merchandise. [1] He seems to have joined Montrose, as soon as he raised the royal standard ; and, as a bold and active partisan, rendered him great service. But, in November, 1644, Gordon, now a colonel, suddenly deserted Montrose, aided the escape of Forbes of Craigievar, one of his prisoners, and reconciled himself to the kirk, by doing penance for adultery, and for the almost equally heinous crime of having scared Mr Andrew Cant,[2] the famous apostle of the Covenant. This, however, seems to have been an artifice, to arrange a correspondence betwixt Montrose and Lord Gordon, a gallant young nobleman, representative of the Huntly family, and inheriting their loyal spirit, though hitherto engaged in the service of the Covenant. Colonel Gordon was successful, and returned to the royal camp with his converted chief. Both followed zealously the fortunes of Montrose, until Lord Gordon fell in the battle of Alford, and Nathaniel Gordon was taken at Philiphaugh. He was one of the ten loyalists, devoted upon that occasion, by the Parliament, to expiate with their blood the crime of fidelity to their

[1] SPALDING, vol. ii. pp. 151, 154, 169, 181, 221. *History of the Family of Gordon*, Edin. 1727, vol. ii. p. 299.

[2] He had sent him a letter, which nigh frightened him out of his wits. —SPALDING, vol. ii. p. 231.

King.   Nevertheless, the covenanted nobles would have probably been satisfied with the death of the gallant Rollock, the sharer of Montrose's dangers and glory,—of Ogilvy, a youth of eighteen, whose crime was the hereditary feud betwixt his family and Argyle,—and of Sir Philip Nisbet, a cavalier of the ancient stamp,—had not the pulpits resounded with the cry, that God required the blood of the malignants to expiate the sins of the people.   " What meaneth," exclaimed the ministers, in the perverted language of Scripture— " What meaneth, then, this bleating of the sheep in my ears, and the lowing of the oxen ? "   The appeal to the judgment of Samuel was decisive, and the shambles were instantly opened.   Nathaniel Gordon was brought first to execution.   He lamented the sins of his youth—once more (and probably with greater sincerity) requested absolution from the sentence of excommunication pronounced on account of adultery—and was beheaded 6th January, 1646.

THE

BATTLE OF PENTLAND HILLS.

WE have observed the early antipathy mutually entertained by the Scottish Presbyterians and the house
of Stuart. It seems to have glowed in the breast even
of the good-natured Charles II. He might have remembered, that, in 1651, the Presbyterians had fought,
bled, and ruined themselves in his cause. But he
rather recollected their early faults than their late repentance; and even their services were combined with the
recollection of the absurd and humiliating circumstances
of personal degradation,[1] to which their pride and folly
had subjected him, while they professed to espouse his

[1] Among other ridiculous occurrences, it is said, that some of
Charles's gallantries were discovered by a prying neighbour. A
wily old minister was deputed by his brethren to rebuke the King
for this heinous scandal. Being introduced into the royal presence,
he limited his commission to a serious admonition, that, upon such
occasions, his Majesty should always shut the windows. The King
is said to have recompensed this unexpected lenity after the Restoration. He probably remembered the joke, though he might have
forgotten the service.

cause. As a man of pleasure, he hated their stern and inflexible rigour, which stigmatized follies even more deeply than crimes ; and he whispered to his confidants, that " Presbytery was no religion for a gentleman." It is not, therefore, wonderful, that, in the first year of his restoration, he formally re-established Prelacy in Scotland ; but it is surprising, that, with his father's example before his eyes, he should not have been satisfied to leave at freedom the consciences of those who could not reconcile themselves to the new system. The religious opinions of sectaries have a tendency, like the water of some springs, to become soft and mild, when freely exposed to the open day. Who can recognise, in our decent and industrious Quakers, and Anabaptists, the wild and ferocious tenets which distinguished those sects, while they were yet honoured with the distinction of the scourge and the pillory ? Had the system of coercion against the Presbyterians been continued until our day, Blair and Robertson would have preached in the wilderness, and only discovered their powers of eloquence and composition, by rolling along a deeper torrent of gloomy fanaticism.

The western counties distinguished themselves by their opposition to the prelatic system. Three hundred and fifty ministers, ejected from their churches and livings, wandered through the mountains, sowing the seeds of covenanted doctrine, while multitudes of fanatical followers pursued them, to reap the forbidden crop. These conventicles, as they were called, were denounced by the law, and their frequenters dispersed by military force. The genius of the persecuted became stubborn, obstinate, and ferocious ; and although indulgences were tardily granted to some Presbyterian ministers, few of the true Covenanters, or Whigs, as they were called, would condescend to compound with a prelatic government, or to listen even to their own favourite doctrine under the auspices of the King. From Richard Cameron, their apostle, this rigid sect acquired the name of Cameronians. They preached and prayed against the indulgence, and against the Presbyterians who availed themselves of it, because their accepting this royal boon was a tacit acknowledgment of the King's supremacy in ecclesiastical matters. Upon these bigoted and persecuted fanatics, and by no means upon the Presbyterians at large, are to be charged the wild anarchical principles of anti-monarchy and assassination, which polluted the period when they flourished.

The insurrection, commemorated and magnified in the following ballad, as indeed it has been in some histories, was, in itself, no very important affair. It began in Dumfries-shire, where Sir James Turner, a soldier of fortune, was employed to levy the arbitrary fines imposed for not attending the Episcopal churches.[1] The people rose, seized his person, disarmed his soldiers, and, having continued together, resolved to march towards Edinburgh, expecting to be joined by their friends

---

[1] Sir James Turner's Memoirs have been published lately. 1830.

in that quarter.   In this they were disappointed; and, being now diminished to half their numbers, they drew up on the Pentland Hills, at a place called Rullien Green.   They were commanded by one Wallace; and here they awaited the approach of General Dalziel, of Binns; who, having marched to Calder, to meet them on the Lanark road, and finding, that, by passing through Collington, they had got to the other side of the hills, cut through the mountains and approached them.   Wallace showed both spirit and judgment: he drew up his men in a very strong situation, and withstood two charges of Dalziel's cavalry; but, upon the third shock, the insurgents were broken and utterly dispersed.   There was very little slaughter, as the cavalry of Dalziel were chiefly gentlemen, who pitied their oppressed and misguided countrymen.   There were about fifty killed, and as many made prisoners.   The battle was fought on the 28th November, 1666; a day still observed by the scattered remnant of the Cameronian sect, who regularly hear a field-preaching upon the field of battle.

I am obliged for a copy of the ballad to Mr Livingston of Airds, who took it down from the recitation of an old woman residing on his estate.

The gallant Grahams, mentioned in the text, are Graham of Claverhouse's horse.

THE

BATTLE OF PENTLAND HILLS.

This Ballad is copied verbatim from the old Woman's
Recitation.

THE gallant Grahams cam from the west,
Wi' their horses black as ony craw ;
The Lothian lads they marched fast,
To be at the Rhyns o' Gallowa.

Betwixt Dumfries town and Argyle,
The lads they marched mony a mile ;
Souters and tailors unto them drew,
Their covenants for to renew.

The Whigs, they, wi' their merry cracks,
Gar'd the poor pedlars lay down their packs ;
But aye sinsyne they do repent
The renewing o' their Covenant.

At the Mauchline muir, where they were review'd,
Ten thousand men in armour show'd ;
But, ere they came to the Brockie's burn,
The half of them did back return.

General Dalyell,[1] as I hear tell,
Was our lieutenant-general ;
And Captain Welsh, wi' his wit and skill,
Was to guide them on to the Pentland hill.

General Dalyell held to the hill,
Asking at them what was their will ;
And who gave them this protestation,
To rise in arms against the nation ?

" Although we all in armour be,
It's not against his majesty ;
Nor yet to spill our neighbour's bluid,
But wi' the country we'll conclude."—

" Lay down your arms, in the King's name,
And ye shall a' gae safely hame ;"—
But they a' cried out wi' ae consent,
" We'll fight for a broken Covenant."—

" O well," says he, " since it is so,
A wilfu' man never wanted woe."—

[1] [General Dalyell—See notes to Old Mortality. Waverley Novels, vol. x.—Ed.]

He then gave a sign unto his lads,
And they drew up in their brigades.

The trumpets blew, and the colours flew,
And every man to his armour drew ;
The Whigs were never so much aghast,
As to see their saddles toom[1] sae fast.

The cleverest men stood in the van,
The Whigs they took their heels and ran ;
But such a raking was never seen,
As the raking o' the Rullien Green.

[1] *Toom*—empty.

THE BATTLE OF LOUDON HILL.

THE Whigs, now become desperate, adopted the
most desperate principles; and retaliating, as far as
they could, the intolerating persecution which they en-
dured, they openly disclaimed allegiance to any monarch
who should not profess Presbytery, and subscribe the
Covenant.   These principles were not likely to con-
ciliate the favour of government; and as we wade
onward in the history of the times, the scenes become
yet darker.   At length, one would imagine the parties
had agreed to divide the kingdom of vice betwixt them;
the hunters assuming to themselves open profligacy and
legalized oppression;   and the hunted, the opposite
attributes of hypocrisy, fanaticism, disloyalty, and midnight assassination.   The troopers and cavaliers became
enthusiasts in the pursuit of the Covenanters.   If
Messrs Kid, King, Cameron, Peden, &c., boasted of
prophetic powers, and were often warned of the approach
of the soldiers by supernatural impulse,[1] Captain John
Creichton, on the other side, dreamed dreams, and saw

---

[1] In the year 1684, Peden, one of the Cameronian preachers,
about ten o'clock at night, sitting at the fire-side, started up to his
feet, and said, " Flee, auld Sandie, [thus he designed himself,]

visions, (chiefly, indeed, after having drunk hard,) in which the lurking-holes of the rebels were discovered to his imagination.[1] Our ears are scarcely more shocked with the profane execrations of the persecutors,[2] than with the strange and insolent familiarity used towards the Deity by the persecuted fanatics. Their indecent modes of prayer, their extravagant expectations of miraculous assistance, and their supposed inspirations, might easily furnish out a tale, at which the good would sigh, and the gay would laugh.[3]

and hide yourself! for Colonel ——— is coming to this house to apprehend you; and I advise you all to do the like, for he will be here within an hour;" which came to pass: and when they had made a very narrow search, within and without the house, and went round the thorn bush, under which he was lying praying, they went off without their prey. He came in, and said, " And has this gentleman [designed by his name] given poor Sandie, and thir poor things, such a fright? For this night's work, God shall give him such a blow, within a few days, that all the physicians on earth shall not be able to cure;" which came to pass, for he died in great misery. —*Life of Alexander Peden.*

[1] See the life of this booted apostle of prelacy, written by Swift, who had collected all his anecdotes of persecution, and appears to have enjoyed them accordingly. [Scott's edition of Swift, vol. x. p. 101.]

[2] " They raved," says Peden's historian, " like fleshly devils, when the mist shrouded from their pursuit the wandering Whigs." One gentleman closed a declaration of vengeance against the conventiclers, with this strange imprecation, " Or may the devil make my ribs a gridiron to my soul!"—*MS. Account of the Presbytery of Penpont.* Our armies swore terribly in Flanders, but nothing to this. *

[3] Peden complained heavily, that, after a heavy struggle with the

* [See Tristram Shandy.]

In truth, extremes always approach each other; and the superstition of the Roman Catholics was, in some degree, revived, even by their most deadly enemies. They are ridiculed, by the cavaliers, as wearing the relies of their saints by way of amulet :—

> " She shewed to me a box, wherein lay hid
> The pictures of Cargil and Mr Kid;
> A splinter of the tree, on which they were slain;
> A double inch of Major Weir's best cane;
> Rathillet's sword, beat down to table knife,
> Which took at Magus' Muir a bishop's life;
> The worthy Welch's spectacles, who saw,
> That windle-straws would fight against the law;
> They, windle-straws, were stoutest of the two,
> They kept their ground, away the prophet flew;
> And lists of all the prophets' names were seen
> At Pentland Hills, Aird Moss, and Rullen Green.
>   " ' Don't think,' she says, ' these holy things are foppery;
> They're precious antidotes against the power of popery.' "
>   *The Cameronian Tooth.*—PENNYCUICK'S *Poems*, p. 110.

The militia and standing army soon became unequal to the task of enforcing conformity, and suppressing conventicles. In their aid, and to force compliance with a test proposed by government, the Highland clans were raised, and poured down into Ayrshire. An armed host of undisciplined mountaineers, speaking a different language, and professing, many of them, another religion,

devil, he had got above him, *spur-galled* him hard, and obtained a wind to carry him from Ireland to Scotland, when, behold! another person had set sail, and reaped the advantage of his *prayer-wind* before he could embark.

were let loose, to ravage and plunder this unfortunate country; and it is truly astonishing to find how few acts of cruelty they perpetrated, and how seldom they added murder to pillage.[1] Additional levies of horse were also raised, under the name of Independent Troops, and great part of them placed under the command of

---

[1] Cleland thus describes this extraordinary army :

—" Those who were their chief commanders,
As such who bore the pirnie standarts,
Who led the van and drove the rear,
Were right well mounted of their gear ;
With brogues, and trews, and pirnie plaids,
With good blue bonnets on their heads,
Which, on the one side, had a flipe,
Adorn'd with a tobacco-pipe,
With durk, and snap-work, and snuff-mill,
A bag, which they with onions fill ;
And, as their strict observers say,
A tup-horn filled with usquebay ;
A slasht-out coat beneath her plaides,
A targe of timber, nails, and hides ;
With a long two-handed sword,
As good's the country can afford.
Had they not need of bulk and bones,
Who fought with all these arms at once ?

Of mortal honestie they're clean,
Nought like religion they retain :
In nothing they're accounted sharp,
Except in bag-pipe, and in harp ;
For a misobliging word,
She'll durk her neighbour o'er the boord,
And then she'll flee like fire from flint,
She'll scarcely ward the second dint ;
If any ask her of her thrift,
Forsooth her nainsell lives by thirt."

CLELAND's *Poems*, Edin. 1697, p. 12.

James Graham of Claverhouse, a man well known to
fame by his subsequent title of Viscount Dundee, but
better remembered, in the western shires, under the
designation of the Bloody Clavers. In truth, he appears
to have combined the virtues and vices of a savage chief.[1]
Fierce, unbending, and rigorous, no emotion of compas-
sion prevented his commanding and witnessing every
detail of military execution against the non-conformists.   Undauntedly brave, and steadily faithful to his
prince, he sacrificed himself in the cause of James, when
he was deserted by all the world.   If we add, to these
attributes, a goodly person, complete skill in martial
exercises, and that ready and decisive character, so essential to a commander, we may form some idea of this
extraordinary character.   The Whigs, whom he perse
cuted, daunted by his ferocity and courage, conceived
him to be impassive to their bullets,[2] and that he had

---

[1] [Compare the character of Claverhouse, as drawn in greater
detail, and with richer colours, long afterwards, in the Tale of Old
Mortality. Waverley Novels, vol. x. pp. 57, 58.   See also Lay
of the Last Minstrel, Introduction and Notes to Canto II.—Ed.]

[2] It was, and is believed, that the devil furnished his favourites,
among the persecutors, with what is called *proof* against leaden bullets, but against those only.   During the battle of Pentland-hills,
Paton of Meadowhead conceived he saw the balls hop harmlessly
down from General Dalziel's boots, and, to counteract the spell,
loaded his pistol with a piece of silver coin.   But Dalziel, having
his eye on him, drew back behind his servant, who was shot dead.
—*Paton's Life.*   At a skirmish in Ayrshire, some of the wanderers defended themselves in a sequestered house, by the side of
a lake.   They aimed repeatedly, but in vain, at the commander of

sold himself, for temporal greatness, to the seducer of mankind. It is still believed that a cup of wine, presented to him by his butler, changed into clotted blood; and that, when he plunged his feet into cold water, their touch caused it to boil. The steed, which bore him, was supposed to be the gift of Satan; and precipices are shown, where a fox could hardly keep his feet, down which the infernal charger conveyed him safely, in pursuit of the wanderers. It is remembered with terror, that Claverse was successful in every engagement with the Whigs, except that at Drumclog, or Loudon Hill, which is the subject of the following ballad. The his

the assailants, an English officer, until, their ammunition running short, one of them loaded his piece with the ball at the head of the tongs, and succeeded in shooting the hitherto impenetrable captain. To accommodate Dundee's fate to their own hypothesis, the Cameronian tradition runs, that in the battle of Killicrankie he fell, not by the enemy's fire, but by the pistol of one of his own servants, who, to avoid the spell had loaded it with a silver button from his coat. One of their writers argues thus : " Perhaps some may think this, anent proof shot, a paradox, and be ready to object here, as formerly, concerning Bishop Sharpe and Dalziel—How can the devil have, or give, power to save life ? Without entering upon the thing in its reality, I shall only observe, 1. That it is neither in his power, or of his nature, to be a saviour of men's lives ; he is called Apollyon, the destroyer. 2. That, even in this case, he is said only to give enchantment against one kind of metal, and this does not save life ; for, though lead could not take Sharpe and Claverhouse's lives, yet steel and silver could do it ; and, for Dalziel, though he died not on the field, yet he did not escape the arrows of the Almighty."— *God's Judgment against Persecutors.* If the reader be not now convinced of *the thing in its reality,* I have nothing to add to such exquisite reasoning.

tory of Burly, the hero of the piece, will bring us immediately to the causes and circumstances of that event.

John Balfour of Kinloch, commonly called Burly,[1] was one of the fiercest of the proscribed sect. A gentleman by birth, he was, says his biographer, " zealous and honest-hearted, courageous in every enterprise, and a brave soldier, seldom any escaping that came in his hands."—*Life of John Balfour*. Creichton says, that he was once chamberlain to Archbishop Sharpe, and, by negligence or dishonesty, had incurred a large arrear, which occasioned his being active in his master's assassination. But of this I know no other evidence than Creichton's assertion, and a hint in Wodrow. Burly (for that is his most common designation) was brother-in-law to Hackston of Rathillet, a wild enthusiastic character, who joined daring courage and skill in the sword to the fiery zeal of his sect. Burly, himself, was less eminent for religious fervour, than for the active and violent share which he had in the most desperate enterprises of his party. His name does not appear among the Covenanters, who were denounced for the affair of Pentland. But, in 1677, Robert Hamilton, afterwards commander of the insurgents at Loudon Hill, and Bothwell Bridge, with several other non-conformists, were assembled at this Burly's house, in Fife. There they were attacked by a party of soldiers, commanded by Captain Carstairs, whom they beat off,

---

[1] [This is another of the heroes of Old Mortality. Waverley Novels, vol. ix. p. 295, &c.—Ed.]

wounding desperately one of his party. For this resistance to authority, they were declared rebels. The
next exploit in which Burly was engaged, was of a
bloodier complexion and more dreadful celebrity. It is
well known, that James Sharpe, Archbishop of St Andrews, was regarded by the rigid Presbyterians, not only
as a renegade, who had turned back from the spiritual
plough, but as the principal author of the rigours exercised against their sect. He employed, as an agent
of his oppression, one Carmichael, a decayed gentleman.
The industry of this man, in procuring information,
and in enforcing the severe penalties against conventi
clers, having excited the resentment of the Cameroni
ans, nine of their number, of whom Burly and his brother-in-law, Hackston, were the leaders, assembled with
the purpose of waylaying and murdering Carmichael;
but, while they searched for him in vain, they received
tidings that the Archbishop himself was at hand. The
party resorted to prayer; after which they agreed unanimously that the Lord had delivered the wicked Haman into their hand. In the execution of the supposed
will of Heaven, they agreed to put themselves under
the command of a leader; and they requested Hackston of Rathillet to accept the office, which he decli-
ned, alleging, that, should he comply with their request,
the slaughter might be imputed to a private quarrel,
which existed betwixt him and the Archbishop. The
command was then offered to Burly, who accepted it
without scruple; and they galloped off in pursuit of

the Archbishop's carriage, which contained himself and his daughter. Being well mounted, they easily overtook and disarmed the prelate's attendants. Burly, crying out, " Judas, be taken !" rode up to the carriage, wounded the postilion, and hamstrung one of the horses. He then fired into the coach a piece, charged with several bullets, so near, that the archbishop's gown was set on fire. The rest, coming up, dismounted, and dragged him out of the carriage, when, frightened and wounded, he crawled towards Hackston, who still remained on horseback, and begged for mercy. The stern enthusiast contented himself with answering, that he would not himself *lay a hand on him.* Burly and his men again fired a volley upon the kneeling old man; and were in the act of riding off, when one, who remained to girth his horse, unfortunately heard the daughter of their victim call to the servant for help, exclaiming, that his master was still alive. Burly then again dismounted, struck off the prelate's hat with his foot, and split his skull with his shable, (broadsword,) although one of the party (probably Rathillet) exclaimed, " *Spare these grey hairs !*"[1] The rest pierced

---

[1] They believed Sharpe to be proof against shot ; for one of the murderers told Wodrow, that at the sight of cold iron his courage fell. They no longer doubted this, when they found in his pocket a small clew of silk, rolled round a bit of parchment, marked with two long words, in Hebrew or Chaldaic characters. Accordingly, it is still averred that the balls only left blue marks on the prelate's neck and breast, although the discharge was so near as to burn his clothes.

him with repeated wounds. They plundered the carriage, and rode off, leaving, beside the mangled corpse, the daughter, who was herself wounded, in her pious endeavour to interpose betwixt her father and his murderers. The murder is accurately represented, in bas relief, upon a beautiful monument, erected to the memory of Archbishop Sharpe, in the Metropolitan Church of St Andrews.[1] This memorable example of fanatic revenge was acted upon Magus Muir, near St Andrews, 3d May, 1679.[2]

Burly was, of course, obliged to leave Fife ; and, upon the 25th of the same month, he arrived in Evandale, in Lanarkshire, along with Hackston, and a fellow called Dingwall, or Daniel, one of the same bloody band. Here he joined his old friend Hamilton, already

---

[1] The murder of Archbishop Sharpe has recently been made the subject of a very noble picture by Mr Wm. Allan, A.R.A. 1830.

[2] The question, whether the Bishop of St Andrews' death was murder, was a shibboleth, or *experimentum crucis*, frequently put to the apprehended conventiclers. Isabel Alison, executed at Edinburgh, 26th January, 1681, was interrogated, before the Privy Council, if she conversed with David Hackston ? " I answered, I did converse with him, and I bless the Lord that ever I saw him ; for I never saw ought in him but a godly pious youth. They asked, if the killing of the Bishop of St Andrews was a pious act ? I answered, I never heard him say he killed him ; but, if God moved any, and put it upon them to execute his righteous judgment upon him, I have nothing to say to that. They asked me, when saw ye John Balfour (Burly,) that pious youth ? I answered, I have seen him. They asked, when ? I answered, these are frivolous questions ; I am not bound to answer them."— *Cloud of Witnesses*, p. 85.

mentioned ; and, as they resolved to take up arms, they were soon at the head of such a body of the " chased and tossed western men," as they thought equal to keep the field.   They resolved to commence their exploits upon the 29th of May, 1679, being the anniversary of the Restoration, appointed to be kept as a holyday, by act of Parliament ; an institution which they esteemed a presumptuous and unholy solemnity.   Accordingly, at the head of eighty horse, tolerably appointed, Hamilton, Burly, and Hackston, entered the royal burgh of Rutherglen ; extinguished the bonfires made in honour of the day ; and burned at the cross the acts of Parliament in favour of Prelacy, and for suppression of conventicles, as well as those acts of council which regulated the indulgence granted to Presbyterians.   Against all these acts they entered their solemn protest, or testimony, as they called it ; and, having affixed it to the cross, concluded with prayer and psalms.   Being now joined by a large body of foot, so that their strength seems to have amounted to five or six hundred men, though very indifferently armed, they encamped upon Loudon Hill.   Claverhouse, who was in garrison at Glasgow, instantly marched against the insurgents, at the head of his own troop of cavalry and others, amounting to about one hundred and fifty men.   He arrived at Hamilton on the 1st of June, so unexpectedly, as to make prisoner John King, a famous preacher among the wanderers ; and rapidly continued his march, carrying his captive along with him, till he came to the village of Drumclog, about a mile east of Loudon Hill, and twelve miles south-west of Hamilton. At some distance from this place, the insurgents were skilfully posted in a boggy strait, almost inaccessible to cavalry, having a broad ditch in their front. Claverhouse's dragoons discharged their carabines, and made an attempt to charge; but the nature of the ground threw them into total disorder. Burly, who commanded the handful of horse belonging to the Whigs, instantly led them down on the disordered squadrons of Claverhouse, who were, at the same time, vigorously assaulted by the foot, headed by the gallant Cleland,[1] and the enthusiastic Hackston. Claverhouse himself was forced to fly, and was in the

---

[1] William Cleland, a man of considerable genius, was author of several poems, published in 1697. His Hudibrastic verses are poor scurrilous trash, as the reader may judge from the description of the Highlanders, already quoted. But, in a wild rhapsody, entitled, " Hollo, my Fancy," he displays some imagination. His anti-monarchical principles seem to break out in the following lines :—

" Fain would I know (if beasts have any reason)
If falcons killing eagles do commit a treason? "

He was a strict non-conformist, and, after the Revolution, became lieutenant-colonel of the Earl of Angus's regiment, called the Cameronian regiment. He was killed 21st August, 1689, in the churchyard of Dunkeld, which his corps manfully and successfully defended against a superior body of Highlanders. His son was the author of the letter prefixed to the Dunciad, and is said to have been the notorious Cleland, who, in circumstances of pecuniary embarrassment, prostituted his talents to the composition of indecent and infamous works; but this seems inconsistent with dates, and the latter personage was probably the grandson of Colonel Cleland.

utmost danger of being taken ; his horse's belly being cut open by the stroke of a scythe, so that the poor animal trailed his bowels for more than a mile. In his flight, he passed King, the minister, lately his prisoner, but now deserted by his guard in the general confusion. The preacher hollowed to the flying commander, " to halt, and to take his prisoner with him ;" or, as others say, " to stay, and take the afternoon's preaching." Claverhouse, at length remounted, continued his retreat to Glasgow. He lost, in the skirmish, about twenty of his troopers, and his own cornet and kinsman, Robert Graham, whose fate is alluded to in the ballad. Only four of the other side were killed, among whom was Dingwall, or Daniel, an associate of Burly in Sharpe's murder. " The rebels," says Creichton, " finding the cornet's body, and supposing it to be that of Clavers, because the name of Graham was wrought in the shirt-neck, treated it with the utmost inhumanity ; cutting off the nose ; picking out the eyes ; and stabbing it through in a hundred places." The same charge is brought by Guild, in his *Bellum Bothuellianum,* in which occurs the following account of the skirmish at Drumclog :—

Mons est occiduus surgit qui celsus in oris,
 Nomine Loudunum,) fossis puteisque profundis,
Quo scatet hic tellus, et aprico gramine tectus :
Huc collecta fuit, numeroso milite cincta,
Turba ferox, matres, pueri, innuptæque puellæ,
Quam parat egregiâ Græmus dispersere turmâ.

Venit, et primo campo discedere cogit ;
Post hos et alios, cœno provolvit inerti ;
At numerosa cohors, campum dispersa per omnem,
Circumfusa ruit ; turmasque, indagine captas,
Aggreditur ; virtus non hic, nec profuit ensis ;
Corripuere fugam, viridi sed gramine tectis,
Precipitata perit fossis pars plurima, quorum
Cornipedes hæsere luto, sessore rejecto :
Tum rabiosa cohors, misereri nescia, stratos
Invadit laceratque viros : hic signifer, eheu !
Trajectus globulo, Grœmus, quo fortior alter,
Inter Scotigenas fuerat, nec justior ullus ;
Hunc manibus rapuere feris, faciemque virilem
Fœdarunt, lingua, auriculis, manibusque resectis,
Aspera diffuso spargentes saxa cerebro.
Vix dux ipse fugâ salvus, namque exta trahebat
Vulnere tardatus sonipes generosus hiante ;
Insequitur clamore cohors fanatica, namque
Crudelis semper timidus si vicerit unquam.

N S. Bellum Bothuellianum.

Although Burly was among the most active leaders
in the action, he was not the commander-in-chief, as
one would conceive from the ballad. That honour belonged to Robert Hamilton, brother to Sir William
Hamilton of Preston, a gentleman, who, like most of
those at Drumclog, had imbibed the very wildest principles of fanaticism. The Cameronian account of the
insurrection states, that " Mr Hamilton discovered a
great deal of bravery and valour, both in the conflict
with, and pursuit of, the enemy ; but when he and some
others were pursuing the enemy, others flew too greedily upon the spoil, small as it was, instead of pursuing

the victory: and some, without Mr Hamilton's knowledge, and against his strict command, gave five of these
bloody enemies quarters, and then let them go: this
greatly grieved Mr Hamilton, when he saw some of
Babel's brats spared, after the Lord had delivered them
to their hands, that they might dash them against the
stones. *Psalm* cxxxvii. 9. In his own account of
this, he reckons the sparing of these enemies, and let-
ting them go, to be among their first stepping aside;
for which he feared that the Lord would not honour
them to do much more for him; and says, that he was
neither for taking favours from, nor giving favours to,
the Lord's enemies."

Burly was not a likely man to fall into this sort of
backsliding. He disarmed one of the Duke of Hamilton's servants who had been in the action, and desired
him to tell his master, he would keep, till meeting,
the pistols he had taken from him. The man described
Burly to the Duke as a little stout man, squint-eyed,
and of a most ferocious aspect; from which it appears
that Burly's figure corresponded to his manners, and
perhaps gave rise to his nickname—*Burly* signifying
strong. He was with the insurgents till the battle of
Bothwell Bridge, and afterwards fled to Holland. He
joined the Prince of Orange, but died at sea during
the expedition. The Cameronians still believe he had
obtained liberty from the Prince to be avenged of those
who had persecuted the Lord's people; but, through his
death, the laudable design of purging the land with

their blood, is supposed to have fallen to the ground. —*Life of Balfour of Kinloch.*

The consequences of the battle of Loudon Hill will be detailed in the introduction to the next ballad.

THE

BATTLE OF LOUDON HILL.

You'l marvel when I tell ye o'
    Our noble Burly, and his train;
When last he march'd up through the land,
    Wi' sax-and-twenty Westland men.

Than they I ne'er o' braver heard,
    For they had a' baith wit and skill;
They proved right well, as I heard tell,
    As they cam up o'er Loudon Hill.

Weel prosper a' the gospel lads,
    That are into the west countrie;
Aye wicked Claver'se to demean,
    And aye an ill deid may he die!

For he's drawn up i' battle rank,
    An' that baith soon an' hastilie;
But they wha live till simmer come,
    Some bludie days for this will see.
2

But up spak cruel Claver'se, then,
    Wi' hastie wit, an' wicked skill ;
" Gae fire on yon Westlan' men ;
    I think it is my sov'reign's will."—

But up bespake his Cornet, then,
    " It's be wi' nae consent o' me '
I ken I'll ne'er come back again,
    An' mony mae as weel as me.

" There is not ane of a' yon men,
    But wha is worthy other three ;
There is na ane amang them a'
    That in his cause will stap to die.

" An' as for Burly, him I knaw ;
    He's a man of honour, birth, and fame
Gie him a sword into his hand,
    He'll fight thysell an' other ten."—

But up spake wicked Claver'se, then,
    I wat his heart it raise fu' hie !
And he has cried that a' might hear,
    " Man, ye hae sair deceived me.

" I never ken'd the like afore,
    Na, never since I came frae hame,

That you sae cowardly here suld prove,
    An' yet come of a noble Græme."—

But up bespake his Cornet, then,
    " Since that it is your honour's will,
Mysell shall be the foremost man,
    That shall gie fire on Loudon Hill—

" At your command I'll lead them on,
    But yet wi' nae consent o' me ;
For weel I ken I'll ne'er return,
    And mony mae as weel as me."—[1]

Then up he drew in battle rank ;
    I wat he had a bonny train !
But the first time that bullets flew,
    Aye he lost twenty o' his men.

Then back he came the way he gaed,
    I wat right soon and suddenly !
He gave command amang his men,
    And sent them back, and bade them flee.

Then up came Burly, bauld an' stout,
    Wi's little train o' Westland men ;

---

[1] [See the account of this battle in Old Mortality. Waverley
Novels, vol. x. pp. 120-125.—ED.]

Wha mair than either aince or twice
  In Edinburgh confined had been.

They hae been up to London sent,
  An' yet they're a' come safely down ;
Sax troop o' horsemen they hae beat,
  And chased them into Glasgow town.

THE

BATTLE OF BOTHWELL BRIDGE.

IT has been often remarked, that the Scottish, notwithstanding their national courage, were always unsuccessful when fighting for their religion. The cause lay, not in the principle, but in the mode of its application. A leader, like Mahomet, who is at the same time the prophet of his tribe, may avail himself of religious enthusiasm, because it comes to the aid of discipline, and is a powerful means of attaining the despotic command, essential to the success of a general. But, among the insurgents, in the reigns of the last Stuarts, were mingled preachers, who taught different shades of the Presbyterian doctrine; and, minute as these shades sometimes were, neither the several shepherds, nor their flocks, could cheerfully unite in a common cause. This will appear from the transactions leading to the battle of Bothwell Bridge.

We have seen that the party, which defeated Claverhouse at Loudon Hill, were Cameronians, whose principles consisted in disowning all temporal authority, which did not flow from and through the Solemn League and Covenant. This doctrine, which is still retained by a scattered remnant of the sect in Scotland, is in theory and would be in practice, inconsistent with the safety of any well-regulated government, because the Covenanters deny to their governors that toleration, which was iniquitously refused to themselves. In many respects, therefore, we cannot be surprised at the anxiety and rigour with which the Cameronians were persecuted, although we may be of opinion, that milder means would have induced a melioration of their principles. These men, as already noticed, excepted against such Presbyterians, as were contented to exercise their worship under the indulgence granted by government, or, in other words, who would have been satisfied with toleration for themselves, without insisting upon a revolution in the state, or even in the church establishment.

When, however, the success at Loudon Hill was spread abroad, a number of preachers, gentlemen, and common people, who had embraced the more moderate doctrine, joined the army of Hamilton, thinking that the difference in their opinions ought no longer to prevent their acting in the common cause. The insurgents were repulsed in an attack upon the town of Glasgow, which, however, Claverhouse, shortly afterwards, thought it necessary to evacuate. They were now nearly in full possession of the west of Scotland, and pitched their camp at Hamilton, where, instead of modelling and disciplining their army, the Cameronians and Erastians (for so the violent insurgents chose to call the more moderate Presbyterians) onlv debated, in council of war, the real cause of their being in arms.   Robert Hamilton, their general, was the leader of the first party ; Mr John Walsh, a minister, headed the Erastians. The latter so far prevailed, as to get a declaration drawn up, in which they owned the King's government ; but the publication of it gave rise to new quarrels.   Each fac-.tion had its own set of leaders, all of whom aspired to be officers; and there were actually two councils of war issuing contrary orders and declarations at the same time ; the one owning the King, and the other designing him a malignant, bloody, and perjured tvrant.

Meanwhile, their numbers and zeal were magnified at Edinburgh, and great alarm excited lest they should march eastward.   Not onlv was the foot militia instantly called out, but proclamations were issued, directing all the heritors, in the eastern, southern, and northern shires, to repair to the King's host, with their best horses, arms, and retainers.   In Fife, and other countries, where the Presbyterian doctrines prevailed, many gentlemen disobeyed this order, and were afterwards severely fined.   Most of them alleged, in excuse, the apprehension of disquiet from their wives.[1]   A re-

---

[1] " Balcanquhall of that ilk alleged, that his horses were robbed, but shunned to take the declaration, for fear of disquiet from his wife.   Young of Kirkton—his ladyes dangerous sickness, and bitter curses if he should leave her, and the appearance of abortion on

spectable force, however, was soon assembled ; and James, Duke of Buccleuch and Monmouth, was sent down, by Charles II., to take the command, furnished with instructions, not unfavourable to the Presbyterians. The royal army now moved slowly forward towards Hamilton, and reached Bothwell moor on the 22d of June, 1679. The insurgents were encamped chiefly in the Duke of Hamilton's park, along the Clyde, which separated the two armies. Bothwell bridge, which is long and narrow, had then a portal in the middle, with gates, which the Covenanters shut, and barricadoed with stones and logs of timber. This important post was defended by three hundred of their best men, under Hackston of Rathillet, and Hall of Haughhead. Early in the morning, this party crossed the bridge, and skirmished with the royal vanguard, now advanced as far as the village of Bothwell. But Hackston speedily retired to his post, at the end of Bothwell bridge.

While the dispositions, made by the Duke of Monmouth, announced his purpose of assailing the pass, the more moderate of the insurgents resolved to offer terms. Ferguson of Kaitloch, a gentleman of landed fortune, and David Hume, a clergyman, carried to the Duke of Monmouth a supplication, demanding free exercise of their religion, a free parliament, and a free general as-

his offering to go from her. And many others pled, in general terms, that their wives opposed or contradicted their going. But the Justiciary Court found this defence totally irrelevant."—Fountainhall's *Decisions*, vol. i. p. 88.

sembly of the church. The Duke heard their demands with his natural mildness, and assured them he would interpose with his Majesty in their behalf, on condition of their immediately dispersing themselves, and yielding up their arms. Had the insurgents been all of the moderate opinion, this proposal would have been accepted, much bloodshed saved, and, perhaps, some permanent advantage derived to their party ; or had they been all Cameronians, their defence would have been fierce and desperate. But, while their motley and misassorted officers were debating upon the Duke's proposal, his field-pieces were already planted on the western side of the river, to cover the attack of the foot guards, who were led on by Lord Livingstone to force the bridge. Here Hackston maintained his post with zeal and courage ; nor was it until all his ammunition was expended, and every support denied him by the general, that he reluctantly abandoned the important pass.[1] When his party was drawn back, the Duke's

[1] There is an accurate representation of this part of the engagement in an old painting, of which there are two copies extant ; one in the collection of his Grace the Duke of Hamilton, the other at Dalkeith House. The whole appearance of the ground, even including a few old houses, is the same which the scene now presents. The removal of the porch, or gateway, upon the bridge, is the only perceptible difference. The Duke of Monmouth, on a white charger, directs the march of the party engaged in storming the bridge, while his artillery gall the motley ranks of the Covenanters. An engraving of this painting would be acceptable to the curious ; and I am satisfied an opportunity of copying it, for that purpose, would be

army, slowly, and with their cannon in front, defiled along the bridge, and formed in line of battle, as they came over the river; the Duke commanded the foot, and Claverhouse the cavalry.

It would seem, that these movements could not have been performed without at least some loss, had the enemy been serious in opposing them. But the insurgents were otherwise employed. With the strangest delusion that ever fell upon devoted beings, they chose these precious moments to cashier their officers, and elect others in their room. In this important operation, they were at length disturbed by the Duke's cannon, at the very first discharge of which the horse of the Covenanters wheeled, and rode off, breaking and trampling down the ranks of their infantry in their flight. The Cameronian account blames Weir of Greenridge, a commander of the horse, who is termed a sad Achan in the camp. The more moderate party lay the whole blame on Hamilton, whose conduct, they say, left the world to debate, whether he was most traitor, coward, or fool. The generous Monmouth was anxious to spare the blood of his infatuated countrymen, by which he incurred much blame among the high-flying royalists. Lucky it was for the insurgents that the battle did not happen a day later, when old General Dalzell, who divided with Claverhouse the terror and hatred of the

readily granted by either of the noble proprietors. 1810. · · · · The picture has been engraved in outline for one of the publications cf the Bannatyne Club. 1830.

Whigs, arrived in the camp, with a commission to su-
persede Monmouth, as commander-in-chief. He is said
to have upbraided the Duke, publicly, with his lenity,
and heartily to have wished his own commission had
come a day sooner, when, as he expressed himself,
" These rogues should never more have troubled the
King or country." [1]   But, notwithstanding the merciful
orders of the Duke of Monmouth, the cavalry made
great havoc among the fugitives, of whom four hundred
were slain.   Guild thus expresses himself :—

Et ni Dux validus tenuisset forte catervas,
Vix quisquam profugus vitam servasset inertem ·
Non audita Ducis verum mandata supremi
Omnibus, insequitur fugientes plurima turba,
Perque agros, passim, trepidâ formidine captos
Obtruncat, sævumque adigit per viscera ferrum.

MS. Bellum Bothuellianum.

[1] Dalzell was a man of savage manners.   A prisoner having railed
at him, while under examination before the Privy Council, calling
him " a Muscovia beast, who used to roast men, the general, in a
passion, struck him with the pomel of his shabble, on the face, till
the blood sprung."—FOUNTAINHALL, vol. i. p. 159.   He had
sworn never to shave his beard after the death of Charles the First.
The venerable appendage reached his girdle, and as he wore always
an old-fashioned buff-coat, his appearance in London never failed
to attract the notice of the children and of the mob.   King Charles
II. used to swear at him, for bringing such a rabble of boys together, to be squeezed to death, while they gaped at his long beard
and antique habit, and exhorted him to shave and dress like a Christian, to keep the poor *bairns*, as Dalzell expressed it, out of danger.
In compliance with this request, he once appeared at court fashion-
ably dressed, excepting the beard ; but, when the King had laughed

The same deplorable circumstances are more elegant-
ly bewailed in Wilson's *Clyde*, a poem, reprinted in
Scottish Descriptive Poems, edited by the late Dr
John Leyden, Edinburgh, 1803 :—

> " Where Bothwell's bridge connects the margin steep,
> And Clyde, below, runs silent, strong, and deep,
> The hardy peasant, by oppression driven
> To battle, deem'd his cause the cause of heaven ;
> Unskill'd in arms, with useless courage stood,
> While gentle Monmouth grieved to shed his blood ;
> But fierce Dundee, inflamed with deadly hate,
> In vengeance for the great Montrose's fate,
> Let loose the sword, and to the hero's shade
> A barbarous hecatomb of victims paid."

The object of Claverhouse's revenge, assigned by
Wilson, is grander, though more remote and less natural, than that in the ballad, which imputes the severity of the pursuit to his thirst to revenge the death of
his cornet and kinsman, at Drumclog ;[1] and to the quar-

---

sufficiently at the metamorphosis, he resumed his old dress, to the
great joy of the boys, his usual attendants.—CREICHTON's *Memoirs*,
p. 102.

[1] There is some reason to conjecture, that the revenge of the
Cameronians, if successful, would have been little less sanguinary
than that of the royalists. Creichton mentions, that they had
erected in their camp, a high pair of gallows, and prepared a quantity of halters, to hang such prisoners as might fall into their hands ;
and he admires the forbearance of the King's soldiers, who, when
they returned with their prisoners, brought them to the very spot
where the gallows stood, and guarded them there, without offering
to hang a single individual. Guild, in the *Bellum Bothuellianum*,

rel betwixt Claverhouse and Monmouth, it ascribes, with great *naïveté*, the bloody fate of the latter. Local tradition is always apt to trace foreign events to the domestic causes, which are more immediately in the narrator's view. There is said to be another song upon this battle, once very popular, but I have not been able to recover it. This copy is given from recitation.

There were two Gordons of Earlstoun, father and son. They were descended of an ancient family in the west of Scotland, and their progenitors were believed to have been favourers of the reformed doctrine, and possessed of a translation of the Bible, as early as the days of Wickliffe. William Gordon, the father, was, in 1663, summoned before the Privy Council, for keeping conventicles in his house and woods. By another act of Council, he was banished out of Scotland, but the sentence was never put into execution. In 1667, Earlstoun was turned out of his house, which was converted into a garrison for the King's soldiers. He was not in the battle of Bothwell bridge, but was met, hastening towards it, by some English dragoons, engaged in the pursuit already commenced. As he refused to surrender, he was instantly slain.—WILSON's *History of Bothwell Rising—Life of Gordon of Earlstoun, in Scottish Worthies*—WODROW's *History*, vol. ii. The son, Alexander Gordon of Earlstoun, I sup-

alludes to the same story, which is rendered probable by the character of Hamilton, the insurgent general.—GUILD's *MSS.*—CREICHTON's *Memoirs*, p. 61.

pose to be the hero of the ballad. He was not a Cameronian, but of the more moderate class of Presbyterians, whose sole object was freedom of conscience, and relief from the oppressive laws against non-conformists. He joined the insurgents shortly after the skirmish at Loudon Hill. He appears to have been active in forwarding the supplication sent to the Duke of Monmouth. After the battle, he escaped discovery, by flying into a house at Hamilton, belonging to one of his tenants, and disguising himself in female attire. His person was proscribed, and his estate of Earlstoun was bestowed upon Colonel Theophilus Ogilthorpe, by the crown, first in security for L.5000, and afterwards in perpetuity.—FOUNTAINHALL, p. 390. The same author mentions a person tried at the Circuit Court, July 10, 1683, solely for holding intercourse with Earlstoun, an intercommuned (proscribed) rebel. As he had been in Holland after the battle of Bothwell, he was probably an accessory to the scheme of invasion, which the unfortunate Earl of Argyle was then meditating. He was apprehended upon his return to Scotland, tried, convicted of treason, and condemned to die; but his fate was postponed by a letter from the King, appointing him to be reprieved for a month, that he might, in the interim, be tortured for the discovery of his accomplices. The council had the unusual spirit to remonstrate against this illegal course of severity. On November 3, 1683, he received a farther respite, in hopes he would make some discovery. When brought to the bar, to be tortured, (for the King had reiterated his commands,) he, through fear, or distraction, roared like a bull, and laid so stoutly about him, that the hangman and his assistant could hardly master him. At last he fell into a swoon, and, on his recovery, charged General Dalzell, and Drummond, (violent Tories,) together with the Duke of Hamilton, with being the leaders of the fanatics. It was generally thought that he affected this extravagant behaviour to invalidate all that agony might extort from him concerning his real accomplices. He was sent, first, to Edinburgh Castle, and, afterwards, to a prison upon the Bass island; although the Privy Council more than once deliberated upon appointing his immediate death. On 22d August, 1684, Earlstoun was sent for from the Bass, and ordered for execution, 4th November, 1684. He endeavoured to prevent his doom by escape ; but was discovered and taken, after he had gained the roof of the prison. The Council deliberated, whether, in consideration of this attempt, he was not liable to instant execution. Finally, however, they were satisfied to imprison him in Blackness Castle, 16th September, 1684, where he remained till after the Revolution, when he was set at liberty, and his doom of forfeiture reversed by act of Parliament. —See FOUNTAINHALL, vol. i. pp. 238, 240, 245, 250, 301, 302.

THE

BATTLE OF BOTHWELL BRIDGE.

———

" O, BILLIE, billie, bonny billie,
    Will ye go to the wood wi' me ?
We'll ca' our horse hame masterless,
    An' gar them trow slain men are we."—

" O no, O no !" says Earlstoun,
    " For that's the thing that mauna be ;
For I am sworn to Bothwell Hill,
    Where I maun either gae or die."—

So Earlstoun rose in the morning,
    An' mounted by the break o' day ;
An' he has joined our Scottish lads,
    As they were marching out the way.

" Now, farewell, father, and farewell, mother,
    And fare ye weel, my sisters three ;
An' fare ye weel, my Earlstoun,
    For thee again I'll never see !"—

So they're awa' to Bothwell Hill,
    An' waly[1] they rode bonnily!
When the Duke o' Monmouth saw them comin',
    He went to view their company.

" Ye're welcome, lads," the Monmouth said,
    " Ye're welcome, brave Scots lads, to me;
And sae are you, brave Earlstoun.
    The foremost o' your company!

" But yield your weapons ane an a';
    O yield your weapons, lads, to me;
For gin ye'll yield your weapons up,
    Ye'se a' gae hame to your country."—

Out then spak a Lennox lad,
    And waly but he spoke bonnily!
" I winna yield my weapons up,
    To you nor nae man that I see."—

Then he set up the flag o' red.
    A' set about wi' bonny blue;[2]

---

[1] *Waly!*—an interjection.

[2] Blue was the favourite colour of the Covenanters; hence the
vulgar phrase of a true blue Whig.   Spalding informs us, that when
the first army of Covenanters entered Aberdeen, few or none
" wanted a blue ribband; the Lord Gordon, and some others of
the Marquis (of Huntly's) family had a ribband, when they were
dwelling in the town, of a red flesh colour, which they wore in
their hats, and called it the *royal-ribband,* as a sign of their love

" Since ye'll no cease, and be at peace,
    See that ye stand by ither true."—

They stell'd[1] their cannons on the height,
    And showr'd their shot down in the howe ;[2]
An' beat our Scots lads even down,
    Thick they lay slain on every knowe.[3]

As e'er you saw the rain down fa',
    Or yet the arrow frae the bow,—

and loyalty to the King. In despite and derision thereof, this blue ribband was worn, and called the *Covenanters' ribband,* by the haill soldiers of the army, who would not hear of the royal ribband, such was their pride and malice."—Vol. i. p. 123. After the departure of this first army, the town was occupied by the barons of the royal party, till they were once more expelled by the Covenanters, who plundered the burgh and country adjacent ; " no fowl, cock, or hen, left unkilled, and the baill house-dogs, messens, [*i.* e. lap-dogs,] and whelps within Aberdeen, killed upon the streets ; so that neither hound, messen, nor other dog, was left alive that they could see. The reason was this,—when the first army came here, ilk captain and soldier had a blue ribband about his craig [*i.* e. neck] ; in despite and derision whereof, when they removed from Aberdeen, some women of Aberdeen, as was alleged, knit blue ribbands about their messens' craigs, whereat their soldiers took offence, and killed all their dogs for this very cause."
—P. 160.

I have seen one of the ancient banners of the Covenanters : it was divided into four compartments, inscribed with the words,— *Christ*— *Covenant*— *King*— *Kingdom.* Similar standards are mentioned in Spalding's curious and minute narrative, vol. ii. pp. 182, 245.

[1] *Stell'd*—Planted—[2] *Howe*—Hollow.—[3] *Knowe*—Knoll.

Sae our Scottish lads fell even down,
    An' they lay slain on every knowe.

" O hold your hand," then Monmouth cry'd,
    " Gie quarters to yon men for me ! "—
But wicked Claver'se swore an oath,
    His Cornet's death revenged sud be.

" O hold your hand," then Monmouth cry'd,
    " If onything you'll do for me ;
Hold up your hand, you cursed Græme,[1]
    Else a rebel to our King ye'll be."—

Then wicked Claver'se turn'd about,
    I wot an angry man was he ;
And he has lifted up his hat,
    And cry'd, " God bless his Majesty ! "—

Than he's awa' to London town,
    Aye e'en as fast as he can dree ;
Fause witnesses he has wi' him ta'en,
    And ta'en Monmouth's head frae his body.

Alang the brae, beyond the brig,
    Monv brave man lies cauld and still ;
But lang we'll mind, and sair we'll rue,
    The bloody battle of Bothwell Hill.

[1] See Note A, p. 241.

APPENDIX.

NOTE A.

Hold up your hand, you cursed **Grame**.—P. 240, v. 3.

IT is very extraordinary, that, in April, 1685, Claverhouse was left out of the new commission of Privy Council, as being too favourable to the fanatics. The pretence was his having married into the presbyterian family of Lord Dundonald. An act of Council was also passed, regulating the payment of quarters, which is stated by Fountainhall to have been done in *odium* of Claverhouse, and in order to excite complaints against him. This charge, so inconsistent with the nature and conduct of Claverhouse, seems to have been the fruit of a quarrel betwixt him and the Lord High Treasurer. FOUNTAINHALL, vol. i. p. 360.

That Claverhouse was most unworthily accused of mitigating the persecution of the Covenanters, will appear from the following simple, but very affecting narrative, extracted from one of the little publications which appeared soon after the Revolution, while the facts were fresh in the memory of the sufferers. The imitation of the scriptural style produces, in passages of these works, an effect not unlike what we feel in reading the beautiful book of Ruth. It is taken from the Life of Mr Alexander Peden,[1] printed about 1720.

[1] The enthusiasm of this personage, and of his followers, invested him, as has been already noticed, with prophetic powers: but hardly any of the stories told of him exceeds that sort of gloomy conjecture of misfortune, which the precarious situation of his sect so greatly fostered. The following passage relates to the battle of Bothwell bridge: " That dis-

" In the beginning of May 1685, he came to the house of John
Brown and Narion Weir, whom he married before he went to Ireland, where he stayed all night ; and in the morning, when he took
farewell, he came out of the door, saying to himself, ' Poor woman,
a fearful morning,' twice over. ' A dark misty morning !' The next
morning, between five and six hours, the said John Brown having
performed the worship of God in his family, was going, with a spade
in his hand, to make ready some peat ground : the mist being very
dark, he knew not until cruel and bloody Claverhouse compassed him
with three troops of horse, brought him to his house, and there ex-
amined him ; who, though he was a man of a stammering speech, yet
answered him distinctly and solidly ; which made Claverhouse to ex-
amine those whom he had taken to be his guides through the muirs, if
ever they heard him preach ? They answered, ' No, no, he was never
a preacher.' He said, ' If he has never preached, meikle he has prayed
in his time ;' he said to John, ' Go to your prayers, for you shall immediately die !'   When he was praying, Claverhouse interrupted him
three times ; one time, that he stopt him, he was pleading that the
Lord would spare a remnant, and not make a full end in the day of

mal day, 22d of June, 1679, of Bothwell-bridge, when the Lord's people
fell and fled before the enemy, he was forty miles distant, near the Border, and kept himself retired until the middle of the day, when some
friends said to him, ' Sir, the people are waiting for sermon.' He answered, ' Let them go to their prayers : for me, I neither can nor will
preach any this day, for our friends are fallen and fled before the enemy,
at Hamilton, and they are hacking and hewing them down, and their
blood is running like water.'"   The feats of Peden are thus commemorated by Fountainhall, 27th of March, 1685 :—" News came to the Privy
Council, that about one hundred men, well armed and appointed, had
left Ireland, because of a search there for such malcontents, and landed
in the west of Scotland, and joined with the wild fanatics.   The Council, finding that they disappointed their forces by skulking from hole to
hole, were of opinion, it were better to let them gather into a body, and
draw to a head, and so they would get them altogether in a snare
They had one Mr Peden, a minister with them, and one Isaac, who commanded them.   They had frighted most part of all the country ministers,
so that they durst not stay at their churches, but retired to Edinburgh,
or to garrison towns ; and it was sad to see whole shires destitute of
preaching, except in burghs. Wherever they came they plundered arms,
and particularly at my Lord Dumfries's house."—FOUNTAINHALL, vol. i.
p. 359.

his anger. Claverhouse said, ' I give you time to pray, and ye are begun to preach ;' he turned about upon his knees, and said, ' Sir, you
know neither the nature of preaching or praying, that calls this preaching.' Then continued without confusion. When ended, Claverhouse
said, ' Take goodnight of your wife and children.' His wife, standing
by with her child in her arms that she had brought forth to him,
and another child of his first wife's, he came to her, and said, ' Now,
Marion, the day is come that I told you would come, when I spake
first to you of marrying me.' She said, ' Indeed, John, I can willingly part with you.'—' Then,' he said, ' this is all I desire, I have
no more to do but die.' He kissed his wife and bairns, and wished
purchased and promised blessings to be multiplied upon them, and
his blessing. Claverhouse ordered six soldiers to shoot him ; the
most part of the bullets came upon his head, which scattered his
brains upon the ground. Claverhouse said to his wife, ' What
thinkest thou of thy husband, now, woman?' She said, ' I thought ever
much of him, and now as much as ever.' He said, ' It were but justice
to lay thee beside him.' She said, ' If ye were permitted, I doubt not
but your crueltie would go that length ; but how will ye make answer for this morning's work?' He said, ' To man I can be an-
swerable ; and for God, I will take him in my own hand.' Claverhouse mounted his horse, and marched, and left her with the
corpse of her dead husband lying there ; she set the bairn on the
ground, and gathered his brains, and tied up his head, and straighted
his body, and covered him in her plaid, and sat down, and wept
over him. It being a very desart place, where never victual grew,
and far from neighbours, it was some time before any friends came
to her ; the first that came was a very fit hand, that old singular
Christian woman, in the Cummer head, named Elizabeth Menzies,
three miles distant, who had been tried with the violent death of her
husband at Pentland, afterwards of two worthy sons, Thomas Weir,
who was killed at Drumclog, and David Steel, who was suddenly shot
afterwards when taken. The said Marion Weir, sitting upon her
husband's grave, told me, that before that, she could see no blood
but she was in danger to faint ; and yet she was helped to be a witness to all this, without either fainting or confusion, except when
the shots were let off her eyes dazzled. His corpse were buried at

the end of his house, where he was slain, with this inscription on his grave-stone :—

' In earth's cold bed, the dusty part here lies,
Of one who did the earth as dust despise !
Here, in this place, from earth he took departure ;
Now he has got the garland of the martyrs.'

" This murder was committed betwixt six and seven in the morning : Mr Peden was about ten or eleven miles distant, having been in the fields all night : he came to the house betwixt seven and eight, and desired to call in the family, that he might pray amongst them ; when praying, he said, ' Lord, when wilt thou avenge Brown's blood ? Oh, let Brown's blood be precious in thy sight! and hasten the day when thou wilt avenge it, with Came-ron's, Cargill's, and many others of our martyrs' names ; and oh ! for that day, when the Lord would avenge all their bloods !' When ended, John Muirhead enquired what he meant by Brown's blood ! He said twice over, ' What do I mean ? Claverhouse has been at the Preshill this morning, and has cruelly murdered John Brown ; his corpse are lying at the end of his house, and his poor wife sitting weeping by his corpse, and not a soul to speak a word comfortably to her.' "

While we read this dismal story, we must remember Brown's situation was that of an avowed and determined rebel, liable as such to military execution ; so that the atrocity was more that of the times than of Claverhouse. That general's gallant adherence to his master, the misguided James VII., and his glorious death on the field of victory, at Killicrankie, have tended to preserve and gild his memory. He is still remembered in the Highlands as the most successful leader of their clans. An ancient gentleman, who had borne arms for the cause of Stuart in 1715, told the Editor, that when the armies met on the field of battle at Sheriff-muir, a veteran chief, (I think he named Gordon of Glenbucket,) covered with scars, came up to the Earl of Mar, and earnestly pressed him to order the Highlanders to charge, before the regular army of Argyle had completely formed their line, and at a moment when the rapid and furious onset of the clans might have thrown them into total disorder. Mar repeatedly answered, it was not yet time ; till the chieftain turned from him in disdain and despair, and, stamping with rage, exclaimed aloud, " O for one hour of Dundee !" [1]

Claverhouse's sword (a straight cut-and-thrust blade) is in the possession of Loid Woodhouselee. In Pennycuick house is preserved the buff-coat, which he wore at the battle of Killicrankie. The fatal shot-hole is under the arm-pit, so that the ball must have been received while his arm was raised to direct the pursuit. However he came by his charm of *proof,* he certainly had not worn the garment usually supposed to confer that privilege, and which was called *the waistcoat of proof, or of necessity.*   It was thus made : " On Christmas dai, at night, a thread must be sponne of flax, by a little virgin girle, in the name of the divell ; and it must be by her woven, and also wrought with the needle.   In the breast, or fore part thereof, must be made, with needle-work, two heads ; on the head, at the right side, must be a hat and a long beard ; the left head must have on a crown, and it must be so horrible that it maie resemble Belzebub ; and on each side of the wastcote must be made a crosse."—Scott's *Discoverie of Witchcraft,* p. 231.

It would be now no difficult matter to bring down our popular poetry, connected with history, to the year 1745.   But almost all the party ballads of that period have been already printed and ably illustrated by Mr Ritson.

[O for one hour of Wallace wight,
Or well-skilled Bruce, to rule the fight, &c.
          Marmion]

END OF HISTORICAL BALLADS.

THE BATTLE OF BOTHWELL BRIGG.

VOCE.

PIANO FORTE.

O billie, billie, bonnie billie,

Will ve gae to the wood wi' me? We'll ca' our horse hame

master - less, And gar them trow · slain men are we.

Oh, no! oh, no! said Earlstoun, For

that's the thing that must never be, For I am Louned to

Bothwell Hill, Where I maun either do or die.

MINSTRELSY

OF THE

SCOTTISH BORDER.

PART SECOND.

𝔎𝔬𝔪𝔞𝔫𝔱𝔦𝔠 𝔅𝔞𝔩𝔩𝔞𝔡𝔰.

SCOTTISH MUSIC.

AN ODE.

BY J. LEYDEN.

TO IANTHE.

AGAIN, sweet siren! breathe again
That deep, pathetic, powerful strain,
   Whose melting tones, of tender woe,
Fall soft as evening's summer dew,
That bathes the pinks and harebells blue,
   Which in the vales of Teviot blow.

Such was the song that soothed to rest,
Far in the green isle of the west,[1]
   The Celtic warrior's parted shade;
Such are the lonely sounds that sweep
O'er the blue bosom of the deep,
   Where shipwreck'd mariners are laid.

Ah! sure, as Hindú legends[2] tell,
When music's tones the bosom swell,

---

[1] The *Flathinnis*, or Celtic paradise.
[2] The effect of music is explained by the Hindús, as recalling to

The scenes of former life return;
Ere, sunk beneath the morning star,
We left our parent climes afar,
    Immured in mortal forms to mourn.

Or if, as ancient sages ween,
Departed spirits, half unseen,
    Can mingle with the mortal throng;
'Tis when from heart to heart we roll
The deep-toned music of the soul,
    That warbles in our Scottish song.

I hear, I hear, with awful dread,
The plaintive music of the dead!
    They leave the amber fields of day ·
Soft as the cadence of the wave,
That murmurs round the mermaid's grave,
    They mingle in the magic lay.

Sweet siren, breathe the powerful strain !
Lochroyan's Damsel[1] sails the main;
    The crystal tower enchanted see!
" Now break," she cries, " ye fairy charms !"—
As round she sails with fond alarms,
    " Now break, and set my true love free!"

our memory the airs of paradise, heard in a state of pre-existence.
— *Vide* Sacontala.
   [1] The Lass of Lochroyan.—*Post.*

Lord Barnard is to greenwood gone,
Where fair *Gil Morrice* sits alone,
   And careless combs his yellow hair:
Ah! mourn the youth, untimely slain!
The meanest of Lord Barnard's train
   The hunter's mangled head must bear.

Or, change these notes of deep despair,
For love's more soothing tender air;
   Sing, how, beneath the greenwood tree,
Brown Adam's[1] love maintain'd her truth,
Nor would resign the exiled youth
   For any knight the fair could see.

And sing the *Hawk of pinion grey,*[2]
To southern climes who wing'd his way,
   For he could speak as well as fly;
Her brethren how the fair beguiled,
And on her Scottish lover smiled,
   As slow she raised her languid eye.

Fair was her cheek's carnation glow,
Like red blood on a wreath of snow;
   Like evening's dewy star her eye;
White as the sea-mew's downy breast,
Borne on the surge's foamy crest,
   Her graceful bosom heaved the sigh.

[1] See the ballad, entitled, *Brown Adam.*
[2] See the *Gay Goss-Hawk.*

In youth's first morn, alert and gay,
Ere rolling years had pass'd away,
  Remember'd like a morning dream,
I heard these dulcet measures float,
In many a liquid winding note,
  Along the banks of Teviot's stream.

Sweet sounds! that oft have soothed to rest
The sorrows of my guileless breast,
  And charm'd away mine infant tears:
Fond memory shall your strains repeat,
Like distant echoes, doubly sweet,
  That in the wild the traveller hears.

And thus, the exiled Scotian maid,
By fond alluring love betray'd
  To visit Syria's date-crown'd shore,
In plaintive strains, that soothed despair,
Did " Bothwell's banks that bloom so fair," [1]
  And scenes of early youth, deplore.

[1] " So fell it out of late years, that an English gentleman, travelling in Palestine, not far from Jerusalem, as he passed through
a country town, he heard, by chance, a woman sitting at her door,
dandling her child, to sing, *Bothwell bank, thou bloomest fair.* The
gentleman hereat wondered, and forthwith, in English, saluted the
woman, who joyfully answered him ; and said she was right glad
there to see a gentleman of our isle : and told him that she was a
Scottish woman, and came first from Scotland to Venice, and from
Venice thither, where her fortune was to be the wife of an officer
under the Turk ; who, being at that instant absent, and very soon

Soft siren, whose enchanting strain
Floats wildly round my raptured brain,
   I bid your pleasing haunts adieu!
Yet, fabling fancy oft shall lead
My footsteps to the silver Tweed,
   Through scenes that I no more must view.[1]

to return, she entreated the gentleman to stay there until his return. The which he did; and she, for country sake, to show herself the more kind and bountiful unto him, told her husband, at his home-coming, that the gentleman was her kinsman; whereupon her husband entertained him very kindly; and, at his departure, gave him divers things of good value."—VERSTIGAN's *Restitution of Decayed Intelligence.* Chap. *of the Surnames of our Antient Families.* Antwerp, 1605.

[1] [Dr Leyden was, when he wrote these verses, on the eve of departing for India—where he died.—ED.]

INTRODUCTION

TO THE

TALE OF TAMLANE.

ON THE

FAIRIES OF POPULAR SUPERSTITION.[1]

" Of airy elves, by moonlight shadows seen,
The silver token, and the circled green."—POPE.

IN a work avowedly dedicated to the preservation of
the poetry and traditions of the " olden time," it would
be unpardonable to omit this opportunity of making
some observations upon so interesting an article of the
popular creed, as that concerning the Elves, or Fairies.
The general idea of spirits, of a limited power, and
subordinate nature, dwelling among the woods and

---

[1] [The reader will do well to compare this early essay with Sir
Walter Scott's fourth Letter on Demonology, 1830, where he will
find the Author's opinions on several points considerably modified ; as
also the Preface and Notes to GRIMM's *Haus-und-kinder* Märchen ; and an Essay on Popular Superstitions, by Mr Southey, in
the 37th Number of the Quarterly Review.—ED.]

mountains, is perhaps common to all nations. But
the intermixture of tribes, of languages, and religion,
which has occurred in Europe, renders it difficult to trace
the origin of the names which have been bestowed upon
such spirits, and the primary ideas which were entertained concerning their manners and habits.

The word *elf*, which seems to have been the original name of the beings afterwards denominated fairies,
is of Gothic origin, and probably signified, simply, a
spirit of a lower order. Thus, the Saxons had not only
dun-elfen, berg-elfen, and *munt-elfen,* spirits of the
downs, hills, and mountains; but also *feld-elfen, wudu-
elfen, sae-elfen,* and *wæter-elfen;* spirits of the fields,
of the woods, of the sea, and of the waters.[1] In Low
German, the same latitude of expression occurs; for
night-hags are termed *aluinnen* and *aluen,* which is
sometimes Latinized *eluæ.* But the prototype of the
English elf is to be sought chiefly in the *berg-elfen,* or
duergar, of the Scandinavians. From the most early
of the Icelandic Sagas, as well as from the Edda itself,
we learn the belief of the northern nations in a race of
dwarfish spirits, inhabiting the rocky mountains, and
approaching, in some respects, to the human nature.

[1] [The writer of the learned Preface to Warton's History of English Poetry, (Edit. 1824,) doubts whether " this catalogue of *Æl-
frics* ever obtained currency among the people." He says, this
is at least rendered doubtful, by its *exact* correspondence with the
Grecian names of *Dryades,* &c. *Elf,* according to this writer,
originally means *running water*—whence the *Elbe;* and here he
notices a curious coincidence with νυμφη and *lympha.*—Ed.]

Their attributes, amongst which we recognise the features of the modern fairy, were, supernatural wisdom and prescience, and skill in the mechanical arts, especially in the fabrication of arms. They are farther described, as capricious, vindictive, and easily irritated. The story of the elfin sword *Tyrfing*, may be the most pleasing illustration of this position. Suafurlami, a Scandinavian monarch, returning from hunting, bewildered himself among the mountains. About sunset he beheld a large rock, and two dwarfs sitting before the mouth of a cavern. The king drew his sword, and intercepted their retreat, by springing betwixt them and their recess, and imposed upon them the following condition of safety :—that they should make for him a falchion, with a baldric and scabbard of pure gold, and a blade which should divide stones and iron as a garment, and which should render the wielder ever vietorions in battle. The elves complied with the requisition, and Suafurlami pursued his way home. Returning at the time appointed, the dwarfs delivered to him the famous sword *Tyrfing ;* then, standing in the entrance of the cavern, spoke thus : " This sword, O king, shall destroy a man every time it is brandished, but it shall perform three atrocious deeds, and it shall be thy bane." The king rushed forward with the charmed sword, and buried both its edges in the rock ; but the dwarfs escaped into their recesses.[1] This en-

---

[1] Perhaps in this, and similar tales, we may recognise something

chanted sword emitted rays like the sun, dazzling all against whom it was brandished; it divided steel like water, and was never unsheathed without slaying a man.—*Hervarar Saga*, p. 9. Similar to this was the enchanted sword *Skoffnung*, which was taken by a pirate out of the tomb of a Norwegian monarch. Many such tales are narrated in the Sagas; but the most distinct account of the *duergar*, or elves, and their attributes, is to be found in a preface of Torfæus to the history of Hrolf Kraka, who cites a dissertation by Einer Gudmund, a learned native of Iceland. " I am firmly of opinion," says the Icelander, " that these beings are creatures of God, consisting, like human beings, of a body and rational soul; that they are of different sexes, and capable of producing children, and subject to all human affections, as sleeping and waking, laughing and crying, poverty and wealth; and that they possess cattle, and other effects, and are obnoxious to death, like other mortals." He proceeds to state, that the females of this race are capable of procreating

---

of real history. That the Fins, or ancient natives of Scandinavia, were driven into the mountains, by the invasion of Odin and his Asiatics, is sufficiently probable; and there is reason to believe that the aboriginal inhabitants understood, better than the intruders, how to manufacture the produce of their own mines. It is therefore possible, that, in process of time, the oppressed Fins may have been transformed into the supernatural *duergar*. A similar transformation has taken place among the vulgar in Scotland, regarding the Picts or Peghs, to whom they ascribe various supernatural attributes.

with mankind; and gives an account of one who bore
a child to an inhabitant of Iceland, for whom she claim
ed the privilege of baptism; depositing the infant for
that purpose, at the gate of the churchyard, together
with a goblet of gold, as an offering.—*Historia Hrolfi
Krakæ, a* TORFÆO.

Similar to the traditions of the Icelanders, are those
current among the Laplanders of Finland, concerning
a subterranean people, gifted with supernatural qualities, and inhabiting the recesses of the earth. Resembling men in their general appearance, the manner of
their existence and their habits of life, they far excel
the miserable Laplanders in perfection of nature, feli-
city of situation, and skill in mechanical arts. From
all these advantages, however, after the partial conversion of the Laplanders, the subterranean people have
derived no farther credit, than to be confounded with
the devils and magicians of the dark ages of Christianity; a degradation which, as will shortly be demon-
strated, has been also suffered by the harmless fairies
of Albion, and, indeed, by the whole host of deities of
learned Greece and mighty Rome. The ancient opinions are yet so firmly rooted, that the Laps of Finland,
at this day, boast of an intercourse with these beings,
in banquets, dances, and magical ceremonies, and even
in more intimate commerce of gallantry. They talk,
with triumph, of the feasts which they have shared in
the elfin caverns, where wine and tobacco, the produc-
tions of the Fairy region, went round in abundance,

and whence the mortal guest, after receiving the kind-
est treatment, and the most salutary counsel, has been
conducted to his tent under an escort of his supernatural entertainers.—*Jessens, de Lapponibus.*

The superstitions of the islands of Feroe, concerning
their *Froddenskemen*, or under-ground people, are derived from the *duergar* of Scandinavia. These beings
are supposed to inhabit the interior recesses of mountains, which they enter by invisible passages. Like the
Fairies, they are supposed to steal human beings, " It
happened," says Debes, p. 354, " a good while since,
when the burghers of Bergen had the commerce of
Feroe, that there was a man in Servaade, called Jonas
Soideman, who was kept by spirits in a mountain during
the space of seven years, and at length came out; but
lived afterwards in great distress and fear, lest they
should again take him away; wherefore people were
obliged to watch him in the night." The same author
mentions another young man who had been carried
away, and, after his return, was removed a second time
upon the eve of his marriage. He returned in a short
time, and related, that the spirit that had carried him
away was in the shape of a most beautiful woman, who
pressed him to forsake his bride, and remain with her;
urging her own superior beauty, and splendid appearance. He added, that he saw the men who were employed to search for him, and heard them call; but that
they could not see him, nor could he answer them, till
upon his determined refusal to listen to the spirit's per-

suasions, the spell ceased to operate. The kidney-shaped West Indian bean, which is sometimes driven upon the shore of the Feroes, is termed by the natives, " the *Fairie's kidney.*"

In these traditions of the Gothic and Finnish tribes, we may recognise, with certainty, the rudiments of elfin superstition ; but we must look to various other causes for the modifications which it has undergone. These are to be sought, first, in the traditions of the East ; 2d, in the wreck and confusion of the Gothic mythology ; 3d, in the tales of chivalry ; 4th, in the fables of classical antiquity ; 5th, in the influence of the Christian religion ; 6th, and finally, in the creative imagination of the 16th century. It may be proper to notice the effect of these various causes, before stating the popular belief of our own time, regarding the Fairies.

I. To the traditions of the East, the Fairies of Britain owe, I think, little more than the appellation, by which they have been distinguished since the days of the Crusade. The term " Fairy," occurs not only in Chaucer, and in yet older English authors, but also, and more frequently, in the Romance language ; from which they seem to have adopted it. Ducange cites the fol lowing passage from Gul. Guiart, in *Historia Fran-cica*, MS.

> " Plusiers parlent de Guenart,
> Du Lou, de L'Asne, de Renait,
> De *Faëries* et de Songes,
> De phantosmes et de mensonges."

The *Lay le Frain*, enumerating the subjects of the Breton Lays, informs us expressly,

Many ther beth of *faïry*.

By some etymologists of that learned class, who not only know whence words come, but also whither they are going, the term *Fairy*, or *Faërie*, is derived from *Faë*, which is again derived from *Nympha*. It is more probable the term is of Oriental origin, and is derived from the Persic, through the medium of the Arabic. In Persic, the term *Peri* expresses a species of imaginary being which resembles the Fairy in some of its qualities, and is one of the fairest creatures of romantic fancy. This superstition must have been known to the Arabs, among whom the Persian tales, or romances, even as early as the time of Mahomet, were so popular, that it required the most terrible denunciations of that legislator to proscribe them. Now, in the enunciation of the Arabs, the term *Peri* would sound *Fairy*, the letter *p* not occurring in the alphabet of that nation ; and, as the chief intercourse of the early crusaders was with the Arabs, or Saracens, it is probable they would adopt the term according to their pronunciation. Neither will it be considered as an objection to this opinion, that in Hesychius, the Ionian term, *Phereas* or *Pheres*, denotes the satyrs of classical antiquity, if the number of words of Oriental origin in that lexicographer be recollected.[1] Of the Persian Peris,

---

[1] [*Faerie* was a general name for *illusion ;* a sense in which it is *always* (?) used by Chaucer. As an appellation for the chin race,

Ousely, in his *Persian Miscellanies*, has described some characteristic traits, with all the luxuriance of a fancy impregnated with the Oriental associations of ideas. However vaguely their nature and appearance are described, they are uniformly represented as gentle, amiable females, to whose character beneficence and beauty are essential. None of them are mischievous or malignant; none of them are deformed or diminutive, like the Gothic fairy. Though they correspond in beauty with our ideas of angels, their employments are dissimilar; and, as they have no place in heaven, their abode is different. Neither do they resemble those intelligences, whom, on account of their wisdom, the Platonists denominated demons; nor do they correspond either to the guardian Genii of the Romans, or the celestial virgins of paradise, whom the Arabs denominate Houri. But the Peris hover in the balmy clouds, live in the colours of the rainbow, and, as the exquisite purity of their nature rejects all nourishment grosser than the odours of flowers, they subsist by inhaling the fragrance of the jessamine and rose. Though their existence is not commensurate with the bonds of

it is certainly of late date; and perhaps a mere corruption—a name given to the agent from his acts. It is certainly not of northern origin. Some of the earliest French tales of *faërie*, acknowledge a Breton source: may not the name itself be Celtic? The Ionic Phcres, of Hesychius, which has been mentioned as a synonym with the Persian Peri, is but a different aspiration of the Attic θηϛ, (German, *thier*,) and which, whether applied to Centaurs or Satyrs, could only have been given to mark their affinity with the animal race.—*Preface to* WARTON, 1824, p. 44.—ED.]

human life, they are not exempted from the common fate of mortals.

With the Peris, in Persian mythology, are contrasted the Dives, a race of beings, who differ from them in sex, appearance, and disposition. These are represented as of the male sex, cruel, wicked, and of the most hideous aspect; or, as they are described by Mr Finch, " with ugly shapes, long horns, staring eyes, shaggy hair, great fangs, ugly paws, long tails, with such horrible difformity and deformity, that I wonder the poor women are not frightened therewith " Though they live very long, their lives are limited, and they are obnoxious to the blows of a human foe. From the malignancy of their nature, they not only wage war with mankind, but persecute the Peris with unremitting ferocity.

Such are the brilliant and fanciful colours with which the imaginations of the Persian poets have depicted the charming race of the Peris ; and, if we consider the romantic gallantry of the knights of chivalry, and of the crusaders, it will not appear improbable, that their charms might occasionally fascinate the fervid imagination of an amorous troubadour. But, further ; the intercourse of France and Italy with the Moors of Spain, and the prevalence of the Arabic, as the language of science in the dark ages, facilitated the introduction of their mythology among the nations of the West. Hence, the romanees of France, of Spain, and of Italy, unite in describing the Fairy as an inferior spirit, in a beautiful

female form, possessing many of the amiable qualities
of the Eastern Peri. Nay, it seems sufficiently clear,
that the romancers borrowed from the Arabs, not merely the general idea concerning those spirits, but even the
names of individuals among them. The Peri *Mergian
Banou,* (see *Herbelot ap. Peri,*) celebrated in the ancient Persian poetry, figures in the European romances,
under the various names of *Mourgue La Faye,* sister
to *King Arthur ; Urgande La Deconnue,* protectress
of *Amadis De Gaul ;* and the *Fata Morgana* of Boi-
ardo and Ariosto. The description of these nymphs,
by the troubadours and minstrels, is in no respect inferior to those of the Peris. In the tale of *Sir Laun-
fal,* in Way's *Fabliaux,* as well as in that of *Sir
Gruelan,* in the same interesting collection, the reader
will find the fairy of Normandy, or Bretagne, adorned
with all the splendour of Eastern description. The
fairy *Melusina,* also, who married Guy de Lusignan,
Count of Poictou, under condition that he should never
attempt to intrude upon her privacy, was of this latter
class. She bore the Count many children, and erected
for him a magnificent castle by her magical art. Their
harmony was uninterrupted, until the prying husband
broke the conditions of their union, by concealing himself, to behold his wife make use of her enchanted bath.
Hardly had *Melusina* discovered the indiscreet intru-
der, than, transforming herself into a dragon, she departed with a loud yell of lamentation, and was never
again visible to mortal eyes; although, even in the

davs of Brantome, she was supposed to be the protectress of her descendants, and was heard wailing, as
she sailed upon the blast round the turrets of the castle
of Lusignan, the night before it was demolished. For
the full story, the reader may consult the *Bibliotheque
des Romans.*[1]

Gervase of Tilbury, (pp. 895 and 989,) assures us,
that, in his days, the lovers of the Fadæ, or Fairies,
were numerous; and describes the rules of their intercourse with as much accuracy, as if he had himself been
engaged in such an affair. Sir David Lindsay also informs us, that a leopard is the proper armorial bearing
of those who spring from such intercourse, because that
beast is generated by adultery of the pard and lioness.
He adds, that Merlin, the prophet, was the first who
adopted this cognizance, because he was " borne of faarie
in adultré, and right sua the first Duk of Guyenne
was born of a *fee ;* and, therefoir, the arms of Guyenne

---

[1] Upon this, or some similar tradition, was founded the notion,
which the inveteracy of national prejudice so easily diffused in Scotland, that the ancestor of the English monarchs, Geoffrey Planta-
genet, had actually married a demon. Bowmaker, in order to explain the cruelty and ambition of Edward I., dedicates a chapter to
show " how the Kings of England are descended from the devil,
by the mother's side."—FORDUN, *Chron.* lib. 9, cap. 6. The
lord of a certain castle, called Espervel, was unfortunate enough to
have a wife of the same class. Having observed, for several years,
that she always left the chapel before the mass was concluded, the
baron, in a fit of obstinacy or curiosity, ordered his guard to detain
her by force ; of which the consequence was, that, unable to support the elevation of the host, she retreated through the air, carrying
with her one side of the chapel, and several of the congregation.

are a leopard."—*MS. on Heraldry, Advocates' Library*, w. 4, 13. While, however, the Fairy of warmer climes was thus held up as an object of desire and of affection, those of Britain, and more especially those of Scotland, were far from being so fortunate ; but retaining the unamiable qualities, and diminutive size of the Gothic elves, they only exchanged that term for the more popular appellation of Fairies.

II. Indeed so singularly unlucky were the British Fairies, that, as has already been hinted, amid the wreck of the Gothic mythology, consequent upon the introduction of Christianity, they seem to have preserved, with difficulty, their own distinct characteristics, while, at the same time, they engrossed the mischievous attributes of several other classes of subordinate spirits, acknowledged by the nations of the north. The abstraction of children, for example, the well-known practice of the modern Fairy, seems, by the ancient Gothic nations, to have rather been ascribed to a species of nightmare, or hag, than to the *berg-elfen*, or *duergar*. In the ancient legend of *St Margaret*, of which there is a Saxo-Norman copy in *Hickes' Thesaurus Linguar. Septen.* and one, more modern, in the Auchinleck MSS., that lady encounters a fiend, whose profession it was, among other malicious tricks, to injure new-born children and their mothers ; a practice afterwards imputed to the Fairies. Gervase of Tilbury, in the *Otia Imperialia*, mentions certain hags, or *Lamiæ*, who entered into houses in the night-time, to oppress the inhabitants while asleep, injure their persons and property, and carry off their children. He likewise mentions the *Dracæ*, a sort of water spirits, who inveigle women and children into the recesses which they inhabit, beneath lakes and rivers, by floating past them, on the surface of the water, in the shape of gold rings or cups. The women, thus seized, are employed as nurses, and, after seven years, are permitted to revisit earth. Gervase mentions one woman, in particular, who had been allured by observing a wooden dish, or cup, float by her, while washing clothes in a river. Being seized as soon as she reached the depths, she was conducted into one of these subterranean recesses, which she described as very magnificent, and employed as nurse to one of the brood of the hag who had allured her. During her residence in this capacity, having accidentally touched one of her eyes with an ointment of serpent's grease, she perceived, at her return to the world, that she had acquired the faculty of seeing the *Dracæ*, when they intermingle themselves with men. Of this power, she was, however, deprived by the touch of her ghostly mistress, whom she had one day incautiously addressed. It is a curious fact, that this story, in almost all its parts, is current in both the Highlands and Lowlands of Scotland, with no other variation than the substitution of Fairies for *Dracæ*, and the cavern of a hill for that of a river.[1]

[1] Indeed, many of the vulgar account it extremely dangerous to touch any thing which they may happen to find, without *saining*

These water fiends are thus characterised by Heywood, in the *Hierarchie*—

> " Spirits, that have o'er water government
> Are to mankind alike malevolent ;
> They trouble seas, flouds, rivers, brookes, and wels,
> Neres, lakes, and love to enhabit watry cells ;
> Hence noisome and pestiferous vapours raise ;
> Besides, they men encounter divers ways.
> At wreckes some present are ; another sort,
> Ready to cramp their joints that swim for sport ;
> One kind of these the Italians *fatæ* name,
> *Fee* the French, we *sibyls*, and the same ;
> Others *white nymphs*, and those that have them seen,
> *Night ladies* some, of which Habundia queen."

Hierarchie of the Blessed Angels, p. 507.

The following Frisian superstition, related by Schott, in his *Physica Curiosa*, p. 362, on the authority of

(blessing) it, the snares of the Enemy being notorious and well attested. A poor woman of Teviotdale, having been fortunate enough, as she thought herself, to find a wooden beetle, at the very time when she needed such an implement, seized it without pronouncing the proper blessing, and, carrying it home, laid it above her bed, to be ready for employment in the morning. At midnight, the window of her cottage opened, and a loud voice was heard, calling upon some one within, by a strange and uncouth name which I have forgotten. The terrified cottager ejaculated a prayer, which, we may suppose, ensured her personal safety ; while the enchanted implement of housewifery, tumbling from the bedstead, departed by the window with no small noise and precipitation. In a humorous fugitive tract, the late Dr Johnson is introduced as disputing the authenticity of an apparition, merely because the spirit assumed the shape of a tea-pot, and of a shoulder of mutton. No doubt, a case so much in point as that we have now quoted, would have removed his incredulity.

Cornelius a Kempen, coincides more accurately with the popular opinions concerning the Fairies, than even the *dracæ* of Gervase, or the water spirits of Thomas Heywood.—" In the time of the Emperor Lotharius, in 830," says he, " many spectres infested Friesland, particularly the white nymphs of the ancients, which the moderns denominate *witte wiven,* who inhabited a subterraneous cavern, formed in a wonderful manner, without human art, on the top of a lofty mountain. These were accustomed to surprise benighted travellers, shepherds watching their herds and flocks, and women newly delivered, with their children ; and convey them into their caverns, from which subterranean murmurs, the cries of children, the groans and lamentations of men, and sometimes imperfect words, and all kinds of musical sounds, were heard to proceed." The same superstition is detailed by Bekker, in his *World Be-witch'd,* p. 196, of the English translation. As the different classes of spirits were gradually confounded, the abstraction of children seems to have been chiefly ascribed to the elves, or Fairies ; yet not so entirely as to exclude hags and witches from the occasional exertion of their ancient privilege. In Germany, the same confusion of classes has not taken place. In the beautiful ballads of the *Erl King,* the *Water King,* and the *Mer-Maid,* we still recognise the ancient traditions of the Goths concerning the *wald-elven,* and the *dracæ.*

A similar superstition, concerning abstraction by de-

mons, seems, in the time of Gervase of Tilbury, to have
pervaded the greatest part of Europe. " In Catalonia,"
says the author, " there is a lofty mountain, named Ca-
vagum, at the foot of which runs a river with golden
sands, in the vicinity of which there are likewise mines
of silver.   This mountain is steep, and almost inacces
sible.   On its top, which is always covered with ice
and snow, is a black and bottomless lake, into which if
a stone be thrown, a tempest suddenly rises ; and near
this lake, though invisible to men, is the porch of the
palace of demons.   In a town adjacent to this mountain, named Junchera, lived one Peter de Cabinam.
Being one day teazed with the fretfulness of his young
daughter, he, in his impatience, suddenly wished that
the devil might take her ; when she was immediately
borne away by the spirits.   About seven years afterwards, an inhabitant of the same city, passing by the
mountain, met a man, who complained bitterly of the burden he was constantly forced to bear.   Upon enquiring
the cause of his complaining, as he did not seem to carry
any load, the man related, that he had been unwarily
devoted to the spirits by an execration, and that they
now employed him constantly as a vehicle of burden.
As a proof of his assertion, he added that the daughter
of his fellow-citizen was detained by the spirits, but
that they were willing to restore her, if her father
would come and demand her on the mountain.   Peter
de Cabinam, on being informed of this, ascended the
mountain to the lake, and, in the name of God, de-

manded his daughter; when a tall, thin, withered figure, with wandering eyes, and almost bereft of understanding, was wafted to him in a blast of wind. After some time, the person, who had been employed as the vehicle of the spirits, also returned, when he related where the palace of the spirits was situated; but added, that none were permitted to enter but those who devoted themselves entirely to the spirits; those who had been rashly committed to the devil by others, being only permitted, during their probation, to enter the porch." It may be proper to observe, that the superstitious idea, concerning the lake on the top of the mountain, is common to almost every high hill in Scotland. Wells, or pits, on the top of high hills, were likewise supposed to lead to the subterranean habitations of the Fairies. Thus Gervase relates, (p. 975,) "that he was informed the swineherd of William Peverell, an English baron, having lost a brood-sow, descended through a deep abyss, in the middle of an ancient ruinous castle, situated on the top of a hill, called Bech, in search of it. Though a violent wind commouly issued from this pit, he found it calm; and pursued his way, till he arrived at a subterraneous region, pleasant and cultivated, with reapers cutting down corn, though the snow remained on the surface of the ground above. Among the ears of corn he discovered his sow, and was permitted to ascend with her, and the pigs which she had farrowed." Though the author seems to think that the inhabitants of this cave might be Antipodes, yet, as many such stories are related of the Fairies, it is probable that this narration is of the same kind. Of a similar nature seems to be another superstition, mentioned by the same author, concerning the ringing of invisible bells, at the hour of one, in a field in the vicinity of Carleol, which, as he relates, was denominated *Laikibraine*, or *Lai ki brait.* From all these tales, we may perhaps be justified in supposing that the faculties and habits ascribed to the Fairies, by the superstition of latter days, comprehend several, originally attributed to other classes of inferior spirits.

III. The notions, arising from the spirit of chivalry, combined to add to the Fairies certain qualities, less atrocious indeed, but equally formidable, with those which they derived from the last-mentioned source, and alike inconsistent with the powers of the *duergar*, whom we may term their primitive prototype. From an early period, the daring temper of the northern tribes urged them to defy even the supernatural powers. In the days of Cæsar, the Suevi were described, by their countrymen, as a people, with whom the immortal gods dared not venture to contend. At a later period, the historians of Scandinavia paint their heroes and champions, not as bending at the altar of their deities, but wandering into remote forests and caverns, descending into the recesses of the tomb, and extorting boons, alike from gods and demons, by dint of the sword and battle-axe. I will not detain the reader by quoting instances in which heaven is thus described as having been literally attempted by storm. He may consult Saxo, Olaus Wormius, Olaus Magnus, Torfæus, Bartholin, and other northern antiquaries. With such ideas of superior beings, the Normans, Saxons, and other Gothic tribes, brought their ardent courage to ferment yet more highly in the genial climes of the south, and under the blaze of romantic chivalry. Hence, during the dark ages, the invisible world was modelled after the material: and the saints, to the protection of whom the knights-errant were accustomed to recommend themselves, were accoutred like *preux chevaliers*, by the ardent imaginations of their votaries. With such ideas concerning the inhabitants of the celestial regions, we ought not to be surprised to find the inferior spirits, of a more dubious nature and origin, equipped in the same disguise. Gervase of Tilbury (*Otia Imperial. ap. Scrip. rer. Brunsvic,* vol. i. p. 797) relates the following popular story concerning a Fairy Knight. " Osbert, a bold and powerful baron, visited a noble family in the vicinity of Wandlebury, in the bishopric of Ely. Among other stories related in the social circle of his friends, who, according to custom, amused each other by repeating ancient tales and traditions, he was informed, that if any knight, unattended, entered an adjacent plain by moonlight, and challenged an adversary to appear, he would be immediately encountered by a spirit in the form of a knight. Osbert resolved to make the experiment, and set out, attended by a single squire, whom he ordered to remain

without the limits of the plain, which was surrounded
by an ancient intrenchment.   On repeating the chal
lenge, he was instantly assailed by an adversary, whom
he quickly unhorsed, and seized the reins of his steed.
During this operation, his ghostly opponent sprung up,
and, darting his spear, like a javelin, at Osbert, wounded him in the thigh.   Osbert returned in triumph with
the horse, which he committed to the care of his servants.   The horse was of a sable colour, as well as his
whole accoutrements, and apparently of great beauty
and vigour.   He remained with his keeper till cock-
crowing, when, with eyes flashing fire, he reared,
spurned the ground, and vanished.   On disarming himself, Osbert perceived that he was wounded, and that
one of his steel boots was full of blood.   Gervase adds,
that as long as he lived, the scar of his wound opened
afresh on the anniversary of the eve on which he encountered the spirit."[1]   Less fortunate was the gallant

---

[1] The unfortunate Chatterton was not, probably, acquainted with
Gervase of Tilbury ; yet he seems to allude, in the *Battle of Has-
tings*, to some modification of Sir Osbert's adventure :—
> " So who they be that ouphant fairies strike,
> Their souls shall wander to King Offa's dike."

The intrenchment, which served as lists for the combatants, is
said by Gervase to have been the work of the Pagan invaders of
Britain.   In the metrical romance of *Arthour and Merlin*, we
have also an account of Wandlesbury being occupied by the Saracens, *i. e.* the Saxons ; for all Pagans were Saracens with the romancers.   I presume the place to have been Wednesbury, in Wilt-
shire, situated on the remarkable mound, called Wandsdike, which
is obviously a Saxon work.—GOUGH's *Camden's Britannia*, pp.
87–95.

Bohemian knight, who, travelling by night with a single companion, came in sight of a fairy host, arrayed under displayed banners. Despising the remonstrances of his friend, the knight pricked forward to break a lance with a champion who advanced from the ranks, apparently in defiance. His companion beheld the Bohemian overthrown, horse and man, by his aërial adversary ; and returning to the spot next morning, he found the mangled corpse of the knight and steed.— *Hierarchie of Blessed Angels*, p. 554.

To the same current of warlike ideas, we may safely attribute the long train of military processions which the Fairies are supposed occasionally to exhibit. The elves, indeed, seem in this point to be identified with the aërial host, termed, during the middle ages, the *Milites Herlikini*, or *Herleurini*, celebrated by Pet. Blesensis, and termed, in the life of St Thomas of Canterbury, the *Familia Helliquinii*. The chief of this band was originally a gallant knight and warrior ; but, having spent his whole possessions in the service of the emperor, and being rewarded with scorn, and abandoned to subordinate oppression, he became desperate, and, with his sons and followers, formed a band of robbers. After committing many ravages, and defeating all the forces sent against him, Hellequin, with his whole troop, fell in a bloody engagement with the imperial host. His former good life was supposed to save him from utter reprobation; but he and his followers were condemned after death, to a state of

wandering, which should endure till the last day. Retaining their military habits, they were usually seen in
the act of justing together, or in similar warlike employments. See the ancient French Romance of *Richard sans Peur*. Similar to this was the *Nacht Lager*,
or midnight camp, which seemed nightly to beleaguer
the walls of Prague,

" With ghastly faces throng'd, and fiery arms,"

but which disappeared upon recitation of the magical
words, *Vezelé, Vezelé, ho ! ho ! ho !*—For similar
delusions, see DELRIUS, pp. 294, 295.

The martial spirit of our ancestors led them to defy
these aërial warriors ; and it is still currently believed,
that he who has courage to rush upon a fairy festival,
and snatch from them their drinking cup or horn, shall
find it prove to him a cornucopia of good fortune, if he
can bear it in safety across a running stream.   Such a
horn is said to have been presented to Henry I., by a
lord of Colchester.—GERVAS TILB. p. 980.   A goblet
is still carefully preserved in Edenhall, Cumberland,
which is supposed to have been seized at a banquet of
the elves, by one of the ancient family of Musgrave ;
or, as others say, by one of their domestics, in the manner above described.   The Fairy train vanished, crying
aloud,

" If this glass do break or fall,
Farewell the luck of Edenhall !"

The goblet took a name from the prophecy, under

which it is mentioned in the burlesque ballad, commonly attributed to the Duke of Wharton, but in reality composed by Lloyd, one of his jovial companions. The duke, after taking a draught, had nearly terminated "the luck of Edenhall," had not the butler caught the cup in a napkin, as it dropped from his grace's hands. I understand it is not now subjected to such risks, but the lees of wine are still apparent at the bottom.

> " God prosper long from being broke,
>   The luck of Edenhall."—*Parody on Chevy Chace.*[1]

Some faint traces yet remain, on the Borders, of a conflict of a mysterious and terrible nature, between mortals and the spirits of the wilds. The superstition is incidentally alluded to by Jackson, at the beginning of the 17th century. The fern seed, which is supposed to become visible only on St John's eve,[2] and at the

[1] [" Prætorius informs us that the member of the German house of *Alveschleben* received a ring from a Nixe, to which the future fortunes of his line were to be attached. *Antherpodemius Plutonicus*, i. p. 113. Another German family, the Ranzaus, held their property by the tenure of a faery spindle."—*Preface to* WARTON, 1824, p. 52.—ED.]

[2] " Ne'er be I found by thee unawed,
     On that thrice-hallow'd eve abroad,
     When goblins haunt, from fire and fen,
     And wood and lake, the steps of men."
                                   COLLIN's *Ode to Fear.*

The whole history of St John the Baptist was, by our ancestors, accounted mysterious, and connected with their own superstitions. The Fairy Queen was sometimes identified with Herodias.—DEL-very moment when the Baptist was born, is held by the vulgar to be under the special protection of the Queen of Faëry. But, as the seed was supposed to have the quality of rendering the possessor invisible at pleasure,[1] and to be also of sovereign use in charms and incantations, persons of courage, addicted to these mysterious arts, were wont to watch in solitude, to gather it at the moment when it should become visible. The particular charms, by which they fenced themselves during this vigil, are now unknown; but it was reckoned a feat of no small danger, as the person undertaking it was exposed to the most dreadful assaults from spirits, who dreaded the effect of this powerful herb in the hands of a cabalist. "Much discourse," says Richard Bivot, "hath been about gathering of fern seed (which is looked upon as a magical herb) on the night of Midsummer-eve; and I remember I was told of one who went to gather it, and the spirits whisk't by his ears like bullets, and sometimes struck his hat, and other parts of his body; in fine, though he apprehended he had gotten a quantity of it, and secured it in papers, and a box besides, when he came home he found all

KII *Disquisitiones Magicæ*, pp. 168, 807. It is amusing to observe with what gravity the learned Jesuit contends, that it is heresy to believe that this celebrated figurante (*saltatricula*) still leads choral dances upon earth!

[1] This is alluded to by Shakspeare, and other authors of his time :—

"We have the receipt of *fern seed*; we walk invisible."
Henry IV. Part 1st, *Act* 2d, *Sc.* 3.

empty. But, most probably, this appointing of times and hours is of the devil's own institution, as well as the fast, that, having once ensnared people to an obedience to his rules, he may with more facility oblige them to a stricter vassalage."—*Pandæmonium*, Lond. 1684, p. 217. Such were the shades, which the original superstition, concerning the Fairies, received from the chivalrous sentiments of the middle ages.

IV. An absurd belief in the fables of classical antiquity lent an additional feature to the character of the woodland spirits of whom we treat. Greece and Rome had not only assigned tutelary deities to each province and city, but had peopled, with peculiar spirits, the Seas, the Rivers, the Woods, and the Mountains. The memory of the Pagan creed was not speedily eradicated, in the extensive provinces through which it was once universally received ; and, in many particulars, it continued long to mingle with, and influence, the original superstitions of the Gothic nations. Hence, we find the elves occasionally arrayed in the costume of Greece and Rome, and the Fairy Queen and her attendants transformed into Diana and her nymphs, and invested with their attributes and appropriate insignia.—DELRIUS, pp. 168, 807. According to the same author, the Fairy Queen was also called *Habundia*. Like Diana, who, in one capacity, was denominated *Hecate*, the goddess of enchantment, the Fairy Queen is identified, in popular tradition, with the *Gyre-Carline, Gay Carline*, or mother witch, of the Scottish peasantry. Of

this personage, as an individual, we have but few
notices. She is sometimes termed *Nicnevin*, and is
mentioned in the *Complaynt of Scotland*, by Lindsay
in his *Dreme*, p. 225, edit. 1590, and in his *Interludes*,
apud PINKERTON's *Scottish Poems*, vol. ii. p. 18. But
the traditionary accounts regarding her are too obscure
to admit of explanation. In the burlesque fragment
subjoined, which is copied from the Bannatyne MS.,
the Gyre-Carline is termed the *Queen of Jowis*, (Jovis,
or perhaps Jews,) and is, with great consistency, married to Mohammed.[1]

[1] " In Tyberius tyme, the trew imperatour,
   Quhen Tynto hills fra skraiping of toun-henis was keipit,
   Thair dwelt ane grit Gyre Carling in awld Betokis bour,
   That levit upoun Christiane menis flesche, and rewheids unleipit;
   Thair wynit ane hir by, on the west syde, callit Blasour,
   For luve of hir lauchane lippis, he walit and he weipit;
   He gadderit ane menzie of modwartis to warp doun the tour;
   The Carling with ane yren club, quhen that Blasour sleipit,
        Behind the heil scho hatt him sic ane blaw,
        Qubil Blasour bled an quart
        Off milk pottage inwart,
        The Carling luche, and let a fart
             North Berwik Law.

" The King of Fary than come, with clhs many ane,
   And sett ane seke, and ane salt, with grit pensallis of pryd;
   And all the doggis fra Dunbar wes thair to Dumblane,
   With all the tykis of Tervey, come to thame that tyd;
   Thay quelle doune with thair gonnes mony grit stane,
   The Carling schup her on ane sow, and is her gaitis gane,
   Gruntying our the Greik sie, and durstna langer byd,
   For bruklyng of bargane, and breiking of browis :

But chiefly in Italy were traced many dim characters of ancient mythology, in the creed of tradition. Thus, so lately as 1536, Vulcan, with twenty of his Cyclops, is stated to have presented himself suddenly to a Spanish merchant, travelling in the night through the forests of Sicily ; an apparition which was followed by a dreadful eruption of Mount Ætna.—*Hierarchie of Blessed Angels*, p. 504. Of this singular mixture, the reader will find a curious specimen in the following tale, wherein the Venus of antiquity assumes the manners of one of the Fays, or Fatæ, of romance. " In the year 1058, a young man of noble birth had been married at Rome, and, during the period of the nuptial feast, having gone with his companions to play at ball, he put his marriage ring on the finger of a broken sta-

> The Carling now for dispyte
> Is mareit with Mahomyte,
> And will the doggis interdyte,
>   For scho is quene of Jowis.

" Sensyne the cochis of Crawmound crew nevir at day
For dule of that devillisch deme wes with Mahoun mareit,
And the henis of Hadingtoun sensyne wald not lay,
For this wild wibroun wich them widlit sa and wareit ;
And the same Noith Berwik Law, as I heir wyvis say,
This Carling, with a fals cast, wald away careit ;
For to luck on quba sa lykis, na langer scho tareit ;
All thie langour for love before tymes fell,
    Lang or Betok was born,
    Sho bred of ane accorne ;
    The laif of the story to morne,
        To you I sall telle."

tue of Venus in the area, to remain while he was engaged in the recreation. Desisting from the exercise, he found the finger, on which he had put his ring, contracted firmly against the palm, and attempted in vain either to break it or to disengage his ring. He concealed the circumstance from his companions, and returned at night with a servant, when he found the finger extended, and his ring gone. He dissembled the loss, and returned to his wife ; but, whenever he attempted to embrace her, he found himself prevented by something dark and dense, which was tangible, though not visible, interposing between them : and he heard a voice saying, ' Embrace me! for I am Venus, whom this day you wedded, and I will not restore your ring.' As this was constantly repeated, he consulted his relations, who had recourse to Palumbus, a priest skilled in necromancy. He directed the young man to go, at a certain hour of night, to a spot among the ruins of ancient Rome, where four roads met, and wait silently till he saw a company pass by, and then, without uttering a word, to deliver a letter, which he gave him, to a majestic being, who rode in a chariot, after the rest of the company. The young man did as he was directed; and saw a company of all ages, sexes, and ranks, on horse and on foot, some joyful and others sad, pass along ; among whom he distinguished a woman in a meretricious dress, who, from the tenuity of her garments, seemed almost naked. She rode on a mule ; her long hair, which flowed over her shoulders, was bound with a golden fillet; and in her hand was a golden rod, with which she directed her mule. In the close of the procession, a tall majestic figure appeared in a chariot, adorned with emeralds and pearls, who fiercely asked the young man, 'What he did there?' He presented the letter in silence, which the demon dared not refuse. As soon as he had read, lifting up his hands to heaven, he exclaimed, ' Almighty God! how long wilt thou endure the iniquities of the sorcerer Palumbus l' and immediately despatched some of his attendants, who, with much difficulty, extorted the ring from Venus, and restored it to its owner, whose infernal banns were thus dissolved."— FORDUNI *Scotichronicon*, vol. i. p. 407, *cura* GOODALL.

But it is rather in the classical character of an infernal Deity, that the Elfin queen may be considered, than as *Hecate*, the patroness of magic; for not only in the romance-writers, but even in Chaucer, are the fairies identified with the ancient inhabitants of the classical hell. Thus Chaucer, in his *Marchand's Tale,* mentions

" Pluto that is king of fayrie—and
Proserpine and all her fayrie."

In the *Golden Terge* of Dunbar, the same phraseology is adopted: Thus,

" Thair was Pluto that elricke incubus
In cloke of grene, his court usit in sable."

Even so late as 1602, in Harsenet's *Declaration of*

Popish Imposture, p. 57, Mercury is called *Prince of the Fairies.*

But Chaucer, and those poets who have adopted his phraseology, have only followed the romance-writers ; for the same substitution occurs in the romance of *Orfeo and Heurodis,* in which the story of Orpheus and Eurydice is transformed into a beautiful romance tale of faëry, and the Gothic mythology engrafted on the fables of Greece. *Heurodis* is represented as wife of *Orfeo,* and Queen of Winchester, the ancient name of which city the romancer, with unparalleled ingenuity, discovers to have been Traciens, or Thrace. The monarch, her husband, had a singular genealogy :—

> " His fader was comen of King Pluto,
> And his moder of King Juno ;
> That sum time were as goddes y-holde,
> For aventours that thai dede and tolde."

Reposing, unwarily, at noon, under the shade of an ymp tree,[1] *Heurodis* dreams that she is accosted by the King of Fairies,

> " With an hundred knights and mo,
> And damisels an hundred also,
> Al on snowe-white stedes ;
> As white as milk were her wedes ;
> Y no seigh never yete bifore,
> So fair creatours y-core :

[1] *Ymp tree.*—According to the general acceptation, this only signifies a grafted tree ; whether it should be here understood to mean a tree consecrated to the imps, or fairies, is left with the reader.

> The kinge badde a cronn on hede,
> It nas of silver, no of golde red,
> Ac it was of a precious ston :
> As bright as the sonne it schon."

The King of Fairies, who had obtained power over the queen, perhaps from her sleeping at noon in his domain, orders her, under the penalty of being torn to pieces, to await him to-morrow under the ymp tree, and accompany him to Fairy-Land. She relates her dream to her husband, who resolves to accompany her, and attempt her rescue :—

> " A morwe the under tide is come,
> And Orfeo hath his armes y-nome,
> And wele ten hundred knights with him,
> Ich y-armed stout and grim ;
> And with the quen wenten he,
> Right upon that ympe tre.
> Thai made scheltrom in iche aside,
> And sayd thai wold there abide,
> And dye ther everichon,
> Er the quen schuld fram hem gon :
> Ac yete amiddes hem ful right,
> The quen was oway y-twight,
> With Fairi forth y-nome,
> Nen wizt never wher she was become."

After this fatal catastrophe, *Orfeo*, distracted for the loss of his queen, abandons his throne, and, with his harp, retires into a wilderness, where he subjects himself to every kind of austerity, and attracts the wild beasts by the pathetic melody of his harp. His state of desolation is poetically described :—

" He that werd the fowe and griis,
Aud on bed the purpur hiis,
Now on hard hethe he lith,
With leves and gresse he him writh :
He that had castells and tours,
Rivers, forests, frith with floweis,
Now, thei it commence to snewe and fiere,
This king mot make his bed in mese ;
He that had y-had knightes of priis,
Bifor him kneland and leuedis,
Now seth he no thing that him liketh,
Bot wild wormes bi him striketh :
He that had y-had plente
Of mete and drinke, of ich deynte,
Now may he al daye digge and wrote,
Er he find his fille of rote.
In somer he liveth bi wilde fruit,
And verien bot gode lite.
In winter may he nothing find,
Bot rotes, grasses, and the rinde.

His here of his berd blac and rowe,
To his girdel stede was growe ;
His harp, whereon was al his gle,
He hidde in anc holwe tre :
And, when the weder was clere and bright,
He toke his harpe to him wel right,
And harped at his owen will,
Into al the wode the soun gan shill,
That al the wild bestes that ther beth
For joie abouten him thai teth ;
And al the foules that there wer,
Come and sete on ich a biere,
To here his harping a fine,
So miche melody was therein."

At last he discovers, that he is not the sole inhabitant of this desert ; for

" He might se him besides,
Oft in hot undertides,
The King of Fani, with his rout,
Com to hunt him al about,
With dim cri and bloweing,
And houndes also with him berking :
Ac no best thai no nome,
No never he nist whider thai bi come.
And other while he might hem se
As a gret ost bi him te,
Wel atourned ten hundred knightes,
Ich y-armed to his rightes,
Of cuntenaunce stout and fers,
With mani desplaid baners ;
And ich his sword y-drawe hold,
Ac never he nist whider thai wold.
And otherwhile he seighe other thing ;
Knightis and leuedis com daunceing,
In queynt atire gisely,
Queyete pas and softlie :
Tabours and trumpes gede hem bi,
And al maner menstraci.—
And on a day he seighe him biside,
Sexti leuedis on hois ride,
Gentil and johf as bird on ris ;
Nought o man amonges hem ther nis ;
And ich a faucoun on hond bere,
And riden on hauken bi o river.
Of game thai found wel gode haunt,
Maulardes, hayroun, and cormoraunt ;
The foules of the water ariseth,
Ich faucoun hem wele deviseth,

Ich faucoun his pray slough,
That seize Orfeo and lough.
' Par fay,' quoth he, ' there is fair game !
Hider Ichil bi Godes name,
Ich was y won swich work to se : '
He aros, and thider gan te ;
To a leuedi hi was y-come,
Bihelde, and hath wel under nome,
And seth, bi all thing, that is
His owhen quen, dam Heurodis ;
Gern hi biheld her, and sche him eke,
Ac nouther to other a word no speke :
For messais that sche on him seighe,
That had been so riche and so heighe,
The tears fel out of her eighe ;
The other leuedis this y-seighe,
And maked her oway to ride,
Sche most with him no longer obide.
' Allas !' quoth he, ' nowe is mi woe,
Whi nil deth now me slo !
Allas ! to long last mi liif,
When y no dare nought with mi wif,
Nor hye to me o word speke ;
Allas whi nil miin hert breke !
Par fay,' quoth he, ' tide what betide,
Whider so this leuedis ride,
The selve way Ichil stieche ;
Of liif, no dethe, me no reche.' "

In consequence, therefore, of this discovery, *Orfeo*
pursues the hawking damsels, among whom he has descried his lost queen. They enter a rock, the king
continues the pursuit, and arrives at Fairy-Land, of
which the following very poetical description is given :

" In at roche the leuedis rideth,
And he after and nought abideth :

When he was in the roche y-go,
Wele thre mile other mo,
He com into a fair contray,
As bright soonne somers day,
Smothe and plain and al grene,
Hill no dale nas none ysene.
Amiddle the lond a castel he seighe,
Rich and reale and wonder heighe;
Al the utmast wal
Was cler and schine of cristal;
An hundred touis ther were about,
Degiselich and bataild stout;
The butrass come out of the diche,
Of rede gold y-arched riche;
The bousour was anowed al,
Of ich maner deuers animal;
Within ther wer wide wones
Al of precious stones,
The werss piler onto biholde,
Was al of burnist gold:
Al that lond was ever light,
For when it schuld be therk and night,
The riche stonnes light gonne,
Bright as doth at none the sonne ·
No man may tel, no thenke in thought,
The riche werk that ther was rought.

————

" Than he gan biholde about al,
And seighe ful liggeand with in the wal,
Of folk that wer thidder y-brought,
And thought dede and nere nought;
Sum stode with outen badde;
Aud some none armes nade;
And sum thurch the bodi hadde wounde;
And sum lay wode y-bounde;
And sum armed on hors sete;
And sum astrangled as thai ete;

And sum war in water adreynt ;
And sum with fire al for schreynt ;
Wives ther lay on childe bedde ;
Sum dede, and sume awedde ;
And wonder fele ther lay besides,
Right as thai slepe her undertides ;
Eche was thus in this warld y-nome,
With fairi thidder y-come.[1]
Ther he seize his owhen wiif,
Dame Heurodis, his liif liif,
Slepe under an ympe tree ;
Bi her clothes he knewe that it was sche.
   " And when he had bihold this mervalis alle,
He went unto the kinges halle ;
Then seigh he ther a semly sight,
A tabernacle blisseful and bright ;
Ther in her maister king sete,
And her quen fair and swete ;
Her crounes, her clothes shine so bright,
That unnethe bihold he them might."

Orfeo and Heurodis, M. S.

Orfeo, as a minstrel, so charms the Fairy King with
the music of his harp, that he promises to grant him
whatever he should ask. He immediately demands his
lost *Heurodis ;* and, returning safely with her to Winchester, resumes his authority ; a catastrophe, less
pathetic indeed, but more pleasing, than that of the
classical story. The circumstances, mentioned in this
romantic legend, correspond very exactly with popular
tradition. Almost all the writers on demonology men-

---

[1] It was perhaps from such description that Ariosto adopted his
idea of the Lunar Paradise, containing every thing that on earth was
stolen or lost.

tion, as a received opinion, that the power of the demons is most predominant at noon and midnight. The entrance to the Land of Faëry is placed in the wilder ness ; a circumstance which coincides with a passage in Lindsay's *Complaint of the Papingo :—*

> "Bot sen my spreit mon from my bodye go,
> I recommend it to the Quene of Fary,
> Eternally into her court to tarry
> In *wilderness* amang the boltis hair."
>
> LINDSAY's *Works*, 1592, p. 222.

Chaucer also agrees, in this particular, with our romancer :—

> " In his sadel he elombe anon,
> And priked over stile and ston,
>   An Elfe Quene for to espie ;
> Til he so long had riden and gone
> That he found in a privie wone
>   The countree of Faerie.

> " Wherein he soughte north and south,
> And often spired with his month,
>   In many a foreste wilde ;
> For in that countree nas ther non,
> That to him dorst ride or gon,
>   Neither wife ne childe."
>
> *Rime of Sir Thopas.*

V. Other two causes, deeply affecting the superstition of which we treat, remain yet to be noticed. The first is derived from the Christian religion, which admits only of two classes of spirits, exclusive of the souls of men—Angels, namely, and devils. This doctrine had a necessary tendency to abolish the distinc-

tion among subordinate spirits, which had been introduced by the superstition of the Scandinavians.   The
existence of the Fairies was readily admitted; but as
they had no pretensions to the angelic character, they
were deemed to be of infernal origin.   The union, also,
which had been formed betwixt the elves and the Pagan
deities, was probably of dissefvice to the former; since
every one knows that the whole synod of Olympus
were accounted demons.

The fulminations of the church were, therefore, early
directed against those, who consulted or consorted with
the Fairies; and, according to the inquisitorial logic,
the innocuous choristers of Oberon and Titania were,
without remorse, confounded with the sable inhabitants
of the orthodox Gehennim; while the rings, which
marked their revels, were assimilated to the blasted
sward on which the witches held their infernal sabbath.
—DELRII *Disq. Mag.* p. 179.   This transformation
early took place; for, among the many crimes for which
the famous Joan of Arc was called upon to answer, it
was not the least heinous, that she had frequented the
Tree and Fountain, near Dompré, which formed the
rendezvous of the Fairies, and bore their name; that
she had joined in the festive dance with the elves, who
haunted this charmed spot; had accepted of their magical bouquets, and availed herself of their talismans, for
the deliverance of her country.—*Vide Acta Judici-
arii contra Johannam D'Arceam, vulgo vocatam
Johanne la Pucelle.*

The Reformation swept away many of the corruptions of the church of Rome ; but the purifying torrent remained itself somewhat tinctured by the superstitious impurities of the soil over which it had passed. The trials of sorcerers and witches, which disgrace our criminal records, become even more frequent, after the Reformation of the church ; as if human credulity, no longer amused by the miracles of Rome, had sought for food in the traditionary records of popular superstition. A Judaical observation of the precepts of the Old Testament, also characterised the Presbyterian reformers : " *Thou shalt not suffer a witch to live,*" was a text, which at once (as they conceived) authorized their belief in sorcery, and sanctioned the penalty which they denounced against it. The Fairies were, therefore, in no better credit after the Reformation than before, being still regarded as actual demons, or something very little better. A famous divine, Doctor Jasper Brokeman, teaches us, in his system of divinity, " that they inhabit in those places, that are polluted with any crying sin, as effusion of blood, or where unbelief or superstitione have gotten the upper hand."—*Description of Feroe.* The Fairies being on such bad terms with the divines, those who pretended to intercourse with them were without scruple punished as sorcerers ; and such absurd charges are frequently stated as exaggerations of crimes, in themselves sufficiently heinous.

Such is the case in the trial of the noted Major Weir, and his sister ; where the following mummery

interlards a criminal indictment, too infamously flagi-
tious to be farther detailed : " 9th April, 1670. Jean
Weir, indicted of sorceries, committed by her when she
lived and kept a school at Dalkeith ; that she took
employment from a woman, to speak in her behalf to
the *Queen of Fairii, meaning the devil;* and that
another woman gave her a piece of a tree, or root, the
next day, and did tell her, that as long as she kept
the same, she should be able to do what she pleased;
and that same woman, from whom she got the tree,
caused her spread a cloth before the door, and set her
foot upon it, and to repeat thrice, in the posture foresaid, these words, '*All her crosses and losses go
alongst the doors,*' which was truly a consulting with
the devil and an act of sorcery, &c. That after the
spirit, in the shape of a woman, who gave her the
piece of tree, had removed, she, addressing herself to
spinning, and having spun but a short time, found more
yarn upon the pirn than could possibly have come there
by good means."[1]—*Books of Adjournal.*

---

[1] It is .observed in the record, that Major Weir, a man of the
most vicious character, was at the same time ambitious of appearing
eminently godly ; and used to frequent the beds of sick persons, to
assist them with his prayers. On such occasions, he put to his
mouth a long staff, which he usually carried, and expressed himself
with uncommon energy and fluency, of which he was utterly inca-
pable when the inspiring rod was withdrawn. This circumstance,
the result, probably, of a trick or habit, appearing suspicious to the
judges, the staff of the Sorcerer was burned along with his person.
One hundred and thirty years have elapsed since his execution, yet
no one has, during that space, ventured to inhabit the house of this

Neither was the judgment of the Criminal Court of Scotland less severe against another familiar of the Fairies, whose supposed correspondence with the court of Elfland seems to have constituted the sole crime for which she was burned alive. Her name was Alison Pearson, and she seems to have been a very noted person. In a bitter satire against Adamson, Bishop of St Andrews, he is accused of consulting with sorcerers, particularly with this very woman ; and an account is given of her travelling through Breadalbane in the company of the Queen of Faëry, and of her descrying, in the court of Elfland, many persons, who had been supposed at rest in the peaceful grave.[1] Among these we find two remarkable personages, the secretary, young Maitland of Lethington, and one of the old Lairds of Buccleuch. The cause of their being stationed in

celebrated criminal. 1803. [This house is engraved as a frontispiece to Sir W. Scott's Letters on Demonology and Witchcraft. 1830.]

[1] " For oght the kirk culd him forbid,
He sped him sone, and gat the thrid;
Ane carling of the Quene of Phareis,
That ewill win geir to elphyne careis ;
Through all Brade Abane scho has bene,
On horsbak on Hallow ewin ;
And ay in seiking certayne nightis,
As scho sayis with sur silly wychirs
And names out nybours sex or sewin,
That we belevit had bene in heawin ;
Scho said scho saw thame weill aneugh,
And speciallie gude auld Balcleuch,
The secretar, and sundrie uther :

Elfland probably arose from the manner of their de-
cease; which, being uncommon and violent, caused the
vulgar to suppose they had been abstracted by the
Fairies. Lethington, as is generally supposed, died a
Roman death during his imprisonment in Leith; and
the Buccleuch, whom I believe to be here meant, was
slain in a nocturnal scuffle by the Kers, his hereditary
enemies. Besides, they were both attached to the cause
of Queen Mary, and to the ancient religion; and were
thence, probably, considered as more immediately obnoxious to the assaults of the powers of darkness.[1] The

> Ane William Symsone, her mother brother,
> Whom fra scho has resavit a buike
> For ony herb scho likes to luke;
> It will instruct hir how to tak it,
> In saws and sillubs how to mak it;
> With stones that meikle mair can doe,
> In leich craft, where scho lays them toe:
> A thowsand maladeis scho has mendit;
> Now being tane, and apprehendit,
> Scho being in the bischops cure,
> And kepit in his castle sure,
> Without respect of worldlie glamer,
> He past into the witches chalmer."
> Scottish Poems of XVI. Century, Edin. 1801.
> vol. ii. p. 320.

[1] Buccleuch was a violent enemy to the English, by whom his
lands had been repeatedly plundered, (See *Introduction, ante,*) and
a great advocate for the marriage betwixt Mary and the Dauphin,
1549. According to John Knox, he had recourse even to threats,
in urging the Parliament to agree to the French match. " The
Laird of Balcleuch," says the Reformer, "a bloody man, with
many God's wounds, swore, they that would not consent should do
worse."

indictment of Alison Pearson notices her intercourse
with the Archbishop of St Andrews, and contains some
particulars, worthy of notice, regarding the court of
Elfland. It runs thus :—" 28th May, 1586. Alison
Pearson, in Byrehill, convicted of witchcraft, and of
consulting with evil spirits, in the form of one Mr
William Sympsoune, her cosin, who she affirmed was
a gritt scollar, and doctor of medicine, that healed her
of her diseases when she was twelve years of age ; having lost the power of her syde, and having a famili-
arite with him for divers years, dealing with charms,
and abuseing the common people by her arts of witchcraft, thir divers yeares by-past.

" *Item*, For hanting and repairing with the gude
neighbours, and Queene of Elfland, thir divers years
by-past, as she had confest ; and that she had friends
in that court, which were of her own blude, who had
gude acquaintance of the Queene of Elfland, which
might have helped her ; but she was whiles well, and
whiles ill, sometimes with them, and other times away
frae them ; and that she would be in her bed haille and
feire, and would not wytt where she would be the morn ;
and that she saw not the Queene this seven years, and
that she was seven years ill handled in the court of Elfland ; that, however, she had gude friends there, and
that it was the gude neighbours that healed her, under
God ; and that she was comeing and going to St Andrews to haile folkes thir many years past.

" *Item*, Convict of the said act of witchcraft, in as

far as she confest that the said Mr William Sympsoune, who was her guidsir sone, borne in Stirleing, who was the King's smith, who, when about eight years of age, was taken away by ane Egyptian into Egypt; which Egyptian was a gyant, where he remained twelve years, and then came home.

" *Item,* That she being in Grange Muir, with some other folke, she, being sick, lay downe; and, when alone, there came a man to her, clad in green, who said to her, if she would be faithful, he would do her good; but she, being feared, cried out, but naebodye came to her; so she said, if he came in God's name, and for the gude of her saule, it was well; but he gaid away: that he appeared to her another time like a lustie man, and many men and women with him; that, at seeing him, she signed herself and prayed, and past with them, and saw them making merrie with pypes, and gude cheir and wine, and that she was carried with them; and that when she telled any of these things, she was sairlie tormentit by them; and that the first time she gaed with them, she gat a sair straike frae one of them, which took all the *poustie*[1] of her syde frae her, and left ane ill-far'd mark on her syde.

" *Item,* That she saw the gude neighbours make their sawes[2] with panns and fyres, and that they gathered the herbs before the sun was up, and they came verie fearful sometimes to her, and flaide[3] her very sair, which made her cry, and threatened they would use her

---

[1] *Poustie*—Power.—[2] *Sawes*—Salves.—[3] *Flaide*—Scared.

worse than before ; and, at last, they took away the power of her haile syde frae her, which made her lye many weeks. Sometimes they would come and sitt by her, and promise all that she should never want, if she would be faithful, but if she would speak and telle of them, they should murther her ; and that Mr William Sympsoune is with them, who healed her, and telt her all things ; that he is a young man not six years older than herself, and that he will appear to her before the court comes ; that he told her he was taken away by them, and he bid her sign herself that she be not taken away, for the teind of them are tane to hell everie year.

" *Item*, That the said Mr William told her what herbs were fit to cure every disease, and how to use them ; and particularlie tauld, that the Bishop of St Andrews laboured under sindrie diseases, sic as the ripples, trembling, fever, flux, &c., and bade her make a sawe, and anoint several parts of his body therewith, and gave directions for making a posset, which she made and gave him."

For this idle story, the poor woman actually suffered death. Yet, notwithstanding the fervent arguments thus liberally used by the orthodox, the common people, though they dreaded even to think or speak about the Fairies, by no means unanimously acquiesced in the doctrine which consigned them to eternal perdition. The inhabitants of the Isle of Man call them the " *good people*, and say they live in wilds and forests, and on mountains, and shun great cities, because of the wickedness acted therein : all the houses are blessed where they visit, for they fly vice. A person would be thought impudently profane, who should suffer his family to go to bed, without first having set a tub, or pail, full of clean water, for those guests to bathe themselves in, which the natives aver they constantly do, as soon as ever the eyes of the family are closed, wherever they vouchsafe to come."—WALDRON's *Works*, p. 126. There are some curious, and perhaps anomalous facts, concerning the history of Fairies, in a sort of Cock-lane narrative, contained in a letter from Moses Pitt to Dr Edward Fowler, Lord Bishop of Gloucester, printed at London in 1696, and preserved in Morgan's *Phœnix Britannicus*, 4to, London, 1732.

Anne Jefferies was born in the parish of St Teath, in the county of Cornwall, in 1626. Being the daughter of a poor man, she resided as servant in the house of the narrator's father, and waited upon the narrator himself, in his childhood. As she was knitting stockings in an arbour of the garden, " six small people, all in green clothes," came suddenly over the garden-wall ; at the sight of whom, being much frightened, she was seized with convulsions, and continued so long sick, that she became as a changeling, and was unable to walk. During her sickness, she frequently exclaimed, " They are just gone out of the window ! They are just gone out of the window ! Do you not see them?" These expressions, as she afterwards declared, related to their disappearing. During the harvest, when every one was employed, her mistress walked out ; and dreading that Anne, who was extremely weak and silly, might injure herself, or the house, by the fire, with some difficulty persuaded her to walk in the orchard till her return. She accidentally hurt her leg, and at her return Anne cured it, by stroking it with her hand. She appeared to be informed of every particular, and asserted, that she had this information from the Fairies, who had caused the misfortune. After this, she performed numerous cures, but would never receive money for them. From harvest time to Christmas, she was fed by the Fairies, and eat no other victuals but theirs. The narrator affirms, that looking one day through the key-hole of the door of her chamber, he saw her eating ; and that she gave him a piece of bread, which was the most delicious he ever tasted. The Fairies always appeared to her in even numbers ; never less than two, nor more than eight, at a time. She had always a sufficient stock of salves and medicines, and yet neither made nor purchased any ; nor did she ever appear to be in want of money. She, one day, gave a silver cup, containing about a quart, to the daughter of her mistress, a girl about four years old, to carry to her mother, who refused to receive it. The narrator adds, that he had seen her dancing in the orchard among the trees, and that she informed him she was then dancing with the Fairies. The report of the strange cures which she performed, soon attracted the attention of both ministers and magistrates. The ministers endeavoured

to persuade her, that the Fairies, by which she was
haunted, were evil spirits, and that she was under the
delusion of the devil. After they had left her, she was
visited by the Fairies, while in great perplexity, who
desired to cause those who termed them evil spirits, to
read that place of Scripture, *First Epistle of John*,
chap. iv. v. 1.—*Dearly beloved, believe not every spirit, but try the spirits, whether they are of God*, &c.
Though Anne Jefferies could not read, she produced
a Bible folded down at this passage. By the magistrates she was confined three months, without food, in
Bodman jail, and afterwards for some time in the house
of Justice Tregeagle. Before the constable appeared
to apprehend her, she was visited by the Fairies, who
informed her what was intended, and advised her to go
with him. When this account was given, on May 1,
1696, she was still alive; but refused to relate any
particulars of her connexion with the Fairies, or the
occasion on which they deserted her, lest she should
again fall under the cognizance of the magistrates.

Anne Jefferies' Fairies were not altogether singular
in maintaining their good character, in opposition to
the received opinion of the church. Aubrey and Lilly,
unquestionably judges in such matters, had a high
opinion of these beings, if we may judge from the
following succinct and businesslike memorandum of
a ghost-seer. " Anno 1670. Not far from Cirencester
was an apparition. Being demanded whether a good
spirit or a bad, returned no answer, but disappeared with

a curious perfume, and most melodious twang. M. W
Lilly believes it was a fairie. So Propertius,

'Omnia finierat; tenues secessit in auras,
Mansit odor, possis scire fuisse Doam!'"

AUBREY'S *Miscellanies*, p. 80.

Webster gives an account of a person who cured
diseases by means of a white powder " To this I shall
only add thus much, that the man was accused for
invoking and calling upon evil spirits, and was a very
simple and illiterate person to any man's judgment, and
had formerly been very poor, but had gotten some pretty
little means to maintain himself, his wife, and diverse
small children, by his cures done with his white powder, of which there were sufficient proofs ; and the
judge asking him how he came by the powder, he told
a story to this effect : That one night, before day was
gone, as he was going home from his labour, being
very sad and full of heavy thoughts, not knowing how
to get meat and drink for his wife and children, he met
a fair woman in fine clothes, who asked him why he
was so sad, and he told her that it was by reason of his
poverty ; to which she said, that if he would follow her
counsel, she would help him to that which would serve
to get him a good living ; to which he said he would
consent with all his heart, so it were not by unlawful
ways : She told him that it should not be by any such
ways, but by doing good, and curing of sick people ;
and so warning him strictly to meet her there the next

night, at the same time, she departed from him, and
he went home. And the next night, at the time appointed, he duly waited, and she (according to promise)
came, and told him that it was well that he came so
duly, otherwise he had missed that benefit that she intended to do unto him, and so bade him follow her,
and not be afraid. Thereupon she led him to a little
hill, and she knocked three times, and the hill opened,
and they went in, and came to a fair hall, wherein was
a Queen sitting in great state, and many people about
her, and the gentlewoman that brought him presented
him to the Queen, and she said he was welcome, and
bid the gentlewoman give him some of the white powder, and teach him how to use it, which she did, and
gave him a little wood box full of the white powder, and
bade him give two or three grains of it to any that were
sick, and it would heal them ; and so she brought him
forth of the hill, and so they parted. And, being asked
by the judge, whether the place within the hill, which
he called a hall, were light or dark, he said, indifferent,
as it is with us in the twilight ; and being asked how
he got more powder, he said, when he wanted, he went
to that hill, and knocked three times, and said every
time, I am coming, I am coming, whereupon it opened,
and he, going in, was conducted by the aforesaid woman to the Queen, and so had more powder given him.
This was the plain and simple story (however it may
be judged of) that he told before the judge, the whole
court, and the jury ; and there being no proofs, but

what cures he had done to very many, the jury did acquit him : and I remember the judge said, when all the evidence was heard, that if he were to assign his punishment, he should be whipped from thence to Fairy-hall ; and did seem to judge it to be a delusion, or an imposture."—WEBSTER's *Displaying of Supposed Witchcraft*, p. 301.

A rustic, also, whom Jackson taxed with magical practices, about 1620, obstinately denied that the good King of the Fairies had any connexion with the devil ; and some of the Highland seers, even in our day, have boasted of their intimacy with the elves, as an innocent and advantageous connexion. One Macoan, in Appin, the last person eminently gifted with the second sight, professed to my learned and excellent friend, Mr Ramsay of Ochtertyre, that he owed his prophetic visions to their intervention.

VI. There remains yet another cause to be noticed, which seems to have induced a considerable alteration into the popular creed of England, respecting Fairies. Many poets of the sixteenth century, and, above all, our immortal Shakspeare, deserting the hackneyed fictions of Greece and Rome, sought for machinery in the superstitions of their native country. " The fays, which nightly dance upon the wold," were an interesting subject, and the creative imagination of the bard, improving upon the vulgar belief, assigned to them many of those fanciful attributes and occupations, which posterity have since associated with the name of Fairy. In such employments, as raising the drooping flower, and arranging the disordered chamber, the Fairies of South Britain gradually lost the harsher character of the dwarfs, or elves. Their choral dances were enlivened by the introduction of the merry goblin *Puck*,[1] for whose freakish pranks they exchanged their original mischievous propensities. The Fairies of Shakspeare, Drayton, and Menuls, therefore, at first exquisite fancy portraits, may be considered as having finally operated a change in the original which gave them birth.[2]

While the fays of South Britain received such attractive and poetical embellishments, those of Scotland,

[1] Robin Goodfellow, or Hobgoblin, possesses the frolicsome qualities of the French *Lutin*. For his full character, the reader is referred to the *Reliques of Ancient Poetry*. The proper livery of this silvan Momus is to be found in an old play. " Enter Robin Goodfellow, in a suit of leather, close to his body, his hands and face coloured russet colour, with a flail."— *Grim the Collier of Croydon, Act* 4, *Scene* 1. At other times, however, he is presented in the vernal livery of the elves, his associates :—

" *Tim.* I have made
Some speeches, sir, in verse, which have been spoke
By a *green Robin Goodfellow*, from Cheapside conduit,
To my father's company."

The City Match, Act 1, *Scene* 6.

[2] The Fairyland and Fairies of Spenser have no connexion with popular superstition, being only words used to denote a Utopian scene of action, and imaginary and allegorical characters ; and the title of the " Fairy Queen" being probably suggested by the elfin mistress of Chaucer's *Sir Thopas*. The stealing of the Red Cross

who possessed no such advantage, retained more of their ancient and appropriate character. Perhaps, also, the persecution which these silvan deities underwent, at the instance of the stricter Presbyterian clergy, had its usual effect, in hardening their dispositions, or at least in rendering them more dreaded, by those among whom they dwelt. The face of the country, too, might have some effect; as we should naturally attribute a less malicious disposition, and a less frightful appearance, to the fays who glide by moonlight through the oaks of Windsor, than to those who haunt the solitary heaths and lofty mountains of the North. The fact at least is certain; and it has not escaped a late ingenious traveller, that the character of the Scottish Fairy is more harsh and terrific than that which is ascribed to the elves of our sister kingdom.—See STODDART'S *View of Scenery and Manners in Scotland.*

Some curious particulars concerning the *Daoine Shie,* or *Men of Peace,* for so the Highlanders call Fairies, may be found in Dr GRAHAME'S " *Sketches of Picturesque Scenery on the Southern Confines of Perthshire.*" They are, though not absolutely malevolent, believed to be a peevish, repining, and envious

---

Knight, while a child, is the only incident in the poem which approaches to the popular character of the Fairy :

——" A Fairy thee unweeting reft ;
Theie as thou sleptst in tender swadling hand,
And her base elfin brood there for thee left :
Such men do changelings call, so changed by Fairies theft."
Book I. Canto 10.

race, who enjoy, in the subterranean recesses, a kind of shadowy splendour. The Highlanders are at all times unwilling to speak of them, but especially on Friday, when their influence is supposed to be particularly extensive. As they are supposed to be invisibly present, they are at all times to be spoken of with respect.

The Fairies of Scotland are represented as a dimi nutive race of beings, of a mixed, or rather dubious nature, capricious in their dispositions, and mischievous in their resentment. They inhabit the interior of green hills, chiefly those of a conical form, in Gaelic termed *Sighan,* on which they lead their dances by moonlight ; impressing upon the surface the marks of circles, which sometimes appear yellow and blasted, sometimes of a deep green hue ; and within which it is dangerous to sleep, or to be found after sunset. The removal of those large portions of turf, which thunderbolts sometimes scoop out of the ground with singular regularity, is also ascribed to their agency. Cattle, which are suddenly seized with the cramp, or some similar disorder, are said to be *elf-shot ;* and the approved cure is, to chafe the parts affected with a blue bonnet, which, it may be readily believed, often restores the circulation. The triangular flints, frequently found in Scotland, with which the ancient inhabitants pro bably barbed their shafts, are supposed to be the weapons of Fairy resentment, and are termed *elf arrowheads.* The rude brazen battle-axes of the ancients,

commonly called *celts*, are also ascribed to their manufacture. But, like the Gothic duergar, their skill is not
confined to the fabrication of arms; for they are heard
sedulously hammering in linns, precipices, and rocky
or cavernous situations, where, like the dwarfs of the
mines, mentioned by Georg. Agricola, they busy themselves in imitating the actions and the various employments of men. The Brook of Beaumont, for example,
which passes, in its course, by numerous linns and
caverns, is notorious for being haunted by the Fairies;
and the perforated and rounded stones which are formed
by trituration in its channel, are termed, by the vulgar,
fairy cups and dishes. A beautiful reason is assigned
by Fletcher for the fays frequenting streams and foun-
tains : He tells us of

> " A virtuous well, about whose flowery banks
> The nimble-footed Fairies dance their rounds,
> By the pale moonshine, dipping oftentimes
> Their stolen children, so to make them free
> From dying flesh and dull mortality."
>
> *Faithful Sheperdess.*

It is sometimes accounted unlucky to pass such
places, without performing some ceremony to avert the
displeasure of the elves. There is, upon the top of
Minchmuir, a mountain in Peebles-shire, a spring called the *Cheese Well*, because, anciently, those who
passed that way were wont to throw into it a piece of
cheese, as an offering to the Fairies, to whom it was
consecrated.

Like the *feld elfen* of the Saxons, the usual dress of
the Fairies is green ; though on the moors, they have
been sometimes observed in heath-brown, or in weeds
dyed with the stoneraw, or lichen.[1]   They often ride
in invisible procession, when their presence is discovered by the shrill ringing of their bridles.   On these
occasions, they sometimes borrow mortal steeds ; and
when such are found at morning, panting and fatigued
in their stalls, with their manes and tails dishevelled
and entangled, the grooms, I presume, often find this
a convenient excuse for their situation ; as the common
belief of the elves quaffing the choicest liquors in the
cellars of the rich (see the story of Lord Duffus, below) might occasionally cloak the delinquencies of an
unfaithful butler.

The Fairies, besides their equestrian processions, are
addicted, it would seem, to the pleasures of the chase.
A young sailor, travelling by night from Douglas, in
the Isle of Man, to visit his sister residing in Kirk
Merlugh, heard the noise of horses, the holloa of a
huntsman, and the sound of a horn.   Immediately
afterwards, thirteen horsemen, dressed in green, and
gallantly mounted, swept past him.   Jack was so much
delighted with the sport, that he followed them, and
enjoyed the sound of the horn for some miles ; and it
was not till he arrived at his sister's house, that he
learned the danger which he had incurred.   I must not
omit to mention, that these little personages are ex-

[1] Hence the hero of the ballad is termed an " elfin grey."

pert jockeys, and scorn to ride the little Manks ponies, though apparently well suited to their size. The exercise, therefore, falls heavily upon the English and Irish horses, brought into the Isle of Man. Mr Waldron was assured by a gentleman of Ballafletcher, that he had lost three or four capital hunters by these nocturnal excursions.—WALDRON'S *Works*, p, 132. From the same author we learn, that the Fairies sometimes take more legitimate modes of procuring horses. A person of the utmost integrity informed him, that having occasion to sell a horse, he was accosted among the mountains by a little gentleman plainly dressed, who priced his horse, cheapened him, and, after some chaffering, finally purchased him. No sooner had the buyer mounted, and paid the price, than he sunk through the earth, horse and man, to the astonishment and terror of the seller; who experienced, however, no inconvenience from dealing with so extraordinary a purchaser.[1]—*Ibid*, p. 135.

---

[1] [" Under each of these six heads of dissertation, a number of curious out-of-the-way relations are compiled from the forgotten repositaries of fabulous marvels. *Many of them will serve for the story of future ballads, and the decoration of yet unwritten metrical romances.* They constitute the elements of British mythology; and *in the hands of a Modern Ovid*, may be shapen into a wild catalogue of metamorphoses, into amusing anecdotes of sorcery, fableries of romance, or tales of wonder, *into a Thousand and One Nights' Entertainment*, or golden legends of shuddering astonishment."— *Critical Review*, November, 1803.—There is something here as much the spirit of prophecy as of criticism.—ED.]

It is hoped the reader will receive, with due respect, these, and similar stories, told by Mr Waldron ; for he himself, a scholar and a gentleman, informs us, " as to circles in grass, and the impression of small feet among the snow, I cannot deny but I have seen them frequently, and once thought I heard a whistle, as though in my ear, when nobody that could make it was near me." In this passage there is a curious picture of the contagious effects of a superstitious atmosphere. Waldron had lived so long among the Manks, that he was persuaded to believe their legends.

The worthy Captain George Burton communicated to Richard Bovet, gent., author of the interesting work, entitled " Pandæmonium, or the Devil's Cloister Opened," the following singular account of a lad called the *Fairy Boy* of Leith, who, it seems, acted as a drummer to the elves, who weekly held rendezvous in the Calton Hill, near Edinburgh.

" About fifteen years since, having business that detained me for some time at Leith, which is near Edinburgh, in the kingdom of Scotland, I often met some of my acquaintance at a certain house there, where we used to drink a glass of wine for our refection ; the woman which kept the house was of honest reputation among the neighbours, which made me give the more attention to what she told me one day about a fairy boy, (as they called him,) who lived about that town. She had given me so strange an account of him, that I desired her I might see him the first opportunity, which she promised; and not long after, passing that way, she told me there was the fairy boy, but a little before I came by; and, casting her eye into the street, said, Look you, sir, yonder he is at play with those other boys; and designing him to me, I went, and, by smooth words, and a piece of money, got him to come into the house with me; where, in the presence of divers people, I demanded of him several astrological questions, which he answered with great subtilty; and, through all his discourse, carried it with a cunning much above his years, which seemed not to exceed ten or eleven.

"He seemed to make a motion like drumming upon the table with his fingers, upon which I asked him, Whether he could beat a drum? To which he replied, Yes, sir, as well as any man in Scotland; for every Thursday night I beat all points to a sort of people that used to meet under yonder hill, (pointing to the great hill between Edenborough and Leith.) How, boy? quoth I, What company have you there? There are, sir, (said he,) a great company both of men and women, and they are entertained with many sorts of musick, besides my drum; they have, besides, plenty of variety of meats and wine, and many times we are carried into France or Holland in a night, and return again, and whilst we are there, we enjoy all the pleasures the country doth afford. I demanded of him how they got under that hill? To which he replied, that there was a great pair of gates that opened to them, though they were invisible to others ; and that within there were brave large rooms, as well accommodated as most in Scotland.—I then asked him, how I should know what he said to be true ?   Upon which he told me he would read my fortune, saying, I should have two wives, and that he saw the forms of them sitting on my shoulders ; that both would be very handsome women.   As he was thus speaking, a woman of the neighbourhood coming into the room, demanded of him, What her fortune should be ?   He told her that she had two bastards before she was married, which put her in such a rage, that she desired not to hear the rest.

" The woman of the house told me that all the people in Scotland could not keep him from the rendezvous on Thursday night ; upon which, by promising him some more money, I got a promise of him to meet me at the same place, in the afternoon, the Thursday following, and so dismist him at that time.   The boy came again, at the place and time appointed, and I had prevailed with some friends to continue with me (if possible) to prevent his moving that night.   He was placed between us. and answered many questions, until, about eleven of the clock, he was got away unperceived by the company; but I, suddenly missing him, hasted to the door, and took hold of him, and so returned him into the same room ; we all watched him, and, of a sudden, he was again got out of doors ; I followed him close, and he made a noise in the street, as if he had been set upon ; but from that time I could never see him.   GEORGE BURTON."

Pandæmonium, or the Devil's Cloister. By Richard Bovet, Gent. Lond. 1684, p. 172.

From the *History of the Irish Bards,* by Mr Walker, and from the glossary subjoined to the lively and ingenious Tale of *Castle Rackrent,* we learn, that the same ideas concerning Fairies are current among the vulgar in that country. The latter authority mentions their inhabiting the ancient tumuli, called barrows, and their abstracting mortals. They are termed " the good people ;" and when an eddy of wind raises loose dust and sand, the vulgar believe that it announces a Fairy procession, and bid God speed their journey.

The Scottish Fairies, in like manner, sometimes reside in subterranean abodes, in the vicinity of human habitations, or, according to the popular phrase, under the " door-stane," or threshold ; in which situation, they sometimes establish an intercourse with men, by borrowing and lending, and other kindly offices. In this capacity they are termed " the good neighbours,"[1] from

[1] Perhaps this epithet is only one example, among many, of the extreme civility which the vulgar in Scotland use towards spirits of a dubious, or even a determinedly mischievous, nature. The arch-fiend himself is often distinguished by the softened title of the " goodman." This epithet, so applied, must sound strange to a southern ear ; but, as the phrase bears various interpretations, according to the places where it is used, so, in the Scottish dialect, the *goodman of such a place* signifies the tenant, or life-renter, in opposition to the laird, or proprietor. Hence, the devil is termed

supplying privately the wants of their friends, and assisting them in all their transactions, while their favours are concealed. Of this the traditionary story of Sir Godfrey Macculloch forms a curious example.

As this Gallovidian gentleman was taking the air on horseback, near his own house, he was suddenly accosted by a little old man arrayed in green, and mounted upon a white palfrey. After mutual salutation, the old man gave Sir Godfrey to understand, that he resided under his habitation, and that he had great reason to complain of the direction of a drain, or common sewer, which emptied itself directly into his chamber of dais.[1] Sir Godfrey Macculloch was a good deal startled at this extraordinary complaint; but, guessing the nature of the being he had to deal with, he assured the old man, with great courtesy, that the

the goodman, or tenant, of the infernal regions. In the book of the Universal Kirk, 13th May, 1594, mention is made of "the horrible superstitoune usit in Galloch, and dyvers parts of the countrie, in not labouring a parcel of ground dedicated to the devil, under the title of the *Guid-Man's Croft.*" Lord Hailes conjectured this to have been the *temnos* adjoining to some ancient Pagan temple. The unavowed, but obvious, purpose of this practice, was to avert the destructive rage of Satan from the neighbouring possessions. It required various fulminations of the General Assembly of the Kirk to abolish a practice bordering so nearly upon the doctrine of the Magi.

[1] The best chamber was thus currently denominated in Scotland, from the French *dais*, signifying that part of the ancient halls which was elevated above the rest, and covered with a canopy. The turf-seats, which occupy the sunny side of a cottage wall, are also termed the *dais*.

direction of the drain should be altered; and caused it to be done accordingly. Many years afterwards, Sir Godfrey had the misfortune to kill, in a fray, a gentleman of the neighbourhood. He was apprehended, tried, and condemned.[1] The scaffold, upon which his head was to be struck off, was erected on the Castle hill of Edinburgh; but hardly had he reached the fatal spot, when the old man upon his white palfrey, pressed through the crowd, with the rapidity of lightning. Sir Godfrey, at his command, sprung on behind him ; the " good neighbour" spurred his horse down the steep bank, and neither he nor the criminal was ever again seen.

The most formidable attribute of the elves, was the practice of carrying away and exchanging children, and that of stealing human souls from their bodies. " A persuasion prevails among the ignorant," says the author of a MS. history of Moray, that " in a consumptive disease, the Fairies steal away the soul, and put the soul of a Fairy in the room of it." This belief prevails chiefly along the eastern coast of Scotland, where a practice, apparently of druidical origin, is used to avert the danger. In the increase of the March moon, withes of oak and ivy are cut, and twisted into wreaths or circles, which they preserve till next March. After that period, when persons are consumptive, or children hectic, they cause them to pass thrice through

---

[1] In this particular, tradition coincides with the real fact ; the trial took place in 1697.

these circles. In other cases the cure was more rough, and at least as dangerous as the disease, as will appear from the following extract :—

" There is one thing remarkable in this parish of Suddie, (in Inverness-shire,) which I think proper to mention. There is a small hill N.W. from the church, commonly called Therdy Hill, or Hill of Therdie, as some term it; on the top of which there is a well, which I had the curiosity to view, because of the several reports concerning it. When children happen to be sick, and languish long in their malady, so that they almost turn skeletons, the common people imagine they are taken away (at least the substance) by spirits, called Fairies, and the shadow left with them; so, at a particular season in summer, they leave them all night themselves, watching at a distance, near this well, and this they imagine will either *end or mend them;* they say many more do recover than do not. Yea, an honest tenant who lives hard by it, and whom I had the curiosity to discourse about it, told me it has recovered some, who were about eight or nine years of age, and to his certain knowledge, they bring adult persons to it; for, as he was passing one dark night, he heard groanings, and, coming to the well, he found a man, who had been long sick, wrapped in a plaid, so that he could scarcely move, a stake being fixed in the earth, with a rope, or tedder, that was about the plaid; he had no sooner inquired what he was, but he conjured him to loose him, and out of sympathy he was pleased to slacken that wherein he was, as I may so speak, swaddled; but, if I right remember, he signified, he did not recover."—*Account of the Parish of Suddie,* apud MACFARLANE'S *MSS.*

According to the earlier doctrine, concerning the original corruption of human nature, the power of demons over infants had been long reckoned considerable, in the period intervening between birth and baptism. During this period, therefore, children were believed to be particularly liable to abstraction by the fairies, and mothers chiefly dreaded the substitution of changelings in the place of their own offspring. Various monstrous charms existed in Scotland, for procuring the restoration of a child which had been thus stolen; but the most efficacious of them was supposed to be, the roasting of the supposititious child upon the live embers, when it was believed it would vanish, and the true child appear in the place, whence it had been originally abstracted.[1] It may be questioned if this experiment could now be made without the animadversion of the law. Even that which is prescribed in the following legend is rather too hazardous for modern use.

[1] Less perilous recipes were sometimes used. The Editor is possessed of a small relic, termed by tradition a toad-stone, the influence of which was supposed to preserve pregnant women from the power of demons, and other dangers incidental to their situation. It has been carefully preserved for several generations, was often pledged for considerable sums of money, and uniformly redeemed from a belief in its efficacy.

" A certain woman having put out her child to
nurse in the country, found, when she came to take it
home, that its form was so much altered that she scarce
knew it ; nevertheless, not knowing what time might
do, took it home for her own.   But when, after some
years, it could neither speak nor go, the poor woman
was fain to carry it, with much trouble, in her arms ;
and one day, a poor man coming to the door, ' God
bless you, mistress,' said he, ' and your poor child ; be
pleased to bestow something on a poor man.'—' Ah !
this child,' replied she, ' is the cause of all my sorrow,'
and related what had happened, adding, moreover, that
she thought it changed, and none of her child.   The
old man, whom years had rendered more prudent in such
matters, told her, to find out the truth, she should make
a clear fire, sweep the hearth very clean, and place the
child fast in his chair, that he might not fall, before it,
and break a dozen eggs, and place the four-and-twenty
half-shells before it ; then go out, and listen at the
door : for, if the child spoke, it was certainly a changeling ; and then she should carry it out, and leave it on
the dunghill to cry, and not to pity it, till she heard its
voice no more.   The woman, having done all things
according to these words, heard the child say, ' Seven
years old was I before I came to the nurse, and four
years have I lived since, and never saw so many milk
pans before.' So the woman took it up, and left it upon
the dunghill to cry, and not to be pitied, till at last she
thought the voice went up into the air ; and coming,

found there her own natural and well-favoured child."
—Grose's *Provincial Glossary*, quoted from " A
Pleasant Treatise on Witchcraft."

The most minute and authenticated account of an
exchanged child is to be found in Waldron's *Isle of
Man*, a book from which I have derived much legendary information. " I was prevailed upon myself,"
says that author, " to go and see a child, who, they
told me, was one of these changelings, and, indeed, I
must own, was not a little surprised, as well as shocked, at the sight. Nothing under heaven could have a
more beautiful face ; but, though between five and six
years old, and seemingly healthy, he was so far from
being able to walk or stand, that he could not so much
as move any one joint ; his limbs were vastly long for
his age, but smaller than any infant's of six months ;
his complexion was perfectly delicate, and he had the
finest hair in the world. He never spoke nor cried, ate
scarce any thing, and was very seldom seen to smile ;
but if any one called him a *fairy-elf*, he would frown,
and fix his eyes so earnestly on those who said it, as if
he would look them through. His mother, or at least
his supposed mother, being very poor, frequently went
out a charcing, and left him a whole day together. The
neighbours, out of curiosity, have often looked in at the
window, to see how he behaved while alone ; which,
whenever they did, they were sure to find him laughing, and in the utmost delight. This made them judge
that he was not without company, more pleasing to

him than any mortals could be ; and what made this
conjecture seem the more reasonable, was, that if he
were left ever so dirty, the woman, at her return, saw
him with a clean face, and his hair combed with the
utmost exactness and nicety."—P. 128.

 Waldron gives another account of a poor woman, to
whose offspring, it would seem, the Fairies had taken
a special fancy. A few nights after she was delivered
of her first child, the family were alarmed by a dreadful cry of " Fire ! " All flew to the door, while the
mother lay trembling in bed, unable to protect her infant, which was snatched from the bed by an invisible
hand. Fortunately, the return of the gossips, after the
causeless alarm, disturbed the Fairies, who dropped the
child, which was found sprawling and shrieking upon
the threshold. At the good woman's second *accouche-*
ment, a tumult was heard in the cowhouse, which drew
thither the whole assistants. They returned, when
they found that all was quiet among the cattle, and lo !
the second child had been carried from the bed, and
dropped in the middle of the lane. But, upon the third
occurrence of the same kind, the company were again
decoyed out of the sick woman's chamber by a false
alarm, leaving only a nurse, who was detained by the
bonds of sleep. On this last occasion, the mother
plainly saw her child removed, though the means were
invisible. She screamed for assistance to the nurse ;
but the old lady had partaken too deeply of the cordials
which circulate upon such joyful occasions, to be easily

awakened. In short, the child was this time fairly carried off, and a withered, deformed creature left in its
stead, quite naked, with the clothes of the abstracted
infant, rolled in a bundle, by its side. This creature
lived nine years, ate nothing but a few herbs, and neither
spoke, stood, walked, nor performed any other func
tions of mortality; resembling, in all respects, the change
ling already mentioned.—WALDRON's *Works, ibid.*

But the power of the Fairies was not confined to un
christened children alone ; it was supposed frequently to
be extended to full-grown persons, especially such as in
an unlucky hour were devoted to the devil by the execration of parents and of masters ;[1] or those who were
found asleep under a rock, or on a green hill, belonging to the Fairies, after sunset, or, finally, to those
who unwarily joined their orgies. A tradition existed,
during the seventeenth century, concerning an ancestor
of the noble family of Duffus, who, " walking abroad
in the fields, near to his own house, was suddenly carried away, and found the next day at Paris in the French

---

[1] This idea is not peculiar to the Gothic tribes, but extends to
those of Sclavic origin. Tooke (*History of Russia,* vol. i. p.
100) relates, that the Russian peasants believe the nocturnal
demon *Kikimoro* to have been a child, whom the devil stole out of
the womb of its mother, because she had cursed it. They also assert,
that if an execration against a child be spoken in an evil hour, the
child is carried off by the devil. The beings, so stolen, are neither
fiends nor men ; they are invisible, and afraid of the cross and holy
water ; but, on the other hand, in their nature and dispositions
they resemble mankind, whom they love, and rarely injure.

king's cellar, with a silver cup in his hand. Being
brought into the king's presence, and questioned by
him who he was, and how he came thither, he told his
name, his country, and the place of his residence ; and
that, on such a day of the month, which proved to be
the day immediately preceding, being in the fields, he
heard the noise of a whirlwind, and of voices, crying,
'*Horse and Hattock !*' (this is the word which the
Fairies are said to use when they remove from any
place,) whereupon he cried '*Horse and Hattock*' also,
and was immediately caught up and transported through
the air, by the Fairies, to that place, where, after he
had drunk heartily, he fell asleep, and before he woke,
the rest of the company were gone, and had left him in
the posture wherein he was found. It is said the King
gave him the cup which was found in his hand, and dismissed him." The narrator affirms, " that the cup was
still preserved, and known by the name of the *Fairy
cup.*" He adds, that Mr Steward, tutor to the then
Lord Duffus, had informed him, that, " when a boy at
the school of Forres, he and his school-fellows were
upon a time whipping their tops in the churchyard,
before the door of the church, when, though the day
was calm, they heard a noise of a wind, and at some
distance saw the small dust begin to rise and turn
round, which motion continued advancing till it came
to the place where they were, whereupon they began to
bless themselves ; but one of their number being, it
seems, a little more bold and confident than his com-

panions, said ' *Horse and Hattock with my top,*' and immediately they all saw the top lifted up from the ground, but could not see which way it was carried, by reason of a cloud of dust which was raised at the same time. They sought for the top all about the place where it was taken up, but in vain ; and it was found afterwards in the churchyard, on the other side of the church."—This puerile legend is contained in a letter from a learned gentleman in Scotland, to Mr Aubrey, dated 15th March, 1695, published in AUBREY's *Miscellanies,* p. 158.

Notwithstanding the special example of Lord Duffus, and of the top, it is the common opinion, that persons, falling under the power of the Fairies, were only allowed to revisit the haunts of men, after seven years had expired. At the end of seven years more, they again disappeared, after which they were seldom seen among mortals. The accounts they gave of their situation differ in some particulars. Sometimes they were represented as leading a life of constant restlessness, and wandering by moonlight. According to others, they inhabited a pleasant region, where, however, their situation was rendered horrible, by the sacrifice of one or more individuals to the devil every seventh year. This circumstance is mentioned in Alison Pearson's indictment, and in the *Tale of the Young Tamlane,* where it is termed, " the paying the kane to hell," or, according to some recitations, " the teind," or tenth. This is the popular reason assigned for the desire of the Fairies to abstract young children, as substitutes for themselves in this dreadful tribute. Concerning the mode of *winning*, or recovering, persons abstracted by the Fairies, tradition differs ; but the popular opinion, contrary to what may be inferred from the following tale, supposes, that the recovery must be effected within a year and a day, to be held legal in the Fairy court. This feat, which was reckoned an enterprise of equal difficulty and danger, could only be accomplished on Hallowe'en, at the great annual procession of the Fairy court.[1] Of this procession the following description is found in Montgomery's *Flyting against Polwart*, apud *Watson's collection of Scots Poems*, 1790, Part III. p. 12.

" In the hinder end of harvest, on All-hallowe'en,
    When our *good neighbours* dois ride, if I read right,
Some buckled on a bunewand, and some on a bean,
    Ay trottand in troups from the twilight ;
Some saidled a she-ape, all grathed into green,
    Some bohland on a hemp-stalk, hovand to the hight ;
The King of Pharie and his court, with the Elf Queen,
    With many elfish incubus was ridand that night.
There an elf on an ape, an ursel begat,
    Into a pot by Pomathorne ;
That bratchart in a busse was born ;
    They fand a monster on the morn,
War faced nor a cat."

---

[1] See the inimitable poem of *Hallowe'en*—
    " Upon that night, when Fairies light
      On Cassilis Downan dance ;
    Or o'er the leas, in splendid blaze,
      On stately coursers prance," &c.—Burns.

The catastrophe of *Tamlane* terminated more successfully than that of other attempts, which tradition still records. The wife of a farmer in Lothian had been carried off by the Fairies, and, during the year of probation, repeatedly appeared on Sunday, in the midst of her children, combing their hair. On one of these occasions she was accosted by her husband; when she related to him the unfortunate event which had separated them, instructed him by what means he might *win* her, and exhorted him to exert all his courage, since her temporal and eternal happiness depended on the success of his attempt. The farmer, who ardently loved his wife, set out on Hallowe'en, and, in the midst of a plot of furze, waited impatiently for the procession of the Fairies. At the ringing of the Fairy bridles, and the wild unearthly sound which accompanied the cavalcade, his heart failed him, and he suffered the ghostly train to pass by without interruption. When the last had rode past, the whole troop vanished, with loud shouts of laughter and exultation; among which he plainly discovered the voice of his wife, lamenting that he had lost her for ever.

A similar, but real incident, took place at the town of North Berwick, within the memory of man. The wife of a man above the lowest class of society, being left alone in the house a few days after delivery, was attacked and carried off by one of those convulsion-fits, incident to her situation. Upon the return of the family, who had been engaged in haymaking, or harvest,

they found the corpse much disfigured. This circumstance, the natural consequence of her disease, led some
of the spectators to think that she had been carried off
by the Fairies, and that the body before them was some
elfin deception. The husband, probably, paid little attention to this opinion at the time. The body was
interred, and after a decent time had elapsed, finding
his domestic affairs absolutely required female super-
intendence, the widower paid his addresses to a young
woman in the neighbourhood. The recollection, however, of his former wife, whom he had tenderly loved,
haunted his slumbers ; and, one morning, he came to
the clergyman of the parish in the utmost dismay, de-
claring that she had appeared to him the preceding night,
informed him that she was a captive in Fairy Land, and
conjured him to attempt her deliverance. She directed him to bring the minister, and certain other persons,
whom she named, to her grave at midnight. Her body
was then to be dug up, and certain prayers recited ;
after which the corpse was to become animated, and
fly from them. One of the assistants, the swiftest
runner in the parish, was to pursue the body ; and, if
he was able to seize it, before it had thrice encircled
the church, the rest were to come to his assistance, and
detain it, in spite of the struggles it should use, and
the various shapes into which it might be transformed.
The redemption of the abstracted person was then
to become complete. The minister, a sensible man,
argued with his parishioner upon the indecency and

absurdity of what was proposed, and dismissed him. Next Sunday, the banns being for the first time proclaimed betwixt the widower and his new bride, his former wife, very naturally, took the opportunity of the following night to make him another visit, yet more terrific than the former. She upbraided him with his incredulity, his fickleness, and his want of affection; and, to convince him that her appearance was no aërial illusion, she gave suck, in his presence, to her youngest child. The man, under the greatest horror of mind, had again recourse to the pastor; and his ghostly counsellor fell upon an admirable expedient to console him. This was nothing less than dispensing with the formal solemnity of banns, and marrying him, without an hour's delay, to the young woman to whom he was affianced; after which no spectre again disturbed his repose.[1]

[1] To these I have now to add the following instance of redemption from Fairy Land. The legend is printed from a broadside still popular in Ireland :—

" Near the town of Aberdeen, in Scotland, lived James Campbell, who had one daughter, named Mary, who was married to John Nelson, a young man of that neighbourhood. Shortly after their marriage, they being a young couple, they went to live in the town of Aberdeen, where he followed his trade, being a goldsmith; they lived loving and agreeable together until the time of her lying-in, when there was female attendants prepared suitable to her situation; when near the hour of twelve at night they were alarmed with a dreadful noise, at which of a sudden the candles went out, which drove the attendants in the utmost confusion; soon as the women regained their half-lost senses, they called in their neighbours, who, after striking up lights, and looking towards the lying-in woman, found her a corpse, which caused great confusion in the family.

Having concluded these general observations upon the Fairy superstition, which, although minute, may not, I hope, be deemed altogether uninteresting, I proceed to the more particular illustrations, relating to *The Tale of the Young Tamlane.*

There was no grief could exceed that of her husband, who, next morning, prepared ornaments for her funeral; people of all sects came to her wake, amongst others came the Rev. Mr Dodd, who, at first sight of the corpse, said, It's not the body of any Christian, but that Mrs Nelson was taken away by the Fairies, and what they took for her was only some substance left in her place. He was not believed, so he refused attending her funeral; they kept her in the following night, and the next day she was interred.

" Her husband, one evening after sunset, being riding in his own field, heard a most pleasant concert of music, and soon after espied a woman coming towards him drest in white; she being veiled, he could not observe her face, yet he rode near her, and asked her very friendly who she was that chose to walk alone so late in the evening? at which she unveiled her face, and burst into tears, saying, I am not permitted to tell you who I am. He knowing her to be his wife, asked her, in the name of God, what disturbed her, or occasioned her to appear at that hour? She said her appearing at any hour was of no consequence; for though you believe me to be dead and buried, I am not, but was taken away by the Fairies the night of my delivery; you only buried a piece of wood in my place; I can be recovered if you take proper means; as for my child, it has three nurses to attend it, but I fear it cannot be brought home; the greatest dependence I have on any person is my brother Robert, who is a captain of a merchant ship, and will be home in ten days hence. Her husband asked her what means he should take to win her? She told him he should find a letter the Sunday morning following, on the desk in his own room, directed to her brother, wherein there would be directions for winning her. Since my being taken from you I have had the attendance of a queen or empress, and if you look over my right shoulder

The following ballad, still popular in Ettrick Forest, where the scene is laid, is certainly of much greater antiquity than its phraseology, gradually modernized as transmitted by tradition, would seem to denote. The

you will see several of my companions ; he then did as she desired, when, at a small distance, he saw a king and queen sitting, beside a moat, on a throne, in splendour.

" She then desired him to look right and left, which he did, and observed other kings on each side of the king and queen, well guarded. He said, I fear it is an impossibility to win you from such a place. No, says she, were my brother Robert here in your place, he would bring me home ; but let it not encourage you to attempt the like, for that would occasion the loss of me for ever ; there is now severe punishment threatened to me for speaking to you ; but, to prevent that, do you ride up to the moat, where (suppose you will see no person) all you now see will be near you, and do you threaten to burn all the old thorns and brambles that is round the moat, if you do not get a firm promise that I shall get no punishment ; I shall be forgiven ; which he promised. She then disappeared, and he lost sight of all he had seen ; he then rode very resolutely up to the moat, and went round it, vowing he would burn all about it if he would not get a promise that his wife should get no hurt. A voice desired him to cast away a book was in his pocket, and then demand his request ; he answered he would not part his book, but grant his request, or they should find the effect of his rage. The voice answered, that upon honour she should be forgave her fault, but for him to suffer no prejudice to come to the moat, which he promised to fulfil, at which he heard most pleasant music. He then returned home, and sent for the Reverend Ʌr Dodd, and related to him what he had seen ; Ʌr Dodd staid with him till Sunday morning following, when, as Ʌr Nelson looked on the desk in his room, he espied a letter, which he took up, it being directed to her brother, who in a few days came home ; on his receiving the letter he opened it, wherein he found the following :—

" ' DEAR BROTHER,—My husband can relate to you my present

Tale of the Young Tamlane is mentioned in the *Complaynt of Scotland;* and the air, to which it was chanted, seems to have been accommodated to a particular dance ; for the dance of *Thom of Lynn,* another

circumstances.   I request that you will (the first night after you ee this) come to the moat where I parted my husband : let nothing daunt you, but stand in the centre of the moat at the hour of twelve at night, and call me, when I, with several others, will surround you ; I shall have on the whitest dress of any in company, then take hold of me, and do not forsake me ; all the frightful methods they shall use let it not surprise you, but keep your hold, suppose they continue till cock-crow, when they shall vanish all of a sudden, and I shall be safe, when I will return home and live with my husband. If you succeed in your attempt, you will gain applause from all your friends, and have the blessing of your ever-loving and affectionate sister,

Ŋary Nelson.

" No sooner had he read the letter than he vowed to win his sister and her child, or perish in the attempt; he returned to his ship, and related to his sailors the consequence of the letter ; he delayed till ten at night, when his loyal sailors offered to go with him, which he refused, thinking it best to go alone. As he left his ship a frightful lion came roaring towards him ; he drew his sword and struck at the lion, which he observed was of no substance, it being only the appearance of one, to terrify him in his attempt ; it only encouraged him, so that he proceeded to the moat, in the centre of which he observed a white handkerchief spread ; on which he was surrounded with a number of women, the cries of whom were the most frightful he ever heard ; his sister being in the whitest dress of any round him, he seized her by the right hand, and said, With the help of God, I will preserve you from all infernal imps ; when of a sudden, the moat seemed to be on the round him.   He likewise heard the most dreadful thunder could be imagined ; frightful birds and beasts seemed to make towards him out of the fire, which he knew was not real ; nothing daunted his courage ; he kept hold of

variation of *Thomalin,* likewise occurs in the same
performance. Like every popular subject, it seems to
have been frequently parodied; and a burlesque ballad,
beginning,

> " Tom o' the Linn was a Scotsman born,"

is still well known.

In a medley, contained in a curious and ancient MS.
cantus, *penes* J. G. Dalyell, Esq. there is an allusion
to our ballad:

> " Sing young Thomlin, be merry, be merry, and twice so merry."

In *Scottish Songs,* 1774, a part of the original tale
was published under the title of *Kerton Ha';* a cor-

---

his sister for the space of an hour and three quarters, when the cocks
began to crow; then the fire disappeared, and all the frightful imps
vanished. He held her in his arms, and fell on his knees, and gave
God thanks for his proceedings that night; he believing her clothing to be light, he put his outside coat on her: she then embraced
him, saying, she was now safe, as he put any of his clothing on
her; he then brought her home to her husband, which occasioned
great rejoicing. Her husband and he began to conclude to destroy
the moat in revenge of the child they had away, when instantly
they heard a voice, which said, you shall have your son safe, and
well, on condition that you will not till the ground within three
perches of the moat, nor damage bushes or brambles round that
place, which they agreed to, when, in a few minutes, the child was
left on his mother's knee, which caused them to kneel and return
thanks to God.

" The circumstance of this terrifying affair was occasioned by
leaving Mrs Nelson, the night of her lying-in, in the care of women
who were mostly intoxicated with liquor. It is requested both sexes
will take notice of the above, and not leave women in distress, but
with people who at such times mind their duty to God."

ruption of Carterhaugh ; and, in the same collection, there is a fragment, containing two or three additional verses, beginning,

" I'll wager, I'll wager, I'll wager with you," &c.

In Johnston's *Musical Museum*, a more complete copy occurs, under the title of *Tom Linn*, which, with some alterations, was reprinted in the *Tales of Wonder*.

The present edition is the most perfect which has yet appeared; being prepared from a collation of the printed copies with a very accurate one in Glenriddel's MSS. and with several recitals from tradition. Some verses are omitted in this edition, being ascertained to belong to a separate ballad, which will be found in a subsequent part of the work. In one recital only, the well-known fragment of the *Wee, wee Man*, was introduced, in the same measure with the rest of the poem. It was retained in the first edition, but is now omitted ; as the Editor has been favoured, by the learn-ed Mr Ritson, with a copy of the original poem, of which it is a detached fragment. The Editor has been enabled to add several verses of beauty and interest to this edition of *Tamlane*, in consequence of a copy obtained from a gentleman residing near Langholm, which is said to be very ancient, though the diction is somewhat of a modern cast. The manners of the Fairies are detailed at considerable length, and in poetry of no common merit.

Carterhaugh is a plain, at the conflux of the Ettrick and Yarrow in Selkirkshire, about a mile above Selkirk, and two miles below Newark Castle ;[1] a romantic ruin, which overhangs the Yarrow, and which is said to have been the habitation of our heroine's father, though others place his residence in the tower of Oakwood. The peasants point out, upon the plain, those electrical rings, which vulgar credulity supposes to be traces of the Fairy revels. Here, they say, were placed the stands of milk, and of water, in which *Tamlane* was dipped, in order to effect the disenchantment ; and upon these spots, according to their mode of expressing themselves, the grass will never grow. Miles Cross, (perhaps a corruption of Mary's Cross,) where fair Janet awaited the arrival of the Fairy train, is said to have stood near the Duke of Buccleuch's seat of Bowhill, about half a mile from Carterhaugh. In no part of Scotland, indeed, has the belief in Fairies maintained its ground with more pertinacity than in Selkirkshire. The most sceptical among the lower ranks only venture to assert, that their appearances, and mischievous exploits, have ceased, or at least become infrequent, since the light of the gospel was diffused in its purity. One of their frolics is said to have happened late in the last century. The victim of elfin sport was a poor man, who, being employed in pulling heather upon Peatlaw, a hill not far from Carterhaugh, had tired of his labour, and laid him down to sleep upon a Fairy ring. When he awakened, he was amazed to find himself in the midst of a populous city, to which, as well as to the

[1] [See notes to the Lay of the Last Minstrel. Canto I.]

means of his transportation, he was an utter stranger.
His coat was left upon the Peatlaw; and his bonnet,
which had fallen off in the course of his aërial journey,
was afterwards found hanging upon the steeple of the
church of Lanark. The distress of the poor man was,
in some degree, relieved, by meeting a carrier whom he
had formerly known, and who conducted him back to
Selkirk, by a slower conveyance than had whirled him
to Glasgow.—That he had been carried off by the
Fairies was implicitly believed by all who did not re-
flect, that a man may have private reasons for leaving
his own country, and for disguising his having inten-
tionally done so.[1]

[1] [" We notice, with particular approbation, a discourse in the 2d
volume, on the *Fairies* of Popular superstition, in which the au
thor takes a much wider range, than was to have been expected
from a collector of Border Ballads; and evinces an extent of reading and sagacity of conjecture, which have never before been applied to this subject. We recommend this treatise, as by far the
most learned, rational, and entertaining, that has yet been made
public, upon the subject of these superstitions."—*Edinburgh Review, No. II.*

" Though we cannot entirely approve the nature and extent of
Mr Scott's plan in ' the Minstrelsy,' yet the fidelity, taste, and
learning, which he has manifested in the execution of it, induce us
to cherish the hope that *he will employ his pen on more important
and useful subjects.* Even from his present labours, indeed, the
curious inquirer may derive some ingenious and entertaining information on several points connected with the antiquities and history
of Great Britain. Prefixed to *The Young Tamlane* is an acute
and philosophical dissertation on the *Fairies of Popular Superstition*," &c.—*Monthly Review, September,* 1803.]

THE YOUNG TAMLANE.

" O I forbid ye, maidens a',
  That wear gowd on your hair.
To come or gae by Carterhaugh,
  For young Tamlane is there.

" There's nane that gaes by Carterhaugh,
  But maun leave him a wad,[1]
Either gowd rings or green mantles,
  Or else their maidenheid.

" Now gowd rings ye may buy, maidens,
  Green mantles ye may spin ;
But, gin ye lose your maidenheid,
  Ye'll ne'er get that agen. "——

But up then spak her, fair Janet,
  The fairest o' a' her kin ;
" I'll cum and gang to Carterhaugh,
  And ask nae leave o' him. "——

[1] *Wad*—Pledge.

Janet has kilted her green kirtle,[1]
　　A little abune her knee;
And she has braided her yellow hair,
　　A little abune her bree.

And when she came to Carterhaugh,
　　She gaed beside the well;
And there she fand his steed standing,
　　But away was himsell.

She hadna pu'd a red red rose,
　　A rose but barely three;
Till up and starts a wee wee man
　　At lady Janet's knee.

Says—" Why pu' ye the rose, Janet?
　　What gars ye break the tree?
Or why come ye to Carterhaugh,
　　Withouten leave o' me?"—

Says—" Carterhaugh it is mine ain;
　　My daddie gave it me;
I'll come and gang to Carterhaugh,
　　And ask nae leave o' thee."

He's ta'en her by the milk-white hand,
　　Among the leaves sae green;

---

[1] The ladies are always represented, in Dunbar's Poems, with
green mantles and yellow hair.—*Maitland Poems*, vol. i. p. 45.

And what they did, I cannot tell—
    The green leaves were between.

He's ta'en her by the milk-white hand,
    Among the roses red ;
And what they did, I cannot say—
    She ne'er return'd a maid.

When she cam to her father's ha',
    She looked pale and wan;
They thought she'd dreed some sair sickness,
    Or been with some leman.[1]

She didna comb her yellow hair,
    Nor make meikle o' her head;
And ilka thing that lady took,
    Was like to be her deid.[2]

It's four and twenty ladies fair
    Were playing at the ba' ;
Janet, the wightest of them anes,
    Was faintest o' them a'.

Four and twenty ladies fair
    Were playing at the chess ;
And out there came the fair Janet,
    As green as any grass.

---

[1] *Leman*—Lover.—[2] *Died*—Death.

Out and spak an auld grey-headed knight
    Lay o'er the castle wa'—
" And ever, alas ! for thee, Janet,
    But we'll be blamed a' l "—

" Now haud your tongue, ye auld grey knight !
    And an ill deid may ye die,
Father my bairn on whom I will,
    I'll father nane on thee. "—

Out then spak her father dear,
    And he spak melk and mild—
" And ever, alas ! my sweet Janet,
    I fear ye gae with child. "—

" And if I be with child, father,
    Mysell maun bear the blame ;
There's ne'er a knight about your ha'
    Shall hae the bairnie's name.

" And if I be with child, father,
    'Twill prove a wondrous birth ;
For weel I swear I'm not wi' bairn
    To any man on earth.

" If my love were an earthly knight,
    As he's an elfin grey,
I wadna gie my ain true love
    For nae lord that ye hae. "—

She prink'd hersell and prinn'd hersell,
 By the ae light of the moon,
And she's away to Carterhaugh,
 To speak wi' young Tamlane.

And when she cam to Carterhaugh,
 She gaed beside the well;
And there she saw the steed standing,
 But away was himsell.

She hadna pu'd a double rose,
 A rose but only twae,
When up and started young Tamlane,
 Says—" Lady, thou pu's nae mae!

" Why pu' ye the rose, Janet,
 Within this garden grene,
And a' to kill the bonny babe,
 That we got us between?"—

" The truth ye'll tell to me, Tamlane
 A word ye mauna lie;
Gin e'er ye was in haly chapel,
 Or sained[1] in Christentie?"—

" The truth I'll tell to thee, Janet,
 A word I winna lie;

---

[1] *Sained*—Hallowed—[*Signed* with the Cross?—ED.]

A knight me got, and a lady me bore,
   As well as they did thee.

" Randolph, Earl Murray, was my sire,
  · Dunbar, Earl March is thine ; [1]
We loved when we were children small,
   Which yet you well may mind.

" When I was a boy just turu'd of nine,
   My uncle sent for me,
To hunt, and hawk, and ride with him,
   And keep him companie.

" There came a wind out of the north,
   A sharp wind and a snell ;
And a deep sleep came over me,
   And frae my horse I fell.

" The Queen of Fairies keppit me,
   In yon green hill to dwell ;
And I'm a fairy, lyth and limb ;
   Fair ladye, view me well.

[1] Both these mighty chiefs were connected with Ettrick Forest and its vicinity. Their memory, therefore, lived in the traditions of the country. Randolph, Earl of Murray, the renowned nephew of Robert Bruce, had a castle at Ha' Guards, in Annandale, and another in Peebles-shire, on the borders of the forest, the site of which is still called Randall's Walls. Patrick of Dunbar, Earl of March, is said, by Henry the Minstrel, to have retreated to Ettrick Forest, after being defeated by Wallace.

" But we, that live in Fairy-land,
    No sickness know, nor pain;
I quit my body when I will,
    And take to it again.

" I quit my body when I please,
    Or unto it repair;
We can inhabit, at our ease,
    In either earth or air.

" Our shapes and size we can convert
    To either large or small;
An old nut-shell's the same to us
    As is the lofty hall.

" We sleep in rose-buds soft and sweet,
    We revel in the stream;
We wanton lightly on the wind,
    Or glide on a sunbeam.

" And all our wants are well supplied
    From every rich man's store,
Who thankless sins the gifts he gets,
    And vainly grasps for more.[1]

[1] *To sin our gifts or mercies,* means, ungratefully to hold them
in slight esteem. The idea, that the possessions of the wicked are
most obnoxious to the depredations of evil spirits, may be illustrated
by the following tale of a *Buttery Spirit,* extracted from Thomas
Heywood :—

" An ancient and virtuous monk came to visit his nephew, an

" Then would I never tire, Janet,
    In Elfish land to dwell ;
But aye, at every seven years,
    They pay the teind to hell ;
And I am sae fat and fair of flesh,
    I fear 'twill be mysell.

" This night is Hallowe'en, Janet,
    The morn is Hallowday ;

innkeeper, and, after other discourse, inquired into his circumstances.   Nine host confessed, that, although he practised all the un-
conscionable tricks of his trade, he was still miserably poor.   The
monk shook his head, and asked to see his buttery, or larder.   As
they looked into it, be rendered visible to the astonished host an im-
mense goblin, whose paunch, and whole appearance, bespoke his
being gorged with food, and who, nevertheless, was gormandizing
at the innkeeper's expense, emptying whole shelves of food, and
washing it down with entire hogsheads of liquor.   ' To the depre-
dation of this visitor will thy viands be exposed,' quoth the uncle,
' until thou shalt abandon fraud and false reckonings.'   The monk
returned in a year.   The host having turned over a new leaf, and
given Christian measure to his customers, was now a thriving man.
When they again inspected the larder, they saw the same spirit, but
wofully reduced in size, and in vain attempting to reach at the full
plates and bottles which stood around him ; starving, in short, like
Tantalus, in the midst of plenty."   Honest Heywood sums up the
tale thus :—

    " In this discourse, far be it we should mean
    Spirits by meat are fatted made, or lean ;
    Yet certain 'tis, by God's permission, they
    May, over goods extorted, bear like sway.

    All such as study fraud, and practise evil,
    Do only starve themselves to plume the devil."
            Hierarchie of the Blessed Angels, p. 577.

And, gin ye dare your true love win,
    Ye hae nae time to stay.

" The night it is good Hallowe'en,
    When fairy folk will ride ;
And they that wad their true-love win,
    At Miles Cross they maun bide."—

" But how shall I thee ken, Tamlane?
    Or how shall I thee knaw,
Amang so many unearthly knights,
    The like I never saw ?"—

" The first company that passes by,
    Say na, and let them gae ;
The next company that passes by,
    Sae na, and do right sae ;
The third company that passes by
    Then I'll be ane o' thae.

" First let pass the black, Janet,
    And syne let pass the brown ;
But grip ye to the milk-white steed,
    And pu' the rider down.

" For I ride on the milk-white steed,
    And aye nearest the town ;
Because I was a christen'd knight,
    They gave me that renown.

" My right hand will be gloved, Janet,
   My left hand will be bare ;
And these the tokens I gie thee,
   Nae doubt I will be there.

" They'll turn me in your arms, Janet,
   An adder and a snake ;
But had me fast, let me not pass,
   Gin ye wad buy me maik. [1]

" They'll turn me in your arms, Janet,
   An adder and an ask ;
They'll turn me in your arms, Janet,
   A bale [2] that burns fast.

" They'll turn me in your arms, Janet,
   A red-hot gad o' airn ;
But haud me fast, let me not pass,
   For I'll do you no harm.

" First dip me in a stand o' milk,
   And then in a stand o' water ;
But had me fast, let me not pass—
   I'll be your bairn's father.

" And, next, they'll shape me in your arms,
   A tod, but and an eel ;

Maik—A Natch ; a Companion.—[2] Bale—A fagot.

But had me fast, nor let me gang,
 As you do love me weel.

" They'll shape me in your arms, Janet,
 A dove, but and a swan ;
And, last, they'll shape me in your arms
 A mother-naked man :
Cast your green mantle over me—
 I'll be myself again."—

Gloomy, gloomy, was the night,
 And eiry[1] was the way,
As fair Janet, in her green mantle,
 To Miles Cross she did gae.

The heavens were black, the night was dark
 And dreary was the place ;
But Janet stood, with eager wish,
 Her lover to embrace.

Betwixt the hours of twelve and one,
 A north wind tore the bent ;
And straight she heard strange elritch sounds
 Upon that wind which went.

About the dead hour o' the night,
 She heard the bridles ring ;

---

[1] *Eiry*—Producing superstitious dread.

And Janet was as glad o' that
    As any earthly thing.

Their oaten pipes blew wondrous shrill,
    The hemlock small blew clear ;
And louder notes from hemlock large,
    And bog-reed, struck the ear ;
But solemn sounds, or sober thoughts,
    The Fairies cannot bear.

They sing, inspired with love and joy,
    Like skylarks in the air :
Of solid sense, or thought that's grave,
    You'll find no traces there.

Fair Janet stood, with mind unmoved,
    The dreary heath upon ;
And louder, louder wax'd the sound,
    As they came riding on.

Will o' Wisp before them went,
    Sent forth a twinkling light ;
And soon she saw the Fairy bands
    All riding in her sight.

And first gaed by the black black steed,
    And then gaed by the brown ;
But fast she gript the milk-white steed,
    And pu'd the rider down.

She pu'd him frae the milk-white steed,
    And loot the bridle fa';
And up there raise an erlish[1] cry—
    " He's won amang us a' ! "—

They shaped him in fair Janet's arms,
    An esk,[2] but and an adder ;
She held him fast in every shape—
    To be her bairn's father.

They shaped him in her arms at last,
    A mother-naked man :
She wrapt him in her green mantle,
    And sae her true love wan !

Up then spake the Queen o' Fairies,
    Out o' a bush o' broom—
" She that has borrow'd young Tamlane,
    Has gotten a stately groom."—

Up then spake the Queen o' Fairies,
    Out o' a bush o' rye—
" She's ta'en awa the bonniest knight
    In a' my cumpanie.

" But had I kenn'd, Tamlane," she says,
    " A lady wad borrow'd thee—

---

[1] *Erlish*—Elritch ; ghastly.—[2] *Esk*—Newt.

I wad ta'en out thy twa grey een,
    Put in twa een o' tree.

" Had I but kenn'd, Tamlane," she says,
    " Before ye came frae hame—
I wad ta'en out your heart o' flesh,
    Put in a heart o' stane.

" Had I but had the wit yestreen
    That I hae coft[1] the day—
I'd paid my kane[2] seven times to hell
    Ere you'd been won away ! "

[1] *Coft*—Bought.—[2] *Kane*—Rent paid in *kind*.

ERLINTON.

NEVER BEFORE PUBLISHED.

THIS ballad is published from the collation of two copies, obtained from recitation. It seems to be the rude original, or perhaps a corrupt and imperfect copy, of *The Child of Elle*, a beautiful legendary tale, published in the *Reliques of Ancient Poetry*. It is singular that this charming ballad should have been translated, or imitated, by the celebrated Bürger, without acknowledgment of the English original. As *The Child of Elle* avowedly received corrections, we may ascribe its greatest beauties to the poetical taste of the ingenious editor. They are in the true style of Gothic embellishment. We may compare, for example the following beautiful verse, with the same idea in an old romance :—

> The baron stroked his dark-brown cheek,
>   And turned his face aside,
> To wipe away the starting tear,
>   He proudly strove to hide!"
>
>   *Child of Elle.*

The heathen Soldan, or Amiral, when about to slay two lovers, relents in a similar manner :—

> " Weeping, he turned his heued awai,
> And his swerde hit fell to grounde."
>
> *Florice and Blauncheflour.*

ERLINTON.

Erlinton had a fair daughter,
   I wat he weird her in a great sin,[1]
For he has built a bigly bower,
   An' a' to put that lady in.

An' he has waru'd her sisters six,
   An' sae has he her brethren se'en,
Outher to watch her a' the night,
   Or else to seek her morn and e'en.

She hadna been i' that bigly bower,
   Na not a night but barely ane,
Till there was Willie, her ain true love,
   Chapp'd at the door, cryin', " Peace within!"—

" O whae is this at my bower door,
   That chaps sae late, or kens the gin?"—[2]

[1] *Weird her in a great sin*—Placed her in danger of committing a great sin.

[2] *Gin*—The slight or trick necessary to open the door; from *engine*.

" O it is Willie, your ain true love,
    I pray you rise and let me in!"—

" But in my bower there is a wake,
    An' at the wake there is a wane;[1]
But I'll come to the green-wood the morn,
    Whar blooms the brier, by mornin' dawn."—

Then she's gane to her bed again,
    Where she has layen till the cock crew thrice,
Then she said to her sisters a',
    " Maidens, 'tis time for us to rise."—

She pat on her back a silken gown,
    An' on her breast a siller pin,
An' she's ta'en a sister in ilka hand,
    And to the green-wood she is gane.

She hadna walk'd in the green-wood,
    Na not a mile but barely ane,
Till there was Willie, her ain true love,
    Wha frae her sisters has her ta'en.

He took her sisters by the hand,
    He kiss'd them baith, and sent them hame,
An' he's ta'en his true love him behind,
    And through the green-wood they are gane.

---

[1] *Wane*—A number of people.

They hadna ridden in the bonnie green ·wood,
　Na not a mile but barely ane,
When there came fifteen o' the boldest knights,
　That ever bare flesh, blood, or bane.

The foremost was an aged knight,
　He wore the grey hair on his chin,
Says, " Yield to me thy lady bright,
　An' thou shalt walk the woods within."—

" For me to yield my lady bright
　To such an aged knight as thee,
People wad think I war gane mad,
　Or a' the courage flown frae me."—

But up then spake the second knight,
　I wat he spake right boustouslie,
" Yield me thy life, or thy lady bright,
　Or here the tane of us shall die."—

" My lady is my warld's meed:
　My life I winna yield to nane;
But if ye be men of your manhead,
　Ye'll only fight me ane by ane."—

He lighted aff his milk-white steed,
　An' gae his lady him by the head,
Say'n, " See ye dinna change your cheer,
　Until ye see my body bleed."—

He set his back unto an aik,
   He set his feet against a stane,
An' he has fought these fifteen men,
   An' killed them a' but barely ane ·
For he has left that aged knight,
   An' a' to carry the tidings hame.

When he gaed to his lady fair,
   I wat he kiss'd her tenderlie ;
" Thou art mine ain love, I have thee bought ;
   Now we shall walk the green-wood free."

THE TWA CORBIES.

THIS Poem was communicated to me by Charles Kirkpatrick Sharpe, Esq., jun. of Hoddom, as written down, from tradition, by a lady. It is a singular circumstance, that it should coincide so very nearly with the ancient dirge, called, *The Three Ravens*, published by Mr Ritson, in his *Ancient Songs ;* and that, at the same time, there should exist such a difference, as to make the one appear rather a counterpart than copy of the other. In order to enable the curious reader to contrast these two singular poems, and to form a judgment which may be the original, I take the liberty of copying the English ballad from Mr Ritson's Collection, omitting only the burden and repetition of the first line. The learned Editor states it to be given " *From Ravenscroft's Melismata. Musical Phansies, fitting the Cittie and Country Humours, to* 3, 4, *and* 5 *Voyces,*" London, 1611, 4to. "It will be obvious," continues Mr Ritson, " that this ballad is much older, not only than the date of the book, but most of the other pieces contained in it." The music is given with the words, and adapted to four voices :—

There were three rauens sat on a tre,
They were as blacke as they might be :

The one of them said to his mate,
" Where shall we our breakefast take ?"—

" Downe in yonder greene field,
There lies a knight slain under his shield ;

" His hounds they lie downe at his feete,
So well they their master keepe ;

" His haukes they flie so eagerlie,
There's no fowle dare come him nie.

" Down there comes a fallow doe,
As great with yong as she might goe.

" She lift up his bloudy hed,
And kist his wounds that were so red.

" She got him up upon her backe,
And carried him to earthen lake.

" She buried him before the prime,
She was dead her selfe ere euen song time.

" God send euery gentleman,
Such haukes, such houndes, and such a leman."

Ancient Songs, 1792, p. 155.

I have seen a copy of this dirge much modernized.

THE TWA CORBIES.[1]

As I was walking all alane,
I heard twa corbies making a mane;
The tane unto the t'other say,
" Where sall we gang and dine to-day ? "—

" In behint yon auld fail[2] dyke,
I wot there lies a new-slain knight;
And naebody kens that he lies there,
But his hawk, his hound, and lady fair.

[1] [" Any person who has read the *Minstrelsy of the Scottish Border* with attention, must have observed what a singular degree of interest and feeling the simple ballad of ' The Twa Corbies ' impresses upon the mind, which is rather increased than diminished by the unfinished state in which the story is left. It appears as if the bard had found his powers of description inadequate to a detail of the circumstances attending the fatal catastrophe, without suffering the interest already roused to subside, and had artfully consigned it over to the fancy of every reader to paint it what way he chose; or else that he lamented the untimely fate of a knight, whose base treatment he durst not otherwise make known than in that short parabolical dialogue. That the original is not improved in the following ballad, (' Sir David Græme,') will too manifestly appear upon perusal. I think it, however, but just to acknowledge, that the idea was suggested to me by reading the ' Twa Corbies.' "— Hogg's *Mountain Bard*, third edition, p. 4.—Ed.]

[2] *Fail*—Turf.

" His hound is to the hunting gane,
His hawk, to fetch the wild-fowl hame,
His lady's ta'en an^ther mate,
So we may mak our dinner sweet.

" Ye'll sit on his white hause-bane,[1]
And I'll pick out his bonny blue een
Wi' ae lock o' his gowden hair,
We'll theek[2] our nest when it grows bare.[3]

" Mony a one for him makes mane,
But nane sall ken where he is gane :
O'er his white banes, when they are bare,
The wind sall blaw for evermair."—

[1] *Hause*—neck.—[2] *Theek*—Thatch.
[3] Various reading—

" We'll theek our nest—it's a' blawn bare."

END OF VOLUME SECOND.

PRINTED BY BALLANTYNE AND CO., PAUL'S WORK, EDINBURGH.

Lightning Source UK Ltd.
Milton Keynes UK
UKOW05f2354131216
289968UK00015B/484/P